To JTMG for 70th Birthday from Henry Cleary Vic 56.

ROYAL
NAVY
LANGUAGE

ROYAL NAVY LANGUAGE

JOHN HARD

The Book Guild Ltd
Sussex, England

The Book Guild Limited
25 High Street
Lewes, Sussex
First published 1991

Set in Baskerville
Typesetting by APS
Salisbury, Wiltshire
Printed in Great Britain by
Antony Rowe Ltd
Chippenham, Wiltshire

British Library Cataloguing in publication Data
Hard, John
Royal Navy Language
1. Great Britain. Royal Navy Language
I. Title
359. 00941

ISBN 0 86332 558 0

CONTENTS

INTRODUCTION

Every profession has its own technical terms, expressions and slang, but the Royal Navy has an unequalled abundance. When one listens in to a conversation aboard a warship for the first time, be it in the wardroom, the messes or places of work, it is almost like hearing a dialect spoken. Much of the language of the Royal Navy is indeed a dialect and there are several reasons for this. One is that the profession of seafaring has been an important and continuous one for most of the nation's history.

When men put to sea in the very early days, they gave the parts of a ship and its equipment the names of objects with which they had been familiar ashore. For instance many of the items of a sailing ship's rigging were given the names of the parts of a horse's harness such as 'bitts', 'bridle' and 'martingale'; some of these terms remain in use today.

The names of animals have also been used; 'camel' for a buoyancy tank, 'cat' for the infamous nine-tailed whip, 'crow's nest' for the masthead lookout shelter and 'donkey' for any mechanical labour saving device. A mast derrick swivel heel fitting is called a 'gooseneck', a boat securing pendant which is suspended from a ship's lower boom is known as a 'lizard' and a three horned post for securing to a jetty is a 'staghorn'. 'Bullring', 'dolphin', 'worm' and 'mouse' are others.

Some names and terms have come directly from old English, some from our immediate foreign neighbours and others borrowed from the more distant parts of the world by sailors in the course of their travels. Many others are connected with persons, places and events in the history of the Royal Navy itself.

Another reason for this unique vocabulary is that the insulated life aboard ship, which men once experienced on extremely long voyages, induced them to invent words and expressions in order to add colour to their mundane everyday lot. Not all of these words and expressions have remained within the bounds of seafaring, indeed a fair number have found their way ashore, although many of these are hardly recognised as having a maritime origin. The sailor has therefore enlarged and enriched the English language.

For the 'landlubber' it is perhaps not at all easy to differentiate between what is professional naval phraseology and what is slang. Many naval terms do not appear in an English dictionary but may well be quoted in official naval publications. A division has therefore been made, and that which is considered as true naval slang is given separately.

With the amount of technological change which has been experienced in the navy during the past hundred years, many terms have necessarily disappeared. The end of sail obviously had a great effect although many of the rigging terms remain. Similarly, the age of the shipborne gun has almost drawn to a close and most of the old gunnery terms have all but gone. However, new innovations and procedures are constantly introducing new terms to make good the losses.

Where the etymology of a word is of particular interest, this is given with an abbreviation of its origin as follows:

Dan.	Danish	MDu.	Middle Dutch
Du.	Dutch	ME.	Middle English
Fr.	French	MFr.	Middle French
G.	German	OE.	Old English
Gk.	Greek	OFr.	Old French
Ice.	Icelandic	ON.	Old Norse
It.	Italian	Pg.	Portuguese
L.	Latin	Sp.	Spanish
LG.	Low German	Sw.	Swedish

1

THE ROYAL NAVY, NAVAL RESERVES AND ASSOCIATED SERVICES

Once 'navy' meant all English ships and seamen, when merchant ships were converted for fighting with 'castles' and weapons loaded on board from the Tower of London. In Blake's day a permanent force of British fighting ships was established. This force, under Charles II was permitted by the Crown to adopt the time honoured title of the Royal Navy.

* * *

BADGE OF THE ROYAL NAVY. This consists of an Admiralty pattern anchor with a rope fouling its stock, shank and arms. It originated in the badge of Lord Howard of Effingham who held the office of Lord High Admiral in the reign of Queen Elizabeth I.

FLEET, THE. The officers, men, ships and shore establishments of the Royal Navy. (OE. 'fleot', a number of ships.)

FLEET AIR ARM (FAA). The arm of the Royal Navy responsible for the operation and maintenance of both fixed wing aircraft and helicopters, in ships and ashore.

The arm was originally the Royal Naval Air Service (RNAS) which was formed unofficially by breaking away from the Royal Flying Corps (RFC) in 1912. In 1918 the RNAS and the RFC were merged to become the Royal Air Force. The 'Fleet Air Arm' of the RAF was then formed specifically to provide aircrew for aircraft carriers. Shortly after, the first course of naval officers joined RAF flying schools for training. Naval aviation eventually came under the direct control of the Admiralty in 1937. The title of Fleet Air Arm was then dropped and the Service became known as the 'Air Branch' of the Royal Navy. In 1953 the title of Fleet Air Arm was re-adopted.

GLOBE AND LAUREL. The badge of the Royal Marines, granted by George IV in 1827 as 'the most proper and distinctive badge'. The meaning was that no badge or colours could contain the names of all the battles in which the Corps had taken part. So numerous were the battle honours of the Corps that over 100 were cited as worthy of inclusion on their colours. The King decreed the device of a globe surrounded by a laurel, the motto 'Per mare per terram' and the single word 'Gibraltar' as a commemoration of the defence of 1704 and a symbol of rock like steadiness under fire.

KING GEORGE'S FUND FOR SAILORS. This fund was set up in 1917 whilst The First World War casualties at sea were mounting. It was established by prominent ship owners, merchants and businessmen, officers of the Royal and Merchant Navies and representatives of marine benevolent institutions. By the end of that year a list of 87 officially recognised charities had been drawn up and donations to the fund reached £207,000. King George V asked for the fund to be named after him and his son Prince Albert became President. Today there are over 160 nautical charities, funds and trusts served by the fund. Much of the work for the fund is done by volunteers, with support from ships and establishments of the RN, organising open days and fetes, and also from the RNR and the Association of Wrens.

MINISTRY OF DEFENCE (NAVY) (MOD(N)). The body responsible for the policy and control of the Royal Navy, formerly the Board of Admiralty.

It was in 1532 that the 'Navy Board' was established in order to control supply and administration. In 1630, 'Lords Commissioners for Executing the Office of the Lord High Admiral' were appointed, which in 1673 became the 'Admiralty Board' with Pepys as first secretary.

On 31st March 1964 the Board of Admiralty met for the last time, shortly to become the Admiralty Board of the Defence Council within a unified MOD. Lords Commissioners became 'Lordships' and Her Majesty the

Queen assumed the title of Lord High Admiral. The Admiralty Board is presided over by a minister, with the First Sea Lord who is the professional head of the Service, together with three other Sea Lords and senior civil servants.

NAVAL ANTHEM. *Rule Britannia* is the official anthem of the Royal Navy. It was written by James Thomson and first performed on 1st August 1740 in honour of the birthday of Princess Augusta.

Rule Britannia displaced the previous naval anthem which was the 18th century naval song *Britons Strike Home*, written by Purcell for the opera *Bonduca* in 1695.

NAVAL CROWN. The badge of the Royal Navy, often mounted on the truck of the ensign staff and jackstaff. It consists of a circlet surmounted by the sterns of four men-of-war, each with three poop lanterns and four square sails, each sail being spread on a mast and yard and fully fitted and sheeted home. The ships and sails are positioned alternately.

NAVAL MARCH. The Naval marches are *Heart of Oak* for the march past and *Nancy Lee* for the advance in review order.

Heart of Oak was the Navy anthem in the 18th and early 19th century. The music was written by William Boyce and the words by David Garrick in 1759 to commemorate the three naval victories of that year; Quebec, Lagos and Quiberon Bay. It was played in British ships going into battle through to Trafalgar:

Come cheer up my lads,
Tis to glory we steer,
To add something more to this glorious year,
Heart of oak are our ships,
Jolly tars are our men. . . . . . .

NAVAL MOTTO. For more than three centuries the motto of the Royal Navy has been 'Fear God and Honour the Queen'. It was taken from Peter 1, chapter 2, verse 17: Honour all men, love the brotherhood, fear God, honour the King.

NAVAL PRAYER. The prayer for the Navy, introduced into the Book of Common Prayer in the revision of 1662, is as follows:

O eternal Lord God, who alone spreadest out the heavens and rulest the raging of the sea; who has compassed the waters with bounds until day and night come to an end; be pleased to receive into thy almighty and most gracious protection the persons of us thy servants, and the Fleet in which we serve. Preserve us from the dangers of the sea, and from the violence of the enemy; that we may be safeguarded unto our most gracious Sovereign Lord, King Charles, and his Dominions. And a security for such as pass on the seas upon their lawful occasions; that the inhabitants of our Empire may in peace and quietness serve thee our God; and that we may return in safety to enjoy the blessings of the land, with the fruits of our labours, and a thankful remembrance of they mercies to praise and glorify thy holy Name, through Jesus Christ our Lord.

NAVY, ARMY AND AIR FORCE INSTITUTES (NAAFI). The organisation used by the Royal Navy to provide canteens in ships and establishments. It caters also for the Army and the Royal Air Force, the naval accounts being kept separate so that the profits or losses cannot be diverted to another service. The NAAFI makes no profit itself, but pays back a rebate on all sales to the 'Ship's Fund' which is used for recreational and benevolent purposes connected with the ship. Part of this rebate is subscribed to the Royal Naval Benevolent Trust by all ships and establishments.

Canteens were run in ships of the Royal Navy in the 19th century under private enterprise, making huge profits at the expense of the men. For this reason, in 1892 the Admiralty placed the running of canteens in the hands of the RN Canteen Board. Integration with similar Army and RAF Boards in 1934 formed the NAAFI.

NAVY LIST, THE. A publication which lists all ships, shore establishments and officers of the Royal Navy and Naval reserves.

NORTH ATLANTIC TREATY ORGANISATION (NATO). The Royal Navy is an integrated part of the NATO alliance, formed in 1949, and as such often exercises with other members, particularly the US Navy. The northern flank of NATO is one of the areas most vulnerable to enemy ingress. Every year units of the Royal Navy operate with the Royal Norwegian Navy in joint exercises designed to test readiness and teamwork.

The RN provides the United Kingdom's contribution to NATO's strategic nuclear deterrent; at least one of its four nuclear powered Polaris ballistic missile submarines is on constant patrol. There are also two NATO Standing Naval Forces of which RN ships form a part of each; STANAVFORLANT, the Atlantic force and STANAVFORCHAN, the channel force. STANAVFORCHAN, formed in 1968 was the first international naval squadron in history and is composed of between five and nine escort ships, of which usually one is RN.

QUEEN ALEXANDRA'S ROYAL NAVAL NURSING SERVICE (QARNNS). The service which staffs the RN hospitals at Gibraltar, Gosport and Plymouth.

Although the first Naval hospitals were built in the middle of the 18th century (the Haslar hospital at Gosport was completed in 1762), no professional nurses were employed in them until 1884 when ten sisters were appointed to Haslar. From this beginning the QARNNS was founded in 1902.

ROYAL CORPS OF NAVAL CONSTRUCTORS. A Civilian body responsible for the design of HM ships and for the supervision of their construction. Members of this Corps are civil servants and are experts in naval architecture, some specialising in mechanical or electrical engineering. Sometimes it is neccessary for them to be appointed to serve in HM ships and on these occasions, although strictly civilians, they do wear uniform.

ROYAL FLEET AUXILLARY (RFA). The ships responsible for supplying the Royal Navy's warships with stores, fuel, ammunition and food. RFA ships, although registered as merchantmen, are fully integrated into the Royal Navy; they are either owned by the Ministry of Defence or under contract. The Ensign of RFA ships is blue with a yellow anchor in the fly.

The RFA was constituted by Royal Charter in 1911, but storeships have accompanied British warships for centuries and were originally known as 'pinks'.

ROYAL FLEET RESERVE (RFR). The reserve into which men are placed for three years following the completion of nine years 'career engagement' service in the Royal Navy.

ROYAL MARINES (RM). The Corps of Royal Marines provides Commando units for amphibious assault operations and also to work world-wide in an infantry role, detachments for service at sea in HM ships and at important shore establishments, specialist amphibious units for raiding and small craft work, a quick reaction force to protect the UK offshore installations and a band service for the Royal Navy and Royal Marines.

The Corps was formed in 1664 as the Duke of York and Albany's Regiment of Foot or Admiral's Regiment, after Charles II's brother, the Duke of York and Lord High Admiral, to provide a permanent 'body of sea soldiers' for assault or landing parties. The title Royal was granted to the Corps in 1802.

ROYAL MARINES RESERVE (RMR). A reserve in which volunteers carry out training annually and at weekends to provide the Royal Marines with a commando trained volunteer force ready to join the regular Corps in an emergency. The RMR was formed in 1963 from the former RMFVR following the disbandment of National Service. There are five units and ten detachments with some seventy officers and 1,100 other ranks.

ROYAL MARITIME AUXILLARY SERVICE (RMAS). A civilian organisation which provides specialist craft for naval purposes other than those provided by the RFA. These are tugs, mooring and salvage vessels, degaussing vessels, cable ships, torpedo recovery vessels and fleet tenders. The vessels have black hulls, grey funnels and fly blue ensigns with a yellow anchor, having two wavy lines beneath, in the fly.

ROYAL NAVAL ASSOCIATION (RNA). An association of ex-naval men for mutual assistance, branches of which are to be found in many districts throughout the country.

ROYAL NAVAL AUXILLARY SERVICE (RNXS). A voluntary non-combatant civilian service, trained for duties which, in the event of war, would release men of the Royal Navy for active service. The service, which was founded in 1962 from members of the Royal Naval Mine-watching Service (itself formed in 1952), has 3,000 members in 71 units around the coasts of the UK and the Channel Islands. Duties include the defence of ports and anchorages, to provide port parties in support of the local Naval Authority and to support the Naval Control of Shipping (NCS) authority.

The RNXS operates some fourteen vessels, fleet tenders and coastal training craft, which have black hulls with light grey upperworks and are prefixed 'XSV' (Auxillary Service Vessel).

ROYAL NAVAL BENEVOLENT SOCIETY (RNBS). A benevolent society for Royal Naval and Royal Marines officers and their families.

Founded in 1739 as the Amicable Navy Society, its original aim was to protect naval officers against exploitation by the Admiralty. It was in effect a trade union and was able to claim the credit for some notable achievements, including the introduction of uniform for naval officers and an increase in pay for unemployed officers.

A few years after formation the society had collected enough money to be in a position to help families in need and it then took on the benevolent role. By 1791, so much money had been collected that it was agreed to discontinue the 'trade union' role and to concentrate on the benevolent work. The name was changed to the RNBS in 1838.

ROYAL NAVAL BENEVOLENT TRUST (RNBT). Established since 1922 as the main benevolent organisation for past and present ratings and ranks of the Royal Navy, Royal Marines and reserves. It provides relief in cases of necessity or distress and gives assistance to those seeking employment on leaving the Service.

ROYAL NAVAL RESERVE (RNR). A reserve which carries out weekly, week-end and annual training for its members to be able to assume nearly all naval roles. The 10th Mine Countermeasures Squadron, part of the NATO defence force, is operated by the RNR.

In 1854, when the fleet mobilised for the Crimean War, only 400 men volunteered for service. Following the war, in 1857, Lieutenant J. H. Brown suggested that a Volunteer reserve be formed, but this was rejected. A Royal Comission was set up in 1858 to look into the manning of the Navy and then J. H. Brown's scheme was implemented.

The RNR was created in 1859, designed to make part-time naval personnel out of merchant seamen. Special drill ships were established throughout the country and by 1862 12,000 had enrolled. By the beginning of this century new skills were required and in 1903 the Royal Navy Volunteer Reserve (RNVR) was introduced, where seafaring experience was not essential; merchant seamen continued to belong to the RNR. In 1958 a unified reserve was formed out of the former RNR and RNVR.

SEA CADET CORPS (SCC). Unlike the Army Cadet Force and Air Training Corps, the SCC is unique in that it is not a pre-Service organisation. The governing body is the Sea Cadet Council, which has charitable status and is supported by the MOD(N). The Royal Navy's assistance includes providing uniforms and equipment on loan and facilities in ships and establishments for occasional training courses.

There are some 400 SCC units in towns and cities throughout the UK, training some 20,000 girls and boys, the girls belonging to Girls Nautical Training contingents within many of these units. More than seventy units also have Marine Cadet detachments. Uniform worn is identical to that worn by officers and men of the Royal Navy, except for distinguishing flashes and badges. The officers and instructors are all unpaid volunteers, the officers holding temporary time-only appointments in the Royal Naval Reserve.

The Corps has the longest continuous history of a youth organisation in the country. It began in 1856 as the Naval Lads Brigade, being founded in Whistable by sailors returning from the Crimean War. By 1899 it was large enough to be formed into a national organisation and named the Navy League Boys Naval Brigade and by the beginning of the Second World War there were 100 units with some 10,000 cadets. In 1942 the Admiralty recognised the value of the Corps as a source of semi-trained manpower for the Fleet. The name of the Corps was changed to the Sea Cadet Corps and placed under the direct control of the Admiral Commanding Reserves (ACR) while still being administered by the Navy League. In 1976 the Navy league was re-named the Sea Cadet Association and the role of ACR was taken over by the Commander-in-Chief Naval Home Command.

SENIOR SERVICE. As such, the Royal Navy is accorded a position of honour on all joint-service ceremonial occassions; on the right of the line in review order and in the van (leading) in marching order.

TRINITY HOUSE. Founded in 1514 and inaugurated by Henry VIII to develop navigational aids and responsible for lighthouses, lightvessels and buoyage around the coasts of England and Wales. Trinity House uses the Red Ensign charged with its own badge in the fly, derived from the Arms of the corporation which themselves date from 1573.

Until 1874, Trinity House examined the officers of the navigation branch of the RN.

WOMEN'S ROYAL MARINES (WRM). The equivalent to the WRNS and carrying out similar duties, but as part of the RM.

WOMEN'S ROYAL MARINES RESERVE (WRMR). Similar to the WRNR, but as part of the RMR.

WOMEN'S ROYAL NAVAL SERVICE (WRNS). The WRNS is an integral part of the Royal Navy but with its own ranks and rates. Officer ranks are commandant, superintendent, chief officer and first, second and third officers, these corresponding to the Royal Navy ranks of commodore to sub-lieutenant. WRNS rates of chief petty officer wren, leading wren and wren, correspond to the Royal Navy rates from chief petty officer to able seaman.

WRNS jobs include air fitter, cinema operator, cook, motor driver, radio operator, stores accountant, weapon analyst and welfare worker.

The Service originated in 1917, but was disbanded in 1919 as a peacetime economy measure. It was re-established in 1939 and such valuable duties were carried out during the Second World War, releasing men for sea service, that it was decided to establish it as part of the Royal Navy in 1949. It was not until 1977 that it came within the Naval Discipline Act; up to that time it had its own disciplinary code.

WOMEN'S ROYAL NAVAL SERVICE RESERVE (WRNSR). As with the Royal Navy Reserve, the training given on drill nights, at weekends and annually provides the WRNS with a trained reserve ready for use if needed.

2

SHIPS AND AIRCRAFT

The zenith in terms of the number of the RN's ships and aircraft was at the end of the Second World War, when there were 8,940 ships (some 50 aircraft carriers alone) and 1,336 front line aircraft. Today the numbers are a mere fraction of those of 1945, in fact the RN is currently suffering from a lack of ships to meet its commitments. However, the quality of the units in service with the fleet is high, providing a potent defence force.

Long gone are the battleships as the 'capital ships' of the fleet; today's capital ships are the nuclear powered fleet submarines. Gone too are the cruisers, although the tonnage of the latest destroyer and frigate types is equal to that of some light cruisers of forty years ago. Other former ship designations such as 'sloop' and 'corvette' have disappeared, but those of 'destroyer' and 'frigate' are still in use. Of course, the functions of today's destroyer and frigate anti-aircraft and anti-submarine escorts are far removed from those performed by their type namesakes of yesteryear.

Conventional aircraft carriers, part of the fleet for half a century, disappeared from the RN in the 1970s, however the light carriers now in service do operate the Sea Harrier aircraft to provide the fleet with air cover. But it is the helicopter which has revolutionised naval warfare in recent years. This aircraft gives the facility for extending a warship's weapons systems to give an 'over the horizon' capability. Today nearly every warship and auxillary is air capable.

There is a saying in the Royal Navy; 'RN sails courtesy of the RFA'; and how very true. Some thirty Royal Fleet Auxillary (RFA) ships sustain the fleet at sea, providing fuel, ammunition, food and naval stores. Although registered as merchantmen, these ships are fully integrated into the RN; they are either owned by the Ministry of Defence or, in the case of some types, under contract. Smaller auxillary vessels such as tugs and fleet tenders are operated by the Royal Maritime Auxillary Service (RMAS).

The RN, in common with other NATO associated organisations, uses abbreviations to describe ships and their role. These are given where appropriate following the type heading.

* * *

ACCOMMODATION VESSEL. An old warship used for harbour training and accommodation. A number of these non-seagoing vessels are employed in the various ports.

AIRCRAFT CARRIER (CVS). The three ships of the *INVINCIBLE* class are the largest British warships built since the Second World War. They are able to act as command ships for anti-submarine groups, each operating about twelve Sea King HAS.5/AEW.3 helicopters and eight Sea Harrier aircraft. A ski jump launching ramp is fitted to improve the operational performance of the Sea Harrier. Displacement is 19,500 tonnes with power provided by four Rolls Royce Olympus TM3B gas turbines giving a maximum speed of some 28 knots. The Crew numbers 1,200.

The main self defence weapon of the carriers is the Sea Dart missile system. During the Falklands War, the missile proved to be versatile but there was concern that it was not sufficient to protect *INVINCIBLE* close in. As a result of this, each of the three ships have been fitted with two or more either Phalanx or Goalkeeper guns and extra 20 mm cannons.

The RN's first aircraft carrier and one the world's earliest was *HMS PEGASUS*. Her original name was the *STOCKHOLM* and she was intended for the Great Eastern Railway's Harwich-Continental passenger service. In 1917, while still on the stocks, she was bought by the Admiralty and completed as a seaplane carrier. The first ship to be designed as an aircraft carrier was *HMS HERMES*, launched in 1919.

ARMAMENT STORE CARRIER (AKF). Two 1,150 tonne ships are operated by the RMAS and are used for supplying armaments to naval establishments.

ASSAULT SHIP (LPD). A purpose built ship, developed from the Landing Ship Dock (LSD) vessels of the Second World War, fitted out as a Naval Group/Brigade HQ and with a flight deck capability for helicopters. There is space for sixteen 50-ton tanks on two vehicle decks and up to six helicopters. A troop of Royal Corps of Signals and a Royal Marines (RM) detachment is carried. At the stern is a docking well to accomodate LCM 9's (Landing Craft Mechanised), each capable of carrying two of the heavy tanks. LCVP's (Landing Craft, Vehicle and Personnel), for carrying men and small vehicles, are carried on davits. The dock walls have enough space to carry 370 RM Commandos normally and on short haul attacks the number can be increased to 700.

There are two ships of the class; *HMS FEARLESS* and *HMS INTREPID*. Displacement is approximately 12,000 tonnes, with power provided by two English Electric turbines to give 21 knots.

AUXILLARY OILER AND REPLENISHMENT SHIP (AOR). A new type of replenishment ship operated by the RFA and also known as a 'one stop AOR'. This is a new concept for RFA ships where all of the fuel and variety of stores required by a warship may be delivered from one ship. Another new concept is that the AOR will be the first RFA type to carry a comprehensive weapon fit, including the Sea Wolf missile system and also be capable of operating Sea King helicopters in the anti-submarine role. Two ships of this 'new Fort' class are being built and the displacement will be 31,500 tonnes.

AVIATION TRAINING SHIP. *HMS ARGOS*, designed to carry six Sea King Helicopters or twelve Sea Harriers. Operated by the RFA, the main distinguishing feature is the large flight deck set upon a mercantile type hull. She displaces 13,000 tonnes.

CANBERRA. Three types of these aircraft; the T4, TT18 and T22 are operated by the Fleet Air Arm for observer training, flight refuelling and target towing. Some of the aircraft themselves provide targets for radar calibration.

The maximum speed of the aircraft, some of which first flew as long ago as the early 1950s, is 500 knots with an endurance of six hours.

DEGAUSSING VESSEL. A vessel carrying electrical equipment to alter or reduce a ship's magnetic signature as a measure against the magnetic mine. Two of these 970 tonne vessels are operated by the RMAS.

DESTROYER, GUIDED MISSILE (DLG), TYPE 42. A guided missile destroyer designed primarily to provide air defence for task group operations. Also known as the *BIRMINGHAM* class (formerly the *SHEFFIELD* class), the ships are all named after cities. They are equipped with the GWS 30 Sea Dart air defence missile system, the Mk 32 Ship Launched Torpedo Weapons System (STWS), the Lynx HAS.5 helicopter, the Vickers Mk 8 4.5 in. gun and 20 mm and 30 mm cannon. Rolls Royce Olympus gas turbines are fitted to give a full power speed in excess of 30 knots, together with Rolls Royce Tyne gas turbines for cruising.

Early Type 42's are known as the Batch 1 and Batch 2 types and number eight ships (originally ten, but two, *SHEFFIELD* and *COVENTRY*, were lost to enemy action in the Falklands War of 1982), with a displacement of 4,000 tonnes. These Batch 1 and 2 types suffered from a lack of internal space for weapons systems. The four more recent Batch 3 ships have therefore been lengthened and broadened and displace 5,000 tonnes.

DESTROYER, GUIDED MISSILE (DLG), TYPE 82. *HMS BRISTOL*, 7,000 tonnes, is the only ship of a class designed as escorts for a new generation of conventional aircraft carriers (CVAs). With the cancellation of CVA01 in the late 1960's, the remaining type 82's were not constructed. The destroyer is armed with the GWS 30 Sea Dart area air defence missile system, for which she was the trials ship in 1972. She is also fitted with the Mk 8 4.5 inch automatic gun and 20 mm and 30 mm cannon. *HMS BRISTOL* is powered by an arrangement of two sets of Standard Range geared steam turbines together with two Bristol-Siddeley marine TMIA gas turbines. She has a speed of 30 knots and carries a complement of 407 officers and ratings.

DESTROYER, TYPE 43. A projected type of new destroyer.
The forerunner of the modern destroyer was originally called a 'torpedo boat destroyer', a fast vessel designed to combat the torpedo boat in the latter half of the last century. This first modern-style destroyer was *HMS HAVOCK*, launched in 1893, combining both gun and three torpedo tubes.

FLEET REPLENISHMENT SHIP (AEFS). The RFA operates four of these large ships. The two ships of the 'Re' class displace 19,310 tonnes and are able to transfer food, ammunition, explosives and stores to warships at sea. The two 14,700 tonnes 'Fort' class are employed in transferring ammunition and stores.

FLEET TENDER. A small RMAS vessel employed to attend on a larger vessel, for duties such as ferrying, stores or armament carrying, diving tender or training. There are numerous tenders, varying in size from 90 to 250 tonnes. Some are also used by the Royal Navy Auxillary Service (RNXS) and some for Sea Cadet Corps training.

FLOTILLA. The main surface forces of the RN are divided into two flotillas. The nine destroyer and frigate squadrons comprise the First Flotilla with the aircraft carriers and assault ships making up the Third Flotilla. (Sp. a fleet of vessels, from 'flota', a fleet.)
Until 1988 the destroyer and frigate squadrons were divided into the First and Second Flotillas. These two flotillas were then combined to form the First Flotilla.

FORWARD REPAIR SHIP. The 10,500 tonnes *RFA DILIGENCE* was originally designed for commercial operations in the North Sea and chartered by the MOD in 1982 to support warships in the Falkland Islands. A feature is the octagonal flight deck for helicopter operations.

FRIGATE (FFH), TYPE 12 (IMPROVED). Also known as the *LEANDER* class after the original lead ship which is no longer in service. These were originally designed as general purpose frigates and were built throughout the 1960's and early 1970's as an updated version of the earlier Type 12 *WHITBY* class. Most have now been converted for more specific roles and are designated under groups: Seawolf, Exocet, etc., according to the armament fit replacing the twin 4.5 inch gun mounting. They are powered by two sets of steam turbines and have a speed of 30 knots. These ships are gradually being disposed of as new Type 42 destroyers come into service; fourteen remain.

FRIGATE (FFH), TYPE 21. The *AMAZON* class of general purpose frigates which were designed and built by Vosper Thornycroft in conjunction with Yarrows; the first commercially designed ships produced for the RN since 1945. They were also the first gas turbine frigates in the RN, being powered by an arrangement of two Rolls Royce Olympus gas turbines, giving a speed of 32 knots and two Rolls Royce Tyne gas turbines for cruising. The displacement is 2,800 tonnes, with main armament consisting of the Exocet missile system, Shipborne Torpedo Weapon System (STWS) and the Lynx helicopter. There are six ships of the class (originally eight but two, *ANTELOPE* and *ARDENT*, were lost through air attacks during the Falklands War of 1982).

FRIGATE (FFH), TYPE 22. The *BROADSWORD* class which were the first RN ships to be designed to the metric system and also the first to be designed around a missile system, the Exocet. They were also the first warships to carry the Seawolf missile and the first to operate two Lynx helicopters. In addition, an anti-submarine torpedo system is fitted (STWS). Displacement of the early Type 22's, known as Batch 1's, is 3,500 tonnes. They are powered by two Rolls Royce Olympus gas turbines to give a full power speed of 30 knots and two Rolls Royce Tyne gas turbines for cruising.

Batch 2's are some 12 metres longer than the Batch 1's and displace, 4,166 tonnes. These also have a different power arrangement of four Rolls Royce Spey gas turbines.

The Type 22's were the first major ships to be built for the RN without any major gun armament, but the latest Batch 3's have an automatic 4.5 inch gun fitted and also the Goalkeeper 30 mm. rapid-fire cannon. Harpoon replaces the Exocet missiles. Different again in the Batch 3's; they are powered by a combination of Spey and Tyne gas turbines.

FRIGATE (FFH), TYPE 23. The latest type of frigate to be built for the RN, known as the 'Duke' class and the first RN escorts capable of carrying large fleet helicopters; the ships are able to carry the Sea King HAS.5 or alternatively two Lynx HAS.3's. They are built entirely of steel and have the vertical-launched version of the Seawolf missile system and The Harpoon anti-surface vessel sea-skimming missile. Seven ships are to be built initially with a second batch of eight expected to follow. The original design included a 4.5 inch automatic gun, but this will now only be fitted to the first batch of ships on cost grounds. Displacement is 3,500 tonnes and power is provided by GEC electric motors and Rolls Royce SMIA gas turbines. The complement is 165 officers and ratings.

The frigates were originally the 4th, 5th and 6th rates; sailing warships mounting from 28 to 50 or 60 guns. They were introduced in the 18th century for use either as auxillaries to the fleet, seeking out and keeping in touch with the enemy, or on trade protection and attack on enemy trade. The first one was built for the RN in 1757, of 315, 30 guns and named *CONSTANT WARWICK*. (Fr. 'frigate' from It. 'frigata', a small galleass.)

GAZELLE HT2. All RN helicopter pilots are trained in this aircraft which has been in service since 1975. It has a maximum speed of 168 knots and an endurance of 2.5 hours.

HUNTER. A shore-based aircraft of which three types are in service with the Fleet Air Arm; the T8C, the T8M and the GA11. They are used for pilot training and to provide target and tracking facilities for warships. The hunter has been used as a training aircraft since 1958 and approximately 40 are still in service. The maximum speed is 590 knots with an endurance of three hours.

ICE PATROL SHIP. The only one of her type, *HMS ENDURANCE* is a special ice-strengthened ship deployed to the South Atlantic for duties which include scientific research and deterrence. She was originally the German built *ANITA DAN*, operated by the Danish shipping company of J. Lauritzen, one of many such ships servicing

Denmark's interests in Greenland and the Faroes. The MOD purchased her in 1967 and she was subsequently converted to carry two helicopters and fitted for ocean survey work. She is painted bright red and is unarmed when operating in Antarctic Treaty waters.

At the time of the Falklands War in 1982, *ENDURANCE* was on the point of being withdrawn. However, a re-appraisal of the RN's role in the South Atlantic has kept her for further service.

JETSTREAM T2/T3. A small number of these aircraft are operated by the Fleet Air Arm as communications aircraft and for observer training. Their maximum speed is 250 knots with an endurance of five hours.

LANDING SHIP, LOGISTIC (LSL). Five RFA ships comprise the *SIR LANCELOT* class of 3,320 tons which are able to transport and land troops, armour, vehicles and stores. Each ship has the capacity to carry sixteen tanks, thirty-four other vehicles and up to 544 troops. Bow and stern doors provide a roll-on-roll-off facility.

During the First World War, the RN developed an armoured landing vessel shaped like a beetle (to become known as a 'beetle boat'), capable of carrying 500 men. It was first used at the landing at Gallipoli and was the forerunner to the Landing Ship, Infantry.

LYNX HAS 2/3. A helicopter developed by Westland/Areospatiale for advanced anti-submarine and other duties and as such is carried in most destroyers and frigates. It is equipped with Ferranti Seaspray search and tracking radar, a derivative of the Blue Fox carried in the Sea Harrier, to give the parent ship an over-the-horizon search capability. It can carry a variety of anti-submarine weapons including Mk 44, Mk 46, or Stingray homing torpedoes, Sea Skua homing missiles and nuclear depth bombs. It is powered by two Rolls Royce Gem turboshafts giving a maximum speed of 140 knots with an endurance of almost three hours. It replaced the 'Wasp' helicopter for service in ships.

MERLIN. The Anglo-Italian EH101 helicopter which is at present under development as a replacement for the Sea King HAS.5/6 and the Lynx HAS.2/3 and due to enter service from 1992. The power from three 2,000 h.p.

engines will, apart from providing greater safety, give the Merlin the ability to operate from a ship's flight deck irrespective of wind and thus without affecting the ship's heading and speed. The aircraft has a maximum speed of 167 knots and an endurance of five hours.

MINES COUNTERMEASURES VESSEL (MCMV). The latest high technology mines countermeasures vessels are the HUNT class. These thirteen vessels are constructed of glass-reinforced fibre materials (GRP) which are non-magnetic and strong enough to withstand the explosive shocks encountered in MCM activities and the largest ships in the world so built. They are capable of both hunting for all types of acoustic and magnetic mines and sweeping for moored varieties, two tasks hitherto having to be carried out by separate minehunter and minesweeper vessels. They displace 725 tonnes, are powered by twin Ruston-Paxman diesels giving a speed of 16 knots and have an armament of a single 40 mm Bofors gun. A camera equipped un-manned PAP-1041 submersible is carried.

The RN has about thirty other MCM vessels divided between minehunters and minesweepers. Between them they can deal with all types of mines. The latest single role minesweepers are the 'River' class of 890 tons which are gradually replacing the ageing *TON* class for operation by the RNR. A new class of single role minehunters, the *SANDOWN* class of 492 tons, are under construction. These have an improved and lightened GRP structure and the latest variable depth sonar. Computer controlled position keeping will be employed using Voith-Schneider cycloidal propellers and bow thrusters.

MOORING, SALVAGE AND BOOM DEFENCE VESSELS. Several of these vessels of approximately 1,000 tons are operated by the RMAS. They are employed in laying buoys and moorings, salvage work and the setting up of booms and nets for harbour and anchorage protection.

OFFSHORE PATROL VESSEL (OPV). The two 1,400 tonne vessels of the *CASTLE* class and the eight 1,000 tonne vessels of the *ISLAND* class are trawler shaped and employed to patrol fishing and natural resource areas including the North Sea. They are powered by two diesel engines, have a speed of 16 knots and are usually armed with a single 40 mm Bofors gun.

PATROL CRAFT. There are three small 700 tonne ships, the *PEACOCK* class, which were built to replace the ageing ex-Ton class minesweepers as patrol craft in Hong Kong waters. They are powered by two diesels, giving a speed of 24 knots and principle gun armament is a single 76 mm Oto-Melara. Three slightly larger 800 tonne vessels of the *PROTECTOR* class, fitted with two 40 mm Bofors guns, are employed as patrol vessels in the Falkland Islands. In Northern Ireland two small 194 tonne craft of the *BIRD* class and armed with a single 40 mm Bofors gun, are used as patrol craft. Two others of the *BIRD* class are assigned to Britannia Royal Naval College Dartmouth.

RESERVE SHIPS. Ships which are surplus to current operational and training requirements are retained at Portsmouth (Reserve Ships Unit) in a dormant state with their armament and machinery sealed. The intention is that such ships may be re-activated and brought forward into service in an emergency.

ROYAL YACHT. The Royal Yacht *BRITANNIA* was designed as a dual purpose vessel; for the peacetime role of conveying members of the Royal Family to any part of the world and for the wartime role of hospital ship. She entered service in 1954, has a displacement of 5,000 tonnes and a ship's company of twenty one officers and 256 ratings who are all specially chosen. Her ornamental binnacle, originally from the earlier *ROYAL GEORGE*, came from the previous Royal Yacht *VICTORIA AND ALBERT* which was built in 1899 and scrapped in 1954.

Custom demands three masts in the Royal Yacht, as when the sovereign is on board the following flags must be worn; Royal Standard at the main, Lord High Admiral's flag at the fore and the Union Flag at the mizzen.

There have been several Royal Yachts in service through recent centuries, in fact the word 'yacht' entered the English language through the presentation to Charles

II by the States General of Holland of the 'jacht' *MARY* (100 tons, eight guns) as a private pleasure vessel.

SEABED OPERATION VESSEL. *HMS CHALLENGER*, a 6,400 tonne diving support ship which is equipped for many types of specialised diving. A 14.2 tonne saturation deep diving bell is lowered through the centre of the ship, equipped to find, inspect and where appropriate recover objects on the sea bed at greater depths than were hitherto possible. The main propellors are five bladed and hung vertically under the hull (Voith-Schneider), three bow thrusters are also fitted. The ship is capable of dynamic positioning, i.e able to maintain position relative to the ocean floor.

The foundation of modern oceanography was laid by the voyage of another *CHALLENGER*, an RN screw corvette, when between 1872 and 1876 she sailed 68,000 miles gathering scientific data.

SEA DEVON C20. The naval version of the De Havilland Dove, used by the Fleet Air Arm since 1955 for communications and fisheries protection duties. The maximum speed is 200 knots with an endurance of three hours.

SEA HARRIER. A fleet reconnaissance and strike (FRS) vertical or short take off and landing (V/STOL) aircraft which is descended from the RAF Harrier GR3. The Mark 1 version (FRS.1) has provided the RN with air defence, reconnaissance and a maritime strike capability since 1980. Approximately fifty five of these aircraft are in service, squadrons being embarked in the CVS's. The main armament carried can be the AIM-9L Sidewinder missile, the sea Eagle missile, or various bombs. In addition, two 30 mm Aden cannon pods are provided. The maximum speed is 625 knots with an endurance of up to two hours. Sea Harrier FRS.1 aircraft are in the process of being updated to FRS.2 to give the capability to carry the Advanced Medium Range Air-to-Air Missile (AMRAAM) and also Blue Vixen radar. Three shore-based Sea Harriers of a T 4N version are used for operational training.

SEA HERON C1/C4. An aircraft which has been in service with the Fleet Air Arm since 1961 and still in use for communications, fisheries protection and surveillance duties. To be replaced by Jetstream aircraft.

SEA KING. This large helicopter has been in service with the RN in an anti-submarine role since 1969. The current Sea King HAS.5 integrates radar, sonar and weapons to provide a complete hunter-killer of submarines. Embarked in the CVSs and some RFAs, it can operate in all weathers to detect, classify and attack the fastest nuclear submarines. Equipment carried includes the Plessey 195 dipping sonar, AW391 search radar and four Mk 44 or Mk 46 homing torpedoes with an option for depth bombs or nuclear depth charges. Modification to HAS.6 is under way, which is an upgrade to convert to the MEL Super-searcher radar and Stingray torpedoes. Powered by two Rolls Royce Gnome turboshafts, the maximum speed is 112 knots, with an endurance of five hours.

During the 1982 Falklands War, the RN Task Force found itself at a distinct disadvantage without any airborne early warning (AEW); the fixed-wing Gannet AEW aircraft had been withdrawn from service upon the demise of the conventional carriers in the 1970s. Escort ships therefore had to be used in an over-the-horizon, primary detection, picket role; one such ship, the Type 42 DLG *HMS SHEFFIELD* was sunk by an enemy aircraft-launched missile. With no suitable fixed-wing aircraft currently available, in order to reinstate a Fleet Air Arm capability, the RN initiated trials using the Sea King to carry the powerful Searchwater radar, as fitted in the RAF's Nimrod aircraft. The result is the highly successful Sea King AEW.2 which entered service in 1985. The radar is carried in a large radome which, when airborne, is extended to give 360 degrees coverage. Embarked in and operating from the CVSs, the aircraft is also able to act in a fighter direction role; guiding the combat air patrols (CAPs) to intercept the enemy until the Sea Harrier closes sufficiently to be able to use its own radar.

In the heavy lift Air Commando role, the normally shore based Sea King HC4 is able to operate from any amphibious ship and also RFAs. It can transport twenty eight fully armed Royal Marines to a battle area, landing them through the cargo door, or transport their equipment or vehicles underslung.

SQUADRON. In the RN the warships are divided into squadrons by type, but it is unusual to find a squadron operating together. Each squadron is commanded by a captain. Fleet Air Arm units are also known as squadrons; those in the 800 series being front line operational units and those in the 700 series being second line training units. (MF. 'esquadron'.)

STANDBY SQUADRON. Certain warships when decommissioned are held in Portsmouth Harbour and kept fully stored and maintained until such time as their disposal is approved. In an emergency these ships are able to return to the Fleet for immediate duty.

SUBMARINE, NUCLEAR POWERED BALLISTIC MISSILE (SSBN). The RN has four of these large submarines of the *RESOLUTION* class, each armed with sixteen Polaris A3 ballistic missiles and also torpedoes. The range of the submarine is approximately 100,000 miles with a submerged speed better than 25 knots. Geared steam turbines are powered by a single pressurised water-cooled nuclear reactor. The displacement is 7,500 tonnes.

At least one SSBN is on constant patrol as the United Kingdom's contribution to NATO's strategic nuclear deterrent. Each submarine has two crews called Port and Starboard; when one is away on patrol, the other is ashore either on leave or training.

The replacements for the Polaris submarines in the latter part of the 1990s will be the four Trident missile carrying *VANGUARD* class nuclear submarines of 15,900 tonnes, at present under construction.

SUBMARINE, NUCLEAR POWERED FLEET (SSN). The RN has fifteen of this type of submarine within four different classes; the *VALIANT*, *CHURCHILL*, *SWIFTSURE* and *TRAFALGAR* classes. They displace between 3,500 and 4,700 tonnes according to class and are armed with homing torpedoes for use against other submarines or surface vessels. The tube launched Sub-Harpoon missile is also carried. These fleet submarines have the ability to operate with surface ships at high speed.

SUBMARINE, PATROL (SSK). A submarine with diesel-electric power, armed with torpedoes. The RN continues to operate a number of these submarines of the 'O' class, the displacement of which is 1,600 tonnes. A new type of SSK, the Vickers type 2400 of 2,400 tons and known as the *UPHOLDER* class is being introduced.

The American J. P. Holland designed the first five submarines built in Britain, the first of which was launched in 1901. These were of 105 tons with a speed of eight and a half knots—seven knots submerged.

SURVEY SHIPS. These ships carry out oceanographic work, especially important to anti-submarine warfare. The largest of the ships in the Survey Flotilla are the three 2,700 tonne ocean-going ships of the *HECLA* class. These are fitted with the most modern equipment which includes satellite navigation control, computerised plotting, magnetometers, gravimeters and echo sounders. Five smaller 1,800 tonne vessels of the *BULLDOG* class, a scaled down version of the *HECLA* class, are employed in coastal surveying.

The charts produced by the RN are primarily for naval use but these are also available to the general public, indeed the world.

The first vessel specifically built for surveying duties was *HMS TRITON*, launched in 1882. She continued in service until 1914.

TANKER, COASTAL. The 'Oil' class of 280 tonne ships are crewed by the RMAS and are employed in transferring fuel oil and diesel fuel from principle to subsidary depots.

TANKER, LARGE FLEET (AOF(L)). The three ships of the 'O1' class, 11,000 tonnes, are able to carry out rapid oiling of warships at cruising speed and also transfer a certain amount of stores. Carrying out a similar role is the smaller *TIDESPRING* of 8,760 tonnes. All are RFA ships.

TANKER, SMALL FLEET (AOF(S)). There are four of these RFA ships, the 'Rover' class of 4,3500 tonnes. Besides refuelling warships at sea they are able to transfer fresh water and stores.

TANKER, SUPPORT (AOS). These five 6,910 tonne RFA ships of the 'Leaf' class are able to transfer oil and aviation fuel to warships at sea.

TARGET SHIP. The *WAKEFUL* is a 900 tonne ship used as a target ship by the Faslane Submarine base. Although an RMAS vessel, she is RN manned.

TORPEDO RECOVERY VESSEL. Several of these vessels, ranging in displacement from 100 to 700 tonnes, are operated by the RMAS for the recovery of exercise and trials torpedoes.

TRIALS SHIP. Various ships from 1,000 to 4,000 tonnes and crewed by the RMAS are employed in sonar trials and weapon testing.

TUG. Tugs are operated by the RMAS and vary in type. The large 1,660 tonne 'Ro' class are designated as 'ocean tugs' and have many uses including the towing of vessels which have paid off and have been sold for scrap. The latest *ADEPT* class of 460 tonne coastal tugs are also known as 'twin unit tractors' (TUTS). The smallest and most numerous are the harbour berthing tugs which vary in size from 40 to 170 tonnes.

3

WEAPONS, DETECTION AND COUNTER-MEASURES SYSTEMS

The age of the missile has dawned and descended upon the Navy in a space of time that has been incredibly short relative to the eras of previous major weapons. The first warship to carry guns was the *Christopher of the Tower* in 1410; she carried three cannons. From then on, the gun reigned supreme for four centuries as the only major weapon at sea. During the 19th century the gun was supplemented by another important ship-borne weapon, the torpedo. Between them, these two weapons became highly developed, particularly guns which grew enormously in size, as did the ships to carry them. However, eventually a revolution occurred; the aircraft carrier appeared and by the end of the Second World War it became obvious that bombs and torpedoes delivered by carrier-borne aircraft were far more effective than the long range gun.

Thus began the demise of the gun; all of the large ones had disappeared by the 1960's, accelerated in the 1970's with the introduction of the ship-to-ship and ship-to-air guided missiles. In the late 1970's the Type 22 frigates were built without any major gun armament at all, reliance being placed entirely on the missile systems embarked.

During the Falklands War of 1982, the usefulness of the 4.5 inch gun, fitted in many of the ships involved, was proved. Also proved was the inadequacy of the ships' close range weapons when enemy anti-ship missiles penetrated their long and intermediate range missile defences. As a result, the latest batch of Type 22 and the new Type 23 frigates now carry the 4.5 inch automatic gun and ships of all types have been fitted with extra close-in-weapons systems, consisting of rapid-fire guns.

And so in the missile age the gun lives on, as does the torpedo which, unlike its free running predecessor, is now a guided missile in its own right.

Until the advent of radio, the only real detection device was the eye; the lookouts either sighted the enemy's smoke, the flash of a gun or the track of a torpedo. Today there is a profusion of radio and acoustic devices, used both to detect the enemy or his weapons and to confuse him, not to mention methods of countering his own detection devices. Some defy description but the acronyms abound.

* * *

ABBEY HILL. A frigate electronic surveillance measures (ESM) system.

ACOUSTIC DECOY. A noise making device, towed by ships to disturb a submarines sonar and to distract homing torpedoes.

ADAAWS. Action Data Automated Weapons System. A computerised Action Information Organisation (AIO) for giving weapon direction facilities. There are various types of ADAAWS, the type fitted in a particular ship being dependent on the group of weapons to be controlled.

ADEN. The 30 mm cannon fitted in the Sea Harrier aircraft.

ADI. Action Data Information. An automated system of handling tactical information received by a ship's radar installation.

AGOUDI SYSTEM. A technique of ejecting air through the barrel of a ship's propellor shaft on to the propellers to confuse listening enemy submarines.

AIO. Action Information Organisation. A system controlled by ratings of the Radar category, which assists in the control of weapons and aircraft. Information is passed to the AIO from many sources such as radar, radio, sonar and visual sighting. The AIO ensures that all information is quickly and clearly displayed for the benefit of the commanding officer.

ALARM. Air Launched Anti-Radar Missile. A new missile under development for equipping the Sea Harrier FRS 2 and Lynx HAS 3/8 for suppressing enemy radar during deep penetration missions. The range is over 10 km.

AMRAAM. Advanced Medium-Range Air-to-Air Missile. At present under development in the USA for equipping the Sea Harrier FRS 2. The range of the missile is 25 km.

ASRAAM. Advanced Short-Range Air-to-Air Missile. A short range version of the AMRAAM at present under development in Europe for equipping the Sea Harrier FRS 2, as a replacement for the Sidewinder. The range of the missile is 5 km.

BATHYTHERMOGRAPH. Equipment fitted to ships to detect variations in water temperature in connection with determining the depth of surface ducts which cause refraction when using Sonar.

BLUE FOX. The search radar carried by the Sea Harrier aircraft which caters for air-to-air intercepts and air-to-surface attack operations.

BLUE KESTREL. The search radar which is to be fitted to the Anglo/Italian EH-101 helicopter to replace the Sea King helicopter. It is a 360 degree scan surveillance radar which exploits advanced digital data and signal processing techniques to cover a range of tasks, including search and rescue, anti-submarine and anti-surface vessel operations and over-the-horizon targeting.

BLUE VIXEN. A radar system designed for the Sea Harrier FRS 2 which gives for the first time a look down, shoot down capability.

BOFORS GUN. A 40 mm gun which originated from Sweden and which has been a standard anti-aircraft and general purpose mounting, both single and twin, in service in the RN since the Second World War. Only the Mk 7 and Mk 9 single mountings remain in service today; first introduced in 1946, the rate of fire in 300 rounds per minute with a range of 4 km.

CAAIS. Computer Assisted Action Information System. An AIO fitted to warships where weapon control is not required, being covered by a separate Weapon System Automation (WSA).

CACS. Command and Computer System. The system which controls and co-ordinates a ship's sensors and weapons, exchanging information with other friendly ships and aircraft by radio data links. The system is replacing ADAAWS and CAAIS.

CHAFF. Thin metal strips, dispensed from a rocket in a cloud, designed to produce false echoes on an enemy missile's radar seeker.

CIWS. Close-In Weapons Systems. A general term for guns employed for 'last ditch' defence, such as GOALKEEPER and PHALANX.

CORVUS LAUNCHER. An eight barrelled launcher fitted in RN ships for the Corvus broadband chaff rocket. The rocket dispenses metallised chaff strips, cut to match the operating frequency of a missile's radar seeker, in a cloud that masks the firing ship or appears in a place some distance from it.

DEPTH CHARGE. An old design, the Mk 11, is still carried in certain ships for use against submarines. A nuclear version is in existence, designed for use by a ship's helicopter at a considerable distance from the parent ship. Also for use by helicopters is the Mod 3 version of the British Aerospace Mk 2 depth bomb.

DIRECTOR. The name for the radar equipment associated with a missile or gunnery system. Before the days of radar, a 'director' consisted of an armoured, manned turret which contained optical range finding equipment.

DMT. Deep Mobile Target. A torpedo like device used for anti-submarine warfare training. It can be programmed to simulate the acoustic and automotive characteristics of a conventional submarine.

ECCM. Electronic Counter-Counter-Measures. The prevention of interference from friendly transmissions of radio and radar.

ECM. Electronic Counter-Measures. This is the use of radar intercept and jamming devices designed to counter enemy target indication, tracking and missile radars.

ESM. Electronic Surveillance Measures. Passive (undetectable) electronic measures used to intercept, analyse, classify and identify enemy radars.

EW. Electronic Warfare. The general term meaning the use of electronic means to confuse or confound the enemy; ECM, ECCM or ESM.

EXOCET MM38. A French made surface-to-surface missile with a sea-skimming approach, in service in RN ships. It has a range of approximately 23 nautical miles (42 km), being propelled by a two stage solid-fuel motor. The warhead contains approximately 363 lbs (165 kg) of high explosive.

The first missile to go into service with the RN was the Seaslug which was fitted in the 'County' class destroyers in the early 1960's. It disappeared when these ships finally paid off in the 1980's.

GOALKEEPER. A 30 mm rapid-fire cannon for close range anti-missile defence. The weapon is automatic with a range of one nautical mile and a rate of fire of 4,200 rounds per minute from seven barrels. The cannon is manufactured in the USA and the associated radar in the Netherlands.

GPMG. General Purpose Machine Gun. A 7.62 mm machine gun fitted on a special mounting in ships but mainly in patrol boats.

GUN, 4.5 INCH (114 MM) Mk 6. First introduced in 1946, this twin turret was once a common standard mounting in many ships, but now only found in the remaining Gun Leander frigates. The rate of fire is 20 rounds per barrel per minute with a range of 10 nautical miles (19 km).

GUN, 4.5 INCH (114 MM) MK 8. This gun, based on the Army's Abbot gun and introduced into the RN in 1971, is single barrelled and fully automatic. It is unmanned in action, the rate of fire is 25 rounds per minute and the range is approximately 12 nautical miles (22 km). The Mk 6 and Mk 8 4.5 inch (114 mm) guns are currently the largest calibre weapons in service.

GWS. Guided Weapon System. The control system for missiles:

GWS 22. The control system for Seacat missiles and, in Type 21 frigates, for gunnery control.

GWS 25. The control system for Sea Wolf missiles, incorporating the types 967 and 968 surveillance radars and the type 910 for guidance.

GWS 30. The control system for Sea Dart missiles, incorporating the type 909 radar for targeting and controlling.

HARPOON. A ship-launched, long range, anti-ship missile system to be fitted to Type 23 frigates. The missile itself is identical to the Sub-Harpoon submarine launched version and the range is 90 km.

IFF (IDENTIFICATION FRIEND OR FOE). A system which enables a radar operator to trigger a transponder in friendly aircraft to display identification marks on his radar scope.

JUBILEE GUARDSMAN. An IFF system fitted in the Sea King Helicopter.

LAPADS. Lightweight Acoustic Processing and Display System. A system which is carried in the Sea King anti-submarine helicopter which consists of passive sonobuoys which transmit to a multi-channel receiver in the aircraft the noises they hear which are analysed by computer.

LASER DAZZLE SIGHT. A dazzle device for use as a close-range deterrent against aircraft or surface craft. Its object is to cause confusion in a non-lethal way.

LIMBO MK 10. A triple-barrelled anti-submarine mortar, first fitted to RN ships in 1961, which has a range of 1,000 yards and is gyro stabilised. It is a development of the 'Squid', itself developed during the Second World War.

LAW 80. A lightweight anti-tank weapon in service with the Royal Marines which is effective against main battle tanks.

MAD. Magnetic Anomoly Detector. An anti-submarine detector fitted in Sea King and Lynx helicopters. The system detects small disturbances caused by submarines in the earth's magnetic field.

MADGE. A microwave guidance system fitted in the Sea Harrier aircraft which gives an aircraft carrier's FLYCO information on an approaching aircraft, including identity, range, height, relative bearing, fuel state, angle of attack and airspeed.

MATILDA. Microwave Analysis, Threat Indication and Launch Direction Apparatus. A countermeasures system linked to the Protean chaff dispenser system.

MINES. Three types of anti-ship mine are available for use in RN; submarine laid ground mine, air-dropped ground mine and acoustic moored mine.

MRS-3. The control system for 4.5 inch guns.

OERLIKON CANNON 30 MM. Two types of mounting employ this close-range weapon. Common in the RN is the GCM-AO3/BMARC, a twin mounting capable of firing 650 rounds per minute per barrel with a range of 2.2 nautical miles. A new single 30 mm mounting, the DS30B, uses the same cannon as that in the twin mounting and is gradually replacing both the Oerlikon 20 mm and Bofors 40 mm single mountings.

OERLIKON CANNON 20 MM. The single 20 mm mounting, type GAM-B01, has been common in most RN ships for a number of years. It has a range of 2.2 nautical miles and a rate of fire of up to 1200 rounds per minute.

ORANGE CROP. A passive ESM (Electronic Surveillance Measures) system carried in the Sea King and Lynx helicopter for identifying targets by their radio or radar transmissions.

OROPESA SWEEP. A towed system employed by minesweepers in order to ensnare mine cables and cut them. The towed cable is kept at a certain inclination relative to the ship by the use of a float and a submerged kite called an 'otter'. Once the mine cable is ensnared, the action of the towed cable draws the cable of the mine to a point on itself where an explosion takes place which cuts the mine cable. The mine is destroyed on the surface by gunfire or by demolition party.

Named after the ship in which it was first tried out in 1918.

OSBORNE SWEEP. See TAG.

OTO-MELARA 76 mm GUN. An Italian made, fully automatic single mounting with a rate of fire of 85 rounds per minute and a range of 9 nautical miles (16 km), fitted in Peacock Class offshore patrol vessels.

PAP-104. A French mine investigation and destruction vehicle carried by the latest minehunter ships. It is in effect a small unmanned, television equipped, remote controlled submarine.

PHALANX. The Vulcan Phalanx Close in Weapon System (CIWS). The system with its fully automatic radar, computer and gun, is designed for use if all other weapon systems have allowed an attacking missile past their defence. It consists of a multiple barrel Gatling type machine gun combined with a 'closed loop' spotting system which tracks both the weapon's own burst of fire and the target and continuously corrects the angular error between them.

It is a US weapon, first installed in the carrier *USS AMERICA* in 1980. The rate of fire is 3,000 rounds per minute with remarkable accuracy; only a metre of dispersion at 1,000 metres range. The ammunition is made up of depleted uranium, much heavier than lead and so possessing more kinetic energy to smash the target to pieces.

The original Gatling gun was the world's first practical machine gun, produced by Richard Jordan Gatling of the USA in 1862. The RN eventually adopted the gun in 1873 as a counter to attack by torpedo boats, produced by W. G. Armstrong of Newcastle-Upon-Tyne under licence. They were used most successfully by shore detachments, notably at the Battle of Tel-el-Kebir in the Anglo-Egyptian War of 1882. Here a naval party had put down a devastating fire where the enemy lost over 2,000 men for only 39 British killed.

POLARIS A3. A submarine launched intermediate-range ballistic missile, developed in the USA and deployed in the four RN SSBN's. It is powered by a two-stage solid propellant rocket motor and has a range of 2,500 nautical miles. A built-in inertial guidance system is fed by geo-ballistic and navigational computers on board the submarine until the moment of launch, after which the missile becomes entirely independant. It is armed with three *Chevaline* 60 kt nuclear warheads, each capable of tracking independently.

RADAR. Radio Detection and Range. A method of detecting ships and aircraft by transmitting radio waves and then receiving the waves bounced back from the target. The distance of a target is calculated by measuring the time taken for a wave to be sent out and returned, the results being displayed visually on a cathode ray tube.

Radar is an American word, adopted by the British during the Second World War. Prior to this it was known as RDF (radio direction finding).

SA-80. A 5.56 mm rifle/sub machine gun in service with the Royal Marines, replacing the 7.62 mm rifle and 9 mm sub machine gun. The ammunition is half the weight of the standard 7.62 mm ammunition.

SEA ARCHER 30. The director control system for the Mk 8 4.5 inch gun fitted in the Batch 3 Type 22 and Type 23 frigates. It is an electro-optical device incorporating a thermal imager, laser rangefinder and a TV camera.

SEA CAT. A close range anti-aircraft missile which can also be used against surface targets within visual range. It is propelled by solid fuel, its range is 4.75 km and its warhead is high explosive.

SEA DART. The missile used in the RN's GWS 30, a third generation air defence weapon system, capable of intercepting high and low flying aircraft and air and surface launched missiles. The Type 909 radar is used for targeting and control. Powered by a solid-fuel booster and a Rolls Royce Odin ramjet sustainer, the missile has a range of 16 nautical miles (30 km) and a warhead of high explosive.

SEA EAGLE. A medium weight, long range, sea skimming anti-ship missile carried by the Sea Harrier aircraft. The range is 30 km.

SEA GNAT. The standard NATO decoy chaff rocket launcher fitted in RN ships.

SEARCHLIGHT. The Type 170 Sonar, associated with the Limbo Mk 10 anti-submarine mortar.

SEARCHWATER. An advanced surveillance radar developed by Thorn-EMI carried by early warning Sea King helicopters. The system was originally developed for RAF Nimrod aircraft, but has been modified for the Sea King to detect aircraft at long range. The aerial is housed outside the Sea King in a 'bucket', a swivelling radome attached to the side of the aircraft.

SEA SEARCHER. A high power, long range radar system fitted to the Sea King HAS 5 helicopter which gives the ability to allow for over-the-horizon targetting of ship-launched missiles.

SEA SKUA. A medium range, semi-active, anti-ship homing missile carried by the Lynx helicopter. It homes on echoes from a target illuminated by the Lynx's Sea Spray radar.

This missile was the first anti-ship missile to sink a ship in combat when an Argentine patrol ship was sunk during the Falklands War.

SEA SPRAY. A lightweight radar, developed by Ferranti, fitted in the Lynx helicopter for detecting and tracking small craft.

SEA URCHIN. A multi-function ground mine.

SEAWOLF. The missile used in the RN's GWS 25, a short-range self defence missile system for use against aircraft and anti-ship missiles. It is propelled by a solid fuel motor, the warhead is high explosive and the range is 10 km. With the Type 910 fire control radar, the system is fully automatic. A vertical-launch version is to be fitted to the 'Duke' class Type 23 frigates.

SHIELD. The Plessey broadband chaff rocket decoy system, fitted in ships for use against a variety of anti-ship missiles.

SIDEWINDER. An infra-red homing air-to-air guided missile which is carried by Sea Harrier aircraft. It has a solid-fuel motor and a high explosive warhead.

The Sidewinder proved to be highly successful during the Falklands War when RN Sea Harriers scored sixteen confirmed kills and one probable with the missile.

SMALL ARMS. A collective term for rifles, sub-machine guns, pistols, etc.

SONAR. Sound Navigation And Ranging system, used for locating submerged submarines by acoustic transmissions. There are many types which may be hull-mounted systems or Variable Depth Sonar (VDS), used by surface ships and submarines. Dipping, or 'dunking' Sonar is also used by ship's helicopters.

The word 'sonar' was invented in 1942 by the US acoustics specialist F V Hunt, intended as a phonetic analogue to 'radar' (RAdio Detection and Ranging). It was originally defined as Sounding Navigation and Ranging, but later changed to Sound Navigation and Ranging.

The American term was adopted by the RN in the early 1950s, prior to which it had been known as 'asdic'.

It is commonly thought that asdic stood for Allied Submarine Detection Investigation Committee, however there is no evidence of any such committee having been in existence. In 1918 the term replaced that of the section heading of supersonics, dealing with acoustic detection experiments at Harwich. It almost certainly stood for pertaining to the Anti-Submarine Division (-ics), the Admiralty department that had initiated the research in this field.

SONOBUOY. An anti-submarine detector which is dropped into the sea from a helicopter. A pattern of Sonobouys are dropped across the presumed track of an enemy submarine and used to detect and amplify the underwater noise. A Sonobuoy scuttles itself after its mission.

SPEARFISH. The latest 21 inch submarine-launched torpedo, the Type 7525, a further development of the Tigerfish. It is wire guided and powered by a gas turbine working with a pumpjet to achieve high speed and a range of 21.6 nautical miles (40 km).

21 inch tubes were first fitted in 'D' class submarines in 1908 and this has been the calibre used ever since.

STARSHELL. A round fired from a gun which upon bursting at altitude gives a prolonged illuminating effect.

STINGRAY. A British 12.75 inch anti-submarine torpedo, similar to the US Mk 46 but having a more sophisticated homing head. It may be launched from the Lynx helicopter or from a ship's STWS.

STWS. Shipborne Torpedo Weapon System. This consists of three tubes mounted on either side of a ship, capable of launching by compressed air lightweight 12.75 inch homing torpedoes of the UK Mk 46 or Stingray type.

SUB HARPOON. A long range (90 km) anti-ship missile which is launched from a submerged submarine. It is fired from a torpedo tube conventionally by compressed air, after which it utilises its built-in turbojet and rocket motors to surface skim towards the target. Guidance is radar programmed and a 500 lb high-explosive or a thermonuclear warhead can be carried.

SUPER RBOC. Super Rapid-Blooming Off-board Countermeasures launching system. A system to launch chaff, flares and other decoy measures against radar or incoming infra-red guided anti-ship missiles.

SUPER SEARCHER. An improved version of the Sea Searcher radar system designed for the Sea King HA 6 helicopter.

TAG. The Sperry Osborne Towed Acoustic Generator. A towed device which generates wideband sound for dealing with acoustic mines, fitted in minesweepers.

TANS. The Decca Tactical Air Navigation System as fitted in the Lynx helicopter.

TIGERFISH. A 21 inch submarine-launched torpedo for use against other submarines or surface ships. This is a homing weapon, wire guided from the submarine in the initial stages of its approach but independantly completing the attack by the use of its own Sonar. Its range is 18.9 nautical miles (35 km).

Two Tigerfish, fired from HM Submarine *CONQUEROR*, sank the Argentine cruiser *GENERAL BELGRANO* on 2 May 1982.

TORPEDO, US MK 46. A 12.75 inch diameter surface ship or air-launched torpedo propelled by a five cylinder liquid fuelled motor and having an active-passive acoustic homing head. The range is 500 yards.

Originally 'torpedo' was the name given to underwater explosive charges which had no means of locomotion. They were in fact mines; cone shaped canisters of zinc, two feet long by 18 inches wide, filled with gunpowder and fired by the breaking of one of a set of glass detonators filled with acid. The 'locomotive torpedo', the forerunner of today's torpedo, was invented by Robert Whitehead in 1866 and was fired from small, fast 'torpedo boats'.

TRIDENT 2D5. A three-stage, solid fuel, submarine-launched ballistic missile which will replace the Polaris system currently deployed in the 'R' class nuclear submarines. The system will be carried in four new *VANGUARD* class SSBN's, each with sixteen launch tubes, with 32 warheads per missile. The range of the missile is 4,000 nautical miles.

VDS. Variable Depth Sonar. The Type 199 system which incorporates a transducer is towed in a closed body behind and below a ship. By allowing the detecting device to operate at various levels, the refractive effect of temperature gradients in the sea is overcome.

WALLOP BARRICADE. A countermeasures system for rapid defence against TV-guided missiles. It uses 57 mm rockets which provide clouds of dense metal smoke.

4

SHORE ESTABLISHMENTS

Until the middle of the 19th century there was no regular Royal Navy, the men were employed as required and paid off when a ship's commission ended. There was therefore little need to accommodate ratings ashore and floating hulks were used as receiving ships for new entries. In 1856 when continuous service engagements were introduced, no move was made to provide accommodation ashore for men awaiting draft or from ships re-fitting etc. One lobby of senior naval officer thought was that the hulks were the best place for the men.

During the years that followed the number of hulks in each of the naval ports increased as, additionally, the specialist training and boys' training ships were established. It was not until the turn of the century that the training ships were replaced by new schools ashore and the commodious barracks built at the ports of Portsmouth, Chatham and Devonport. All of the new shore establishments were commissioned as HM ships, in most cases taking the names of their predecessors afloat. The Royal Marines still use the term 'barracks' but RN barracks are now called 'accommodation centres'.

* * *

AEW HASLAR. The Admiralty Experimental Works at Haslar near Gosport which is concerned with the study of ship hull forms in the search for improving efficiency and also the testing of propellors and other equipment. Two ship tanks, respectively 475 and 886 feet in length and a large manoevering tank 400 feet long by 200 feet wide and 18 feet deep in which artificial sea states can be generated, are housed in the establishment for the testing of models.

In 1846 William Froude, at the age of 36, retired from his employment as civil engineer to devote the rest of his life to the study of ship behaviour. His early experiments with models were made in open water, mainly in the River Dart, but they could not be carried with sufficient accuracy although they did form the basis for later work. What he required was a large testing tank to provide controlled conditions.

Eventually in 1870 he was granted £2000 by the Admiralty to construct a covered model tank on his own land at Chelston Cross near Torquay and from 1882 the establishment was known as the AEW. Froude died in 1879 and his son Robert, who then took over his father's work, supervised the move in 1886 of the AEW to a new site at Hasler where it exists today.

AML HOLTON HEATH. The Admiralty Material Laboratory near Poole in Dorset.

ATTURM INSTOW. The Royal Marines Amphibious Trials and Training Unit at Instow near Plymouth.

BICKLEIGH BARRACKS. The base near Plymouth for 42 Commando Royal Marines.

BRITANNIA RNC. The Royal Naval College at Dartmouth where the initial training of all RN and WRNS officers and also naval officers from other countries is carried out.

In 1854, *HMS ILLUSTRIOUS* was allocated by the Admiralty as a training ship for boys. The training of the young ratings was a success and it was decided that young officers should be trained in a similar manner. And so in 1857 the Admiralty introduced a new scheme for the training of naval cadets. At first the cadets were mixed up with the ratings, but after a short time the ratings were transferred to another training ship.

The scheme became so successful that a larger ship soon became necessary and in 1858 the three-decker sailing ship of the line *BRITANNIA* was allocated. This was followed in 1869 by another three-decker, the *PRINCE OF WALES* and re-named *BRITANNIA*, which after a time in Portsmouth and a short stay in Portland, moved to the River Dart in Devon. She was later joined by the two-decker *HINDUSTAN* which was moored ahead and connected by a light bridge. In 1905 the training was moved ashore there at Dartmouth and the BRITANNIA RNC was founded. WRNS officer training moved from RNC Greenwich to BRNC Dartmouth in 1976.

CTCRM LYMPSTONE. The Royal Marines Commando Training Centre at Lympstone near Devon.

DEVONPORT DOCKYARD. The Royal Dockyard at Plymouth is situated on the Hamoaze overlooking Cornwall and is the largest ship repair yard in the British Isles. It was extensively reorganised in 1967 when it was allocated part of the responsibility for maintaining SSN's. It has an under-cover frigate re-fit complex and was the first dockyard with the feature of ships being able to enter or leave a complex under their own power.

Devonport Dockyard was originally founded as Plymouth Dockyard in 1689. Plymouth, being two miles away, was inconvenient as accommodation for the dockyard workers and so the local township of Plymouth Dock was established. The town first adopted the name Devonport in 1824, although the dockyard itself retained the earlier name. Eventually, in 1843 at the time of a visit made by Queen Victoria, the name of Devonport was transferred to the dockyard.

GIBRALTAR RNH. The Royal Naval Hospital at Gibraltar. It was opened in 1908 and was run by the Army until 1963 when the RN assumed responsibility for medical services on the Rock.

GREENWICH RNC. The Royal Naval College at Greenwich accommodates the Joint Service Defence College, the Royal Naval Staff College and the Department of Nuclear Science and Technology.

Originally the site of one of Queen Elizabeth's palaces, the college was formerly the Royal Naval Hospital, Greenwich, the inception of which was due to a decision of Queen Mary, wife of William III, to commemorate the Battle of Barfleur, fought in 1694. That year King William made a grant of part of the royal grounds at Greenwich for that purpose. The hospital opened in 1705 and was more of a rest home for wounded seamen pensioned off, the counterpart of the Army's

Chelsea Hospital. In 1869 all of the then existing inmates were given out-pensions and in 1873 the hospital became the RNC for the higher education of officers.

The Naval Staff College was moved there from Portsmouth Dockyard in 1919.

GUNWHARF. Formerly HMS VERNON the torpedo and underwater establishment in Portsmouth Harbour. VERNON was decomissioned in 1986, but the site still plays an important role in the Portsmouth Command under the control of NELSON and is officially known as NELSON (Gunwharf). It is the Fleet centre for Sonar and Mine warfare and the Fleet and Portsmouth Command Clearance Diving Teams are based there. Also accommodated are the RN Saturation Diving Team and the Experimental Diving Unit.

In 1867 a special section of the *EXCELLENT* gunnery school was formed for the study of torpedo warfare and the application of electrics to gunnery. The section was housed in the old frigate *VERNON*, a tender to the *EXCELLENT*. It soon became clear that torpedoes and electrics were more important than a mere offshoot of gunnery and in 1876 *VERNON* became an entirely separate and independent command. When the *EXCELLENT* establishment moved ashore to Whale Island and the gunnery school proved successful there, a similar plan was made for *VERNON*, this establishment moving ashore to the old gun wharf in Portsmouth Harbour.

HASLAR RNH. The Royal Naval Hospital at Gosport. Building began in 1746 and the first patients were admitted in 1753.

HMS CALEDONIA. The Royal Marine Engineering School at Rosyth.

HMS CALLIOPE. The headquarters of the Tyne Divsion of the RNR in Gateshead.

HMS CALPE. The RNR Communications Headquarters Unit at Gibraltar.

HMS CAMBRIA. The headquarters of the South Wales Division of the RNR at East Docks in Cardiff.

HMS CAMBRIDGE. The Royal Navy's Gunnery School at Wembury near Plymouth where all missile, gunnery, small arms and military training is carried out. The Devonport Command field gun crew train here.

The old sailing ship *CAMBRIDGE*, with the *FOUDROYANT* attached, was once moored at Devonport as the Gunnery School for the Western Divisions, the counterpart of the *EXCELLENT* at Portsmouth.

HMS CAMPERDOWN. The headquarters of the Tay Division of the RNR in Dundee.

HMS CAROLINE. The headquarters of the Ulster Division of the RNR in Belfast.

CAROLINE is in fact a real ship. Launched as a crusier in 1914, she eventually became a drill ship for the RNVR in 1926. She is the sole survivor of the Battle of Jutland.

HMS CENTURION. The shore establishment at Gosport which deals with pay and allowances, drafting and also provides personnel and management information from the computer systems installed there.

HMS CERES. The RNR Communications Training Centre in Leeds.

HMS CLAVERHOUSE. The headquarters of the Forth Division of the RNR in Edinburgh.

HMS COCHRANE. The Fleet Accommodation Centre at Rosyth which was purpose-built in 1968.

The establishment is named after Admiral Thomas Cochrane, 10th Earl of Dundonald. In the early stages of his career in the Royal Navy he made enemies of his superiors and when promoted to command in 1801, instead of being given the usual sloop-of-war, he was snubbed by being appointed to the brig *SPEEDY*, armed with only 4-pounder guns. However, with his great skill and daring, he captured so many Spanish ships that the 32-gun frigate *EL GAMO* was sent out especially to look for him. Cochrane escaped, but on the next occasion of meeting the *EL GAMO* he captured her, a feat which brought him world fame.

Following an alleged complicity in a Stock Exchange swindle, he was disgraced and his RN rank and honours were taken away from him. He then went on to become a 'sailor of fortune', first taking command of the Chilean Navy in 1818, the Peruvian Navy in 1820 and in 1823 the Brazilian Navy, achieving huge successes against the Spanish and Portuguese and doing much towards helping the countries gain their independence. Some years later, in England, the previous charges against him were withdrawn and he was re-instated in the RN as an admiral.

HMS COLLINGWOOD. The RN weapon engineering and explosives school situated between Portsmouth and the Royal Naval Air Station at Lee-on-Solent. Weapon Electrical Mechanical (WEM) ratings and some Marine Engineering Mechanical (MEM) ratings are trained there.

This shore establishment was originally built in 1939 to train new entry 'hostilities only' ratings of the seaman branch. It is named after Admiral Lord Collingwood who led the lee line fleet at Trafalgar and took over command on the death of Lord Nelson.

HMS DAEDALUS. The Royal Naval Air Station at Lee-on-Solent where technical training of the Fleet Air Arm is carried out. It is at this station that the Fleet Air Arm Command Field Gun Crew train.

Opened in 1917 as HM Naval Seaplane School. Following the amalgamation of the RNAS and the RFC to form the RAF, the station was taken over by the Air Ministry. In 1939 the navy again took control of the base when it was commissioned HMS DAEDALUS.

HMS DALRIADA. The Inverkip Headquarters Unit of the RNR in Greenock.

HMS DEFIANCE. The submarine base at Devonport which is part of the Fleet Maintenance complex there. It is the home of the Second Submarine Squadron consisting of SSN and SSK boats.

Following the success of *VERNON* as the torpedo school moored in Portsmouth Harbour, the *DEFIANCE* became the Western Divisions' counterpart in Plymouth Harbour in 1884.

HMS DOLPHIN. The submarine base at Gosport which is the home of the First Submarine Squadron, all non-nuclear boats. The RN Submarine School is situated here as is the Submarine Escape School and the Submarine Museum.

The previous *HMS DOLPHIN* was an old sailing ship which from 1906 to 1923 provided headquarters facilities to the first submarine boat station which was established at Gosport in 1905.

HMS DRAGON. The RNR Communications Training Centre in Swansea.

HMS DRAKE. The Fleet Accommodation Centre at Devonport Naval Base.

The original buildings there, some of which still exist, were named Naval Barracks Keyham and completed in 1889. They eventually acquired the name HMS VIVID after the Commander-in-Chief's yacht. In 1934 the barracks were commissioned as HMS DRAKE, the 24th ship to bear the name.

HMS DRYAD. The Maritime Tactical School situated ten miles to the north of Portsmouth on the South Downs. Radar and Electronic Warfare (EW) training is carried out here.

HMS DRYAD was originally commissioned in 1906 as the Royal Navy's Navigation School which was transferred to HMS MERCURY in 1977.

HMS EAGLET. The headquarters of the Mersey Division of the RNR at Princes Dock in Liverpool.

HMS FOREST MOOR. A Fleet Communications and Transmitting Station situated at Darley near Harrogate in Yorkshire.

HMS FORWARD. The RNR Communications Training Centre in Birmingham.

HMS FLYING FOX. The headquarters of the Severn Division of the RNR in Bristol.

HMS GANNET. The Royal Naval Air Station at Prestwick International Airport which operates Sea King helicopters.

GANNET was commissioned in 1971, taking over the former USAF base at Prestwick. The previous GANNET was RNAS Eglington in Northern Ireland, commissioned in 1943 and closed in 1958.

HMS GRAHAM. The headquarters of the Clyde Division of the RNR in Glasgow.

HMS HALLAM. The RNR Communications Training Centre in Sheffield.

HMS HERON. The Royal Naval Air Station at Yeovilton in Somerset, the headquarters of the Flag Officer Naval Air Command. The station houses the Aircraft Direction School, the Air Training Section, the Sea Harrier training Ski-jump, the RN Flight Safety Centre and the Fleet Air Arm Museum. 3 Commando Brigade Air Squadron Royal Marines are also located here.

The airfield has been on this site since the Fleet Air Arm commenced fighter training there in 1940.

HMS HOWARD. The 'ship' to which RN officers and ratings are assigned when serving as liason personnel with the Royal Canadian Navy in Ottawa.

HMS INSKIP. A Royal Naval Communications and Transmitting Station situated on the Fylde Peninsula, near Preston in Lancashire.

The station was commissioned in 1958. It was originally the Royal Naval Air Station HMS NIGHTJAR.

HMS MALABAR. The RN establishment on Ireland Island, Bermuda.

The Royal Dockyard on Ireland Island, established in 1814, was closed in 1951.

HMS MERCIA. The RNR Communications Training Centre in Coventry.

HMS MERCURY. The RN Communications and Navigation School near Petersfield. It is due to close in 1992.

Commissioned in 1941 and the twelfth ship to bear the name *MERCURY*.

HMS NELSON. The Fleet Accommodation Centre for the Portsmouth area situated in Portsmouth Naval Base. It also houses the RN school of Educational and Training Technology and the Dental Training School.

Under the control of NELSON are the decommissioned gunnery and torpedo establishments EXCELLENT and VERNON, now known as NELSON (Whale Island) and NELSON (Gunwharf). (See WHALE ISLAND and GUNWHARF.)

Originally the Portsmouth Royal Naval Barracks (RNB), completed in 1903 to accommodate the men from the old depot ships *VICTORY* and *WELLINGTON* in the harbour there. The barracks were named VICTORY by order of Edward VII as it was thought that Nelson's flagship was about to decay. However, the ship was saved for restoration and so there were two VICTORY's known as '*VICTORY* ship' and 'VICTORY barracks'. Eventually in 1974 the shore establishment was renamed NELSON.

HMS NEPTUNE. The submarine base at Faslane on the Clyde.

The establishment was commissioned in 1967 following the Nassau Agreement on the Polaris for the Royal Navy. The barracks there, to which all personnel are appointed, is named NEPTUNE but the whole of the Clyde base is known as the NEPTUNE Complex, which includes the dockyard area, the Armament Depot at Coulport on Loch Long and other associated areas. The 3rd Submarine Squadron, made up of SSN and SSK boats, is based there and also the 10th Squadron; the SSBN Polaris boats. NEPTUNE houses the RN Polaris School, the Submarine Attack Teacher and the Propulsion Plant Control Trainer.

HMS NORTHWOOD. The RNR Headquarters Unit at Northwood in Middlesex. The unit operates in support of CINCFLEET and CINCHAN regular and NATO forces based at HMS WARRIOR.

HMS OSPREY. The Royal Naval Air Station at Portland and also the base establishment for all naval personnel serving at the naval base there. HM Ships carry out sea training from Portland and there is a Fleet Maintenance Group there, but no dockyard facilities.

The Air Station was commissioned in 1959 and has always been involved with helicopter operations, there being no main runway.

HMS PALATINE. The RNR Communications Training Centre in Preston.

HMS PARAGON. The RNR Communications Training Centre in Stockton.

HMS PELLEW. The RNR Communications Training Centre in Exeter.

HMS PHOENIX. The Fleet Damage Control and NBC (Nuclear, Biological and Chemical) School at Portsmouth, actually now a part of NELSON.

HMS PRESIDENT. The headquarters of the London Division of the RNR at King's Reach in London.

PRESIDENT is in fact a floating ship. Launched in 1918 as *HMS SAXIFRAGE*, a 'flower' class sloop, she was re-named *PRESIDENT* after the First World War to become the nominal base ship of the Admiralty in London and also a drill ship for the RNVR.

HMS RALEIGH. The training establishment for all new entrants to the RN. Basic (Part I) training is given to all ratings before they begin their Part II training in the specialist schools. Seaman Operation branch ratings remain in RALEIGH for their Part II training.

Until the middle of the 19th century no training ships for new entries existed; a boy went straight to sea, to be placed under the wing of an old hand. As a result of the Admiralty Committee on manning of 1853, two ships for training young seamen were allocated; *ILLUSTRIOUS* at Portsmouth in 1854 and *IMPLACABLE* at Devonport in 1855. A Royal Commission on manning in 1859 recommended further training ships and four large ships were set aside for the training of boys: *ST VINCENT* at Portsmouth, *BOSCOWAN* at Portland and *IMPREGNABLE* and *GANGES* at Devonport. Later in 1869 *FORMIDABLE* lay off Portishead Pier in North Somerset (Avon) as an additional boys' training ship. Eventually, schools ashore replaced all of these ships. The *GANGES*, because of her teak construction, lasted the longest, ending her career at Shotley, Suffolk before finally being broken up in 1929.

The main new entry shore establishments for many years were the GANGES at Shotley and ST VINCENT at Portsmouth. RALEIGH was first commissioned in 1940 as a shore training establishment for RN seamen, but was later taken over temporarily by the United States Navy for pre-invasion operations and accommodation. In 1971 the site was completely re-developed to cater for all entrants to the RN and in 1981 WRNS new entry training moved from DAUNTLESS at Burghfield near Reading to RALEIGH. Following the closure of PEMBROKE RN Barracks at Chatham, the RN Supply School was established in RALEIGH in 1983.

HMS ROOKE. The shore establishment at Gibralter which provides base support facilities for visiting warships.

The establishment is named after Admiral Sir George Rooke who defeated the Spanish and captured 'the Rock' in 1704. The dry dock and mole at Gibraltar were constructed in 1900. The dockyard, the last of the foreign dockyards, was closed in 1984.

HMS ROYAL ARTHUR. The RN Ratings Leaderships School at Corsham in Wiltshire.

During the Second World War ROYAL ARTHUR was the name of the new entry induction centre at Corsham and later in the former Butlin's holiday camp at Skegness.

HMS SAKER. The 'ship' to which RN officers and ratings are assigned when serving as liason personnel with the United States Navy in Washington.

HMS SALFORD. The RNR Communications Training Centre in Manchester.

HMS SCOTIA. The Rosyth Headquarters Unit of the RNR in Dunfermline, Fife.

HMS SEAHAWK. The Royal Naval Air Station at Culdrose, near Helston in Cornwall on the Lizard Peninsular. This, the largest RNAS, is the parent station for four operational Sea King Squadrons and all helicopter flying training is carried out there.

SEAHAWK was commissioned in 1947 as the Naval Air Fighter School. In 1953 it became the centre for operational anti-submarine and observer training.

HMS SHERWOOD. The RNR Communications Training Centre in Nottingham.

HMS SOUTHWICK. The Southwick Headquarters Unit of the RNR in Portsmouth.

HMS SULTAN. The RN school of Marine Engineering near Gosport.

SULTAN was commissioned in 1956 having been built on the site of a former First World War airfield.

HMS SUSSEX. The headquarters of the Sussex Division of the RNR in Hove.

HMS TAMAR. The headquarters of the Captain-in-Charge Hong Kong, formerly the Army's Wellington Barracks which were transferred to the RN in 1946 and since rebuilt.

The original *HMS TAMAR* was a barque-rigged troopship secured to a buoy off the dockyard. In 1913 she was moved alongside the West Wall and remained there until she was scuttled in advance of the Japanese occupation in 1941.

HMS TEMERAIRE. The RN School of Physical Training in Burnaby Road, Portsmouth.

The original School was founded at Pitt Street, Portsmouth in 1903 and moved to new premises in 1988.

HMS THUNDERER. The RN Engineering College at Manadon where the education and training of engineer officers to degree level is carried out. In addition, students are able to take further courses in naval or areonautical engineering, underwater technology, marine defence technology and computer sciences.

The college was originally established at Keyham near Plymouth in 1880. Keyham steam yard with a massive complex of storehouses and foundries had been completed in 1853. The college moved to its present site in 1940 and commissioned as THUNDERER.

HMS VICTORY. The Flagship of the Commander-in-Chief Naval Home Command, still in commission and permanently preserved in dry dock in Portsmouth Naval Base.

Launched at Chatham in 1778 *VICTORY* is famous as Nelson's flagship at the Battle of Trafalgar in 1801. She remained afloat until 1922 when she was moved to her present position.

HMS VIVID. The Maritime Headquarters of the Flag Officer Plymouth in his NATO role of COMPLYMCHAN and COMCENTLANT at Mount Wise between Plymouth and Devonport.

HMS VULCAN. The Naval Reactor Test Establishment at Dounreay, Caithness.

HMS WARRIOR. The joint Headquarters of the Commander-in-chief Fleet and NATO Maritime Headquarters at Northwood in Middlesex.

The land which is now the Northwood HQ was originally purchased by the Air Ministry in 1937 for a

Royal Air Force HQ. When the need for a NATO command centre arose, this proved to be a suitable place.

HMS WESSEX. The headquarters of the Solent Division of the RNR at Eastern Docks in Southampton.

HMS WILDFIRE. The RNR Communications Training Centre in Chatham.

INM ALVERSTOKE. The Institute of Naval Medicine which was formed in 1969. Situated near the RN Hospital at Haslar in Gosport it carries out research in naval medicine and provides operational medical research and specialised medical training.

PLYMOUTH RNH. The Royal Naval Hospital at Stonehouse which was built between 1758 and 1762.

PORTSMOUTH NAVAL BASE. A major base and operating port of the Royal Navy, containing a Fleet Maintenance Group facility. There are three basins there which all have several docks leading off them and there is also a floating dry dock.

The former Royal Dockyard at Portsmouth, closed in 1984, was in existence for over 700 years, the first British dry dock being established there in 1496.

RM CONDOR. Royal Marines CONDOR at Arbroath in Scotland, where 45 Commando Group is located.

Prior to the Royal Marines moving here this was HMS CONDOR, a Royal Naval Air Station and thus is the only RM establishment with a ship name.

RM DEAL. Royal Marines Deal in Kent, the headquarters of the RM Band Service which provide the bands for certain RN shore establishments and HM Yacht *BRITANNIA*.

Bands had existed in the Royal Navy from a very early day, though composed mostly of foreigners. It was not until 1846 that the Admiralty officially recognised the naval rating of 'bandsman'. So many Royal Marines were attracted to the naval bands that in 1903 the provision of bands for service both in ships and ashore was entrusted to the Corps and the School of Music formed at Eastney. The school remained there until 1930 when it was transferred to Deal. All large ships carried RM bands until the demise of these vessels.

RM EASTNEY. Royal Marines Eastney near Portsmouth, the administration centre for RM Training and Reserves. The Corps Museum is also located here.

RM NORTON MANOR CAMP. Situated near Taunton in Somerset, this is the base of 40 Commando Royal Marines.

RM POOLE. Royal Marines Poole where all RM amphibious training is carried out.

ROSYTH DOCKYARD. The Royal Dockyard at Rosyth is situated above the Forth Bridge on the northern shore of the firth near Inverkeithing. It is a re-fitting base for nuclear submarines and frigates. The frigate complex incorporates a syncrolift which has replaced the three 1,000 ton floating docks.

Becoming first operational in 1916, the dockyard played a major part in the repair of the ships damaged in the Battle of Jutland. Between the wars it was placed in care and maintenance and re-opened in 1938. In 1963 the location was chosen as the first re-fitting base for nuclear submarines, the first of which arrived for refit in 1970.

ROYAL CLARENCE YARD. HM Victualling Depot at Gosport.

ROYAL ELIZABETH YARD. HM Victualling Depot at Kirkliston in Scotland.

ROYAL WILLIAM YARD. HM Victualling Depot at Plymouth.

STONEHOUSE BARRACKS. Situated at Plymouth, this Royal Marines establishment is the Headquarters of 3 Commando Brigade RM and the Mountain and Arctic Warfare Cadre RM. These, the first of the RM barracks, were built in 1784.

WHALE ISLAND. Formerly HMS EXCELLENT, the Gunnery and Naval Leadership School in Portsmouth Harbour. EXCELLENT was de-commissioned in 1976 but the island still plays an important role in the Portsmouth Command under the control of NELSON and is officially called NELSON (Whale Island). Currently using the facilities there are the Portsmouth Command Field Gun Crew, the RN Regulating School, the Ship Firefighting School, the RN Divisional and Management

School and also facilities are provided for HM Yacht *BRITANNIA*.

During the Napoleonic Wars, British gunnery was greatly superior to the French and Spanish. All battles were fought at such close range that it was almost impossible to miss the target. Because the enemy were largely blockaded in their ports, the British captains were well practised in ship handling and their ship's companies in working their ships and guns, they fired at least three broadsides to the enemy's two.

The American War of 1812, however taught the Royal Navy a lesson. The Americans had very few ships, but they were good ships, on the whole armed with more big guns which were accurate to longer ranges. They trained their crews to load and fire as fast as the British and also to aim their guns carefully. The captains handled their ships so as to keep the range open. Thus the Royal Navy suffered a number of defeats.

Nothing was done to remedy the state of the navy's gunnery until 1829 when Commander George Smith sent a plan for improvement to the Admiralty. He suggested that an establishment be set up for the training of gun's crews and for the testing and evaluation of new gunnery equipment. As a result, in 1830 the 74-gun *EXCELLENT*, which had been Collingwood's ship at the battle of St. Vincent in 1797, was moored in a position in Portsmouth harbour off the north corner of the dockyard. From here the guns could be fired across the mudflats without endangering anyone. In 1843 the *EXCELLENT* was replaced by the *BOYNE*, herself being replaced by the *QUEEN CHARLOTTE* in 1859. The old ship was broken up in 1835, but all were called *EXCELLENT*.

Close by the ship were two mudbanks, called on the chart 'Waley', which the Admiralty had bought in 1853 for use by the gunnery school and in 1859 a rifle range was constructed on one of them. By 1864 the names of the islands had been changed to the better sounding 'Big Whale Island' and 'Little Whale Island' and a 'house that Jack built' erected on one of them. In the following years the land between the two islands was reclaimed and the whole of 'Whale Island' extended by the use of convict labour. A thousand convicts were engaged to level off with spoil from the new dockyard extention. Finally in 1891 the old ship paid off and all hands came ashore.

5

RANKS, RATES AND JOBS

Edward the Confessor in 1040 instituted the system under which the Cinque Ports, in return for exemption from taxation, appointment of judges, etc., furnished the Crown with a given number of vessels for war purposes. All these were provided with the mariners to manage them, while the fighting was done by soldiers who were embarked for the purpose. The officers of the soldiers were commissioned by the King.

In the process of time the ship's officers, the master, purser, gunner, boatswain, carpenter, etc., received the equivalent of a commission, namely a warrant from the different authorities upon whom the administration of naval affairs, from time to time, depended. Later, the 'standing officers', the purser, boatswain, carpenter, gunner and cook, received their warrants from the Admiralty direct, as the executive board, while the master, surgeon, chaplain and inferior officers were warranted by the Navy Office.

In the 15th century the methods of fighting began to slowly change and the soldiers were eventually no longer required. However, those of the soldier officers who had been most intimately connected with the sea attached themselves entirely to the naval service. Gradually they assumed the functions of command of ships as well as men, until by the early part of the 19th century they had absorbed all of the naval executive functions and posts connected. Some classes of the warrant officers; masters, surgeons, chaplains, schoolmasters, paymasters and finally engineers, all passed to commissioned rank. Other classes; master-at-arms, sailmaker, ropemaker, armourer, armourer's mate and ship's cook, dropped back 'before the mast' to become 'petty officers'.

As for the hands, in a sailing ship the cream of the able and ordinary seamen worked aloft on the masts. Older able and ordinary seamen worked on the forecastle and quarterdeck. Then there were the waisters; infirm or old seamen and landsmen, who worked in the waist of the ship carrying out menial tasks such as swabbing decks and hauling. Daymen, or idlers, where the artisans; they worked regular hours during the day and were not allocated to parts of ship or watches.

These jobs of the crew remained more or less static for centuries, but then steam came along, superceding wind for motive power, and the new rating of stoker was introduced. The eventual effect of this was that most of the skills of the true sailor were no longer required. However, he was far from redundant; as time progressed further into the technological age he was required to combine new skills with those of seafaring.

* * *

ABLE SEAMAN (AB). The rating next above ordinary seaman and below that of leading seaman, one who is 'able' to carry out all of the duties of a seaman. There is no distinguishing badge of rate.

Originally an 'able rate' referred to a man who was able to 'hand, reef and steer'.

ACTING RATE. Advancements to leading rate and petty officer are on an acting basis, a man being required to serve for 12 months from date of rating before being confirmed in the advanced rate.

ACTIVE LIST. The list of officers actively employed in the Royal Navy.

In the 19th century the Navy was suffering from the long stagnation of the officers' promotion lists; senior officers would still be deemed active at advanced ages and could be called for service. There were three purges of captains; in 1847, 1851 and again in 1864, but it was not until 1870 that the Navy List was divided into 'active' and 'retired' officers.

ADMIRAL. The rank above that of vice-admiral and below that of admiral-of-the-fleet. One broad band of gold lace with three narrower ones above are worn on the uniform cuffs. (OF. 'amiral' from the arabic 'amiral-bahr', prince or commander of the sea.)

In 1649, at the time of Oliver Cromwell as Protector of the Kingdom, the Council of State appointed Army officers as 'Generals at Sea' to command the Navy. During the reign of Charles II the name was changed to 'Admiral' in order to distinguish the Navy from the Army.

ADMIRAL-OF-THE-FLEET. The most senior rank in the RN. One broad band of gold lace with four narrower ones above are worn on the uniform cuffs.

Up to 1863, with a few special exceptions, the rank was held only by the senior admiral in the Navy. By that time the Army had three field-marshalls and so from then on three admirals-of-the-fleet were allowed. In 1870 it was decided to retire admirals-of-the-fleet at age 70, leaving three always on the active list. The number on both active and retired lists increased as a result of promotions during the First and Second World Wars. All admirals-of-the-fleet on the retired list in 1940 were replaced on the active list to conform with Army practice in respect of field-marshalls who never retired. Admirals-of-the-fleet therefore now remain on the active list for life.

ADMIRALTY BOARD. This board is responsible to the Sovereign and Parliament for the administration of the Royal Navy. The government is represented on this board by the Under-Secretary of State for Defence and the Under-Secretary of State (Royal Navy). They are assisted by the naval members of the board, all admirals or vice-admirals, each of which is allotted certain responsibilities in the general administration of the Royal Navy.

Formerly the 'Board of Admiralty', originally established as the 'Navy Board' in the 16th Century to control the administration of the Navy. In 1964 a unified Ministry of Defence was formed, within which the Board of Admiralty became the Admiralty Board of the Defence Council.

ADVANCEMENT. The progress of a rating through the rates to petty officer.

AIRCRAFT CONTROLLER. An officer of the seaman branch responsible for the guidance and safety of aircraft in a ship.

AIR ENGINEERING OFFICER (AEO). Responsible for the operational performance of aircraft and air weapons.

ANCHOR WATCH. A party utilised, when at anchor in bad weather, to watch for signs of the anchor dragging.

ANTI-AIR WARFARE OFFICER (AAWO). The officer in a ship carrying air defence weapons of fixed wing aircraft, delegated with authority to conduct the air battle. He is subordinate to the Principle Warfare Officer (PWO).

ARTIFICER. A skilled rating of the Engineering Branch who is trained in one of nine categories within three sub-branches:

MEA	Marine Engineering Artificer (Electrical or Mechanical).
WEA	Weapon Engineering Articifer (Action Data, Communications and Electronic Warfare, Ordnance Control or Weapon Data).
AEA	Air Engineering Articifer (Mechanical, Radio or Weapon Electrical).

ARTIFICER APPRENTICE. In 1906 *HMS FISGARD* was commissioned as a training ship for boy artificers. The title of these trainees was changed to artificer apprentice in 1920.

ASSISTANT CHIEF OF DEFENCE STAFF (ACDS). Three senior Ministry of Defence appointments are held by rear-admirals as ACDS to deal with naval affairs. Their individual titles are ACDS Operational Requirements (Sea Systems), ACDS (Programmes) and ACDS (Overseas).

ASSISTANT CHIEF OF NAVAL STAFF. A rear-admiral appointed to the staff of the Chief of Naval Staff.

AVIATION OFFICER. The officer responsible for aviation in a frigate or other warship carrying a helicopter.

BOARDING OFFICER. An officer of sub-lieutenant rank or above directed to take charge of a boarding party.

BOARDING PARTY. A party detailed to board another ship or vessel.

BOATSWAIN'S MATE. Pronounced 'Bo'sun's Mate'. Really an assistant to the Quartermaster. His jobs include the passing of orders over the ship's broadcast system, making pipes using the boatswain's call and assisting in gangway security.

When navigation was chiefly confined to the coast the 'boatswain' was in charge of the ship and sailors. Then, as the needs of navigation increased, the master, of superior skill, filled the place and the boatswain became merely a storekeeper chosen from the older sailors. Later, with the growth of a permanent force, the boatswain rose again in importance; he and the newly appointed gunner being next to the captain and master, the chief fighting officers in a ship. When he gave the necessary orders for the motion of the ship, his mates passed them on.

Eventually came steam, with the engineer superceding the boatswain as responsible for motive power, the latter only being left looking after the boats and ground tackle. The centuries old title of boatswain was abolished in the 1970s, but the job of the boatswain's mate is still in being. (Boatswain from OE 'bat', boat and 'swan', servant from ON 'sveinn', boy.)

BOATSWAIN'S YEOMAN. A seaman specialist in sailmaking and other seamanship skills. A key senior rating in survival at sea, firefighting, damage control and a variety of evolutions such as towing disabled ships.

CABLE PARTY. A party of special sea dutymen who are mustered when it is required for the ship to anchor or weigh anchor, come to or leave a buoy, or when entering or leaving harbour.

CAPTAIN. The rank above that of commander and below that of rear-admiral. Four narrow bands of gold lace are worn on the uniform cuffs. Also the title of the commanding officer of any naval ship, irrespective of his rank. A ship of sufficient importance to warrant command by a full captain is known as a 'post' ship; the captain being known as a 'post' captain. (F. 'capitaine' from L. 'caput', head.)

The rank dates from the 14th century but in those days the captain was a military officer, not a ship's captain in the modern sense; the master was the nearest equivalent.

CAPTAIN (D). The senior captain of a destroyer squadron, the squadron commander. Similarly, Captain (F) for a frigate squadron, Captain (H) for the surveying flotilla and Captain (SM) for a submarine squadron.

CAPTAIN OF THE SIDE. The rating in charge of the side party, responsible for the general appearance of the ship's side.

CAPTAIN OF THE TOP. The petty officer in charge of a part of ship.

The term 'top' comes from the days of sail; it was a sort of platform surrounding the head of the lower mast and projecting on all sides, serving to extend the shrouds and for the convenience of the men.

The crew of a 'ship of the line' with three masts, were divided into foc'slemen, foretopmen, maintopmen, mizzentopmen, quarterdeckmen, waisters and daymen or idlers. The topmen worked aloft on the masts and yards.

CAPTAIN'S SECRETARY. The officer in charge of the Captain's Office.

CASING PARTY. The party employed outside on the 'deck' of a submarine when entering or leaving harbour.

CATERING ACCOUNTANT. A rating of the Supply and Secretariat Branch trained in provision accounting and storeroom control.

CHAPLAIN. Chaplains serve in shore establishments and in the larger warships. They have officer status and may wear an officers' style uniform with no badges of rank, but this is optional. Until the First World War chaplains belonged only to the Church of England, but since then Roman Catholic and non-conformist chaplains have entered the Fleet.

Chaplains have served in ships from very early times, but originally they were classed as ratings despite their social position and education. In 1812 a 'chaplain's charter' was introduced, giving the chaplain a code of duties and, although still regarded as a civilian, he was accepted into the wardroom. It was at this time that the custom was abolished under which warrant officers, petty officers and men had been compelled to support chaplains in both pay and pensions by a contribution of fourpence per individual per month.

Later, in 1843, it was decided that the status of the chaplain should be that of commissioned officer, at the same time as other odd members of the crew including the schoolmaster, but with no rank and no uniform. A uniform was introduced in 1914 but few liked it, it was discontinued in 1918 and resurrected again in 1939.

CHAPLAIN OF THE FLEET. The head of the Chaplain's branch has been known since 1879 as the 'Chaplain of the Fleet'. Since 1902 he has also held, under the Archbishop of Canterbury, the title of Archdeacon of the Royal Navy.

CHARGE CHIEF PETTY OFFICER (CCPO). A higher rate of CPO, introduced in 1985 for artificers only, intended to overcome a shortage of a technical management.

CHIEF BOATSWAINS MATE. A senior rating of the seaman group responsible for upper deck maintenance. Also known as the 'buffer'.

CHIEF COMMANDANT WRNS. The Princess Anne, the rank being equivalent to rear-admiral.

CHIEF COMMUNICATIONS YEOMAN (CCY). A chief petty officer who is in charge of the tactical communications department in a ship.

CHIEF NAVAL INSTRUCTOR OFFICER. A senior appointment held by a rear-admiral; the head of the Instructor Branch.

CHIEF OFFICER. A WRNS rank equivalent to Commander RN.

CHIEF OF FLEET SUPPORT. A member of the Admiralty Board and responsible for the maintenance and repair of the fleet and for all logistic support. He holds the rank of vice-admiral.

CHIEF OF NAVAL PERSONNEL. The Second Sea Lord who is a member of the Admiralty Board and responsible for the recruiting and administration of officers, ratings, the Royal Marines and the WRNS, including the Reserves, and all matters relating to them regarding manning, training and welfare. He holds the rank of admiral.

CHIEF OF NAVAL STAFF. The First Sea Lord who is a member of the Admiralty Board and is the principle adviser to the government on naval affairs. He holds the rank of admiral and is assisted by the Vice-Chief of Naval Staff.

CHIEF OF STAFF TO COMMANDER ALLIED NAVAL FORCES SOUTHERN EUROPE. A Senior NATO appointment held by a vice-admiral of the Royal Navy.

CHIEF OF STAFF TO COMMANDER-IN-CHIEF. Both of the Commanders-in-Chief; C-in-C Fleet and C-in-C Naval Home Command, each have one rear-admiral appointed as chief of staff.

CHIEF PETTY OFFICER (CPO). The rating above that of petty officer and below that of warrant officer. It was instituted in 1853 following an Admiralty Committee report on manning. Three gilt buttons are worn across each cuff, but no other arm badges. Badges denoting branch or specialist qualification are worn on the jacket collar, except in the case of articifer CPOs.

CHIEF RADIO SUPERVISOR (CRS). A chief petty officer who is in charge of the radio department in a ship.

CHIEF STAFF OFFICER (ENGINEERING) TO COMMANDER-IN-CHIEF FLEET. A senior appointment held by a rear-admiral.

CHIEF STRATEGIC SYSTEMS EXECUTIVE. A senior appointment held by a rear-admiral.

CLEARANCE DIVER. Divers trained in demolition, rendering mines safe, underwater rescue and salvage and examination of ships below waterline.

COMMANDANT. A WRNS rank equivalent to Commodore RN.

COMMANDANT GENERAL ROYAL MARINES (CGRM). A lieutenant-general RM who commands the Corps of Royal Marines. He is not a member of the Admiralty Board but he advises the Board on all amphibious and RM matters.

COMMANDANT ROYAL COLLEGE OF DEFENCE STUDIES. A senior appointment held by an admiral. The college is situated in Belgrave Square, London and is attended by senior officers and officials from the UK, the Commonwealth, NATO and certain other nations. A rear-admiral is also appointed as Senior Naval Member.

COMMANDER. The rank above that of lieutenant-commander and next below captain. Three narrow bands of gold lace are worn on the uniform cuffs. In a large ship, the executive branch commander is the second in command and is known as 'the Commander' (see also EXECUTIVE OFFICER). The commanding officer of a small warship such as a frigate is an officer of commander's or lieutenant-commander's rank. (OF. 'comander' from L. 'comander', 'com' and 'mandare', to entrust.)

Up until the middle of the 18th century the captain of a non-post ship had to qualify as master and carry out his own navigation, whereas a post ship carried a fully qualified master. In 1746 'second master' was introduced into non-post ships to relieve the captain of the navigation duties. From this, in 1794, the title 'commander' came into use.

COMMANDER (AIR). The head of the Air Department in an aircraft carrier, who is responsible for all air operations from the ship.

COMMANDER BRITISH NAVAL STAFF WASHINGTON. A rear-admiral appointment, which also combines the duties of Naval Attache Washington and UK National Liason Representative to SACLANT.

COMMANDER (E). The Marine Engineering Officer in a large warship. (See also MARINE ENGINEERING OFFICER.)

COMMANDER-IN-CHIEF (C-IN-C). There are two C-in-C commands in the RN. C-in-C Fleet, who has his HQ at Northwood near London, has command of all operational ships, submarines and embarked aircraft. C-in-C Fleet also holds the NATO posts of Allied Commander-in-Chief Channel (CINCHAN) and Commander-in-Chief Eastern Atlantic (CINCEASTLANT). C-in-C Naval Home Command commands all naval shore establishments in the UK (except for naval air stations) and is responsible for training.

COMMISSION. The document issued by the sovereign to officers by which they hold their accredited status.

COMMODORE. The rank of Commodore is not a promotional rank but an acting one conferred temporarily on a captain who is in command of a number of ships or a particular responsibility. Certain of the large shore establishments have a commodore in command. One broad band of gold lace is worn of the cuffs and a broad pennant is worn in his ship or shore establishment.

COMMODORE AMPHIBIOUS WARFARE. The Senior Naval Officer responsible for the afloat side of amphibious operations, in charge of the ships involved and the embarked forces.

COMMODORE CLYDE. The Senior Naval Officer of the submarine bases on the River Clyde.

COMMODORE MINOR WAR VESSELS AND MINE WARFARE. A post which combines Captains Fishery Protection and Mine Countermeasures.

COMMUNICATIONS OFFICER. The officer in a ship who is responsible for all the communications, both tactical and radio.

COMMUNICATIONS TECHNICIAN. A senior rating specialist in operating computing and radio equipment with particular regard to the reception and analysis of foreign transmissions. Categories are:

CT (L) Communications Technician (Linguist)
CT (A) Communications Technician (Analyst)

The CT branch was formed in 1978 from a restructuring of the Radio Operator (Special) branch of the Communications Group.

CONTROLLER OF THE ROYAL NAVY. A member of the Admiralty Board and responsible for the design, development and production of ships, weapons and equipment. He holds the rank of vice-admiral.

COOK. A rating of the Supply and Secretariat Branch trained in the preparation of all food including bread baking.

A curious custom, one which existed until the 1820s, was that when a ship paid off, none of the officers could leave the ship until the cook had struck the paying-off pennant at sunset. If for some reason he was absent, no other person could perform the duty.

COOKS OF THE MESS. The hands in a mess who take turns to clean out the mess, collect the beer ration, make stand-easy tea and, where meals are taken in the mess, collect parts of the meal from the galley and clean up after meals.

The term is retained from the days when ratings were detailed to act literally as 'cooks of the mess'. Their job was to draw or buy fresh provisions for individual messes, prepare the food in their own mess and take it to the galley for cooking.

CORPORAL OF THE GANGWAY. A marine allocated to duty with the gangway staff in a ship carrying a marine detachment.

COXSWAIN. (Pronounced 'coxsun'.) In a small ship in which no Master-at-Arms or ratings of the Regulating Branch are carried, a senior rating is nominated to carry out regulating duties and is known as the 'coxswain'.

The term comes from the fact that for centuries the senior member of a boat's crew has been called the 'coxswain'. 'Cockswayne' (ME.) was the original title from the days when ship's boats were called 'cockboats' or 'cocks'. ('Swayne' from OE. 'swan', servant, from ON. 'sveinn', boy.) When destroyers and submarines entered service they became known as 'boats' (and still are), the senior petty officer in each of these thus became the 'coxswain'.

DAMAGE CONTROL PARTY. A body of duty ratings responsible for the routine closing and opening of watertight openings at night and morning, and for carrying out rounds of the ship during silent hours to ensure that watertight integrity is maintained.

DISRATED. To lose one's rate.

DIVISIONAL OFFICER (DO). Each division of a ship's company is under the charge of an officer who is responsible for the administration, training, advancement, welfare and general efficiency of everyone in it.

DENTAL OFFICER. Dental officers rank from surgeon-captain (D) to surgeon-lieutenant (D), but there is no equivalent to commodore. Pink cloth is worn between the bands of rank distinction lace (see MEDICAL OFFICER).

Until 1904, when a few civilian dental surgeons were appointed in certain shore estalishments, little interest was taken in the dental condition of naval personnel. Neglect and dental diseases was rife and any emergency treatment was undertaken by the medical officer. During the 1914-18 war a number of civilian dental surgeons were employed afloat, being granted temporary commissions in the RNVR. From a nucleus of these a permanent dental branch was formed in 1920.

DEPUTY ASSISTANT CHIEF OF STAFF (OPERATIONS) ON THE STAFF OF THE SUPREME ALLIED COMMANDER EUROPE. A senior NATO appointment held by a rear-admiral of the Royal Navy.

DEPUTY CHIEF OF DEFENCE STAFF (SYSTEMS). A senior Ministry of Defence appointment held by a rear-admiral.

DEPUTY CONTROLLER WARSHIPS CHIEF NAVAL ENGINEER OFFICER. A senior appointment held by a vice-admiral.

DEPUTY SUPREME ALLIED COMMANDER ATLANTIC. A senior NATO appointment held by a vice-admiral of the Royal Navy.

DIRECTOR. A number of officers of the rank of captain or colonel (RM) are appointed to posts in Ministry of Defence departments as directors. Each of these heads of departments is responsible for policy and procedure throughout the Service. There are some thirty directorates which deal with all aspects of the Service.

DIRECTOR GENERAL. There are seven rear-admirals who hold senior appointments as director generals, each with a particular responsibility. They are:

Director General Aircraft (Naval)
Director General Fleet Support, Policy and Services
Director General Future Material Projects
Director General Marine Engineering
Director General Naval Manpower and Training
Director General Naval Personal Services
Director General Ship Refitting

DIRECTOR WRNS. The active head of the Women's Royal Naval Service, a post usually held by the rank of commandant.

DUTY DISCIPLINARY PETTY OFFICER. A PO employed for disciplinary duties which include calling the hands, inspecting libertymen, taking requestmen and defaulters before the Officer-of-the-Watch and rounds at night. In a small ship these duties would be carried out by the Duty Petty Officer. Prior to 1914 he was known as the 'ship's corporal'.

DUTY HANDS. A number of hands from the duty part of the watch, utilised for any work required out of working hours where only a small party is required.

DUTY PART. The duty part of the watch in harbour who are required to remain on board, ready to carry out any work necessary or to deal with any emergency. The fire party, damage control party and the duty hands are provided from the duty part.

DUTY PETTY OFFICER. A PO responsible for the employment of the duty watch or part should they be required, the fire and emergency party and taking charge of men under punishment. In a small ship he may also undertake regulating duties.

EMERGENCY LIST OFFICER. A supplementary list officer who, on leaving the service, is required to serve on this list for four years.

ENGINEERING MECHANIC. A semi-skilled rating of the Engineering Branch who is trained in one of seven categories within three sub branches:

MEM Marine Engineering Mechanic (Electrical or Mechanical).

WEM Weapon Engineering Mechanic (Radio or Ordnance).

AEM Air Engineering Mechanic (Mechanical, Radio or Weapon Electrical).

The rating of 'stoker' was instituted in 1826 at the beginning of the coal burning days, later to become 'stoker mechanic' in 1883. 'Stoker' was not dropped until 1955 when the new title of engineering mechanic was introduced.

ENGINEERING OFFICER. An officer trained in one of five categories within three sub branches:

MEO Marine Engineering Officer (Surface Ship or Submarine).

WEO Weapons Engineering Officer (Surface Ship or Submarine).

AEO Air Engineering Officer.

EXECUTIVE BRANCH. The seaman branch.

EXECUTIVE OFFICER. The seaman officer in a ship who is next to the captain, appointed to carry out executive duties. He is responsible to the captain for the fighting efficiency of the ship and the general organisation and routine of the ship's company. He may be of any rank from commander to sub-lieutenant according to the size of the ship. In ships where the executive officer is of commander's rank he is known as 'the Commander'; otherwise he is known as 'the First Lieutenant'. In ships where the executive officer is a commander, another officer of the seaman specialisation is known as 'the First Lieutenant'. (See also FIRST LIEUTENANT.)

FIELD GUN CREW. As a regular and popular feature of the annual Royal Tournament, 18-man crews from Portsmouth, Devonport and Naval Air Command compete in dismantling a field gun and limber which has a combined weight of almost one ton. In preparation the crews carry out a four month training period prior to the competition.

The display, first completed in 1907, was originally designed to commemorate an event during the Boer War. In 1899 the Army was under pressure and requested the RN to provide some guns to assist in the defence of Ladysmith. Two 4.7 inch guns were borrowed from the cruiser *HMS TERRIBLE* and taken on board *HMS POWERFUL* to Durban. Here, under the command of Captain Lambton RN, these guns, together with four 12 pounders, were transported initially by rail and then across difficult terrain to Ladysmith. They played a vital role in keeping the enemy at bay until, after a siege lasting 120 days, the town was relieved in 1900. Later that year, seamen of *HMS POWERFUL* displayed a 4.7 inch gun and a battery of 12 pounders in the arena of the Royal Tournament and the seeds for the famous competition were sown.

FIRE PARTY. A body of duty ratings, competent to deal in the first instance with any fire. They sleep in a special place so as to be readily available.

FIRST LIEUTENANT. The executive officer in a ship, who is next to the captain, is known by this title when his rank is lower than that of commander. (See also EXECUTIVE OFFICER.)

Until the 19th century all officers other than post captains were of lieutenant rank. In a ship they were titled according to their relative status; e.g. the officer next to the captain was known as the 'first lieutenant', the next was called the 'second lieutenant' and so on depending on the number borne. When the intermediate ranks of commander and lieutenant commander were later introduced, the 'lieutenant' titles were dropped, with the exception of that of 'first lieutenant' which remained.

FIRST OFFICER. A WRNS rank equivalent to lieutenant commander RN.

FIRST SEA LORD. See CHIEF OF NAVAL STAFF.

FLAG CAPTAIN. The captain of a flagship.

FLAG LIEUTENANT. The adjutant of a flag officer. Aiguilettes (ropes of gold lace) are worn on the left shoulder.

FLAG OFFICER. An officer of the rank of rear-admiral or above who holds a senior post within the naval command structure. He wears his flag in his flagship or establishment to denote his presence in command.

FLAG OFFICER FLOTILLA ONE. Responsible for the operational readiness of the First Flotilla, the RN's destroyer and frigate force. A rear-admiral appointment.

FLAG OFFICER FLOTILLA TWO. Responsible for operations and the tactical development of the First Flotilla. A rear-admiral appointment.

Until 1988 the destroyer and frigate force was divided into two flotillas; the First and Second each with their respective flag officers. These two flotillas were then combined to form the First Flotilla, but the two flag officers continue to exercise command whilst retaining their original titles.

FLAG OFFICER GIBRALTAR. Responsible for the operational control of ships in the Gibraltar sea area and for the support of ships there. He also has the title of Gibraltar Naval Base Commander and holds the NATO post of COMGIBMED. A rear-admiral appointment.

FLAG OFFICER NAVAL AVIATION. Responsible for all naval aviation matters afloat and ashore. A rear-admiral appointment.

Until March 1990 the title was Flag Officer Naval Air Command who was responsible for the Fleet Air Arm, with the Flag Officer Third Flotilla being responsible for the aircraft carriers. The new title combines both responsibilities.

FLAG OFFICER PLYMOUTH. Responsible for the operational control of RN ships in the Plymouth sea area. This is a vice-admiral appointment which also carries the additional resonsibilities of Port Admiral Devonport and the NATO posts of Commander Central Sub Area Eastern Atlantic and Commander Plymouth Sub Area Channel.

FLAG OFFICER PORTSMOUTH. Responsible for the operational control of RN ships in the Portsmouth sea area and Naval Base Commander. This is a rear-admiral appointment and includes the Head of Establishment of the Fleet Maintenance and Repair Organisation.

FLAG OFFICER ROYAL YACHTS. A rear-admiral who is appointed as master of HM Royal Yacht *BRITANNIA*.

FLAG OFFICER SEA TRAINING. A rear-admiral, based at Portland Naval Base, who is responsible for all of the operational sea training of the fleet.

FLAG OFFICER SCOTLAND AND NORTHERN IRELAND. The commander of RN operations in the northern part of the UK. It is a vice-admiral appointment which includes the duties of Port Admiral Rosyth and the NATO posts of Commander Sub Area Eastern Atlantic and Commander NORE Sub Area Channel.

FLAG OFFICER SUBMARINES. A real-admiral who is the head of the Submarine Branch. He also holds the NATO appointment of COMSUBEASTLANT.

FLAG OFFICER THIRD FLOTILLA. Responsible for the operational effectiveness of the larger warships such as the aircraft carriers and assault ships, with particular concern with the anti-submarine element of these forces.

This is a rear-admiral appointment which also includes the NATO post of Commander Anti-Submarine Striking Force. (COMASWSTRIKFOR).

FLIGHT DECK OFFICER. The officer in charge of helicopter flight deck operations in a ship, a duty often performed by the Instructor Officer.

GANGWAY STAFF. Watchkeepers of the gangway in harbour, which include the officer-of-the-watch, quartermaster and boatswain's mate. One marine acts as 'corporal of the gangway' in a ship which carries a marine detachment.

GENERAL LIST OFFICER. An officer trained as a midshipman and sub-lieutenant at Britannia Royal Naval College, Dartmouth, having entered direct from school, university or selected as a rating called an UPPER YARDMAN.

HAND. Seaman, man.

Apart from the wheel and the capstan, until 1805 there was no machinery in use on board ship. All of the work, including the movement of guns, was done by manual labour. The members of a ship's company were therefore known as 'hands'.

HEAD OF DEPARTMENT. A ship's company is divided into departments according to branch relating to a particular task, e.g. marine engineering department. The senior officer of a department is known as the 'head' of the department and is responsible to the captain for its efficiency.

HELMSMAN. A rating stationed at the ship's wheel and responsible for steering the ship.

HYDROGRAPHER TO THE NAVY. A rear-admiral who controls the RN's survey vessels and is responsible for the continuous updating of all the Admiralty charts.

INSTRUCTOR OFFICER. Instructor officers are carried in all of the larger ships and establishments. Apart from their instructional duties they are available for consultation with all personnel on educational matters. METOC is also another of their responsibilities, which is the term for the combined sciences of Meteorology and Oceanography.

Education officers have been carried in ships since the 17th century, their original duty being to instruct young officers. In 1837 they were called Naval Instructors to distinguish them from the Seamans' Schoolmaster, which was a new petty officer rate then introduced for the instruction of ratings. The Seaman's Schoolmaster was given warrant rank in 1916 and, two years later, the title of Naval Instructor was changed to Instructor Officer. In 1946 the two types education officer became one under the general title of Instructor Officer.

INTERNAL SECURITY PLATOON. A party of men which can be called out at any time to help civil authorities restore law and order.

JUNIOR. A rating under the age of 17½ years. This rating has been in being since 1956, when the rating of boy (under 18 years) was abolished.

The boy rating had been in the RN for 300 years, known at action stations in sailing days as 'powder monkeys', they supplied charges and powder from the magazines to the gun crews.

JUNIOR RATE. A rating below that of petty officer.

KEYBOARD SENTRY. A watchkeeping rating who is stationed at the ship's main keyboard, responsible for the safety, issue and return of all keys.

LEADING HAND. See LEADING SEAMAN.

LEADING HAND OF THE MESS. A leading hand who is appointed to take charge of the conduct and general running of a junior rate's mess.

LEADING RATE. A general term to describe the equivalent of leading seaman in other branches.

LEADING SEAMAN. The rating above able seaman and below petty officer, the senior of the 'junior rates' and equivalent to a corporal in the Army.

This rating was introduced into the RN following an Admiralty Committee report on manning produced in 1853. At the same time the rating of chief petty officer was introduced and the rating of 'landsman' (inexperienced seaman) was abolished and replaced by that of ordinary seaman second class.

LIEUTENANT. (Pronounced 'lef-tenant'). An officer next below the rank of lieutenant-commander and ranking with a captain in the Army. Two narrow bands of gold lace are worn on the uniform cuffs. (F. 'tenant', holding and 'lieu', in place of, in the respect of originally deputising for the captain.)

Lieutenants were introduced in 1631. Due to Pepys, youths were carefully selected and sent to sea under royal patronage. After rating in turn to ordinary and able seaman, they eventually served for two years as petty officers before taking an oral examination in the Tower of London. If successful they received commissions to serve as lieutenants. These officers then gradually assumed the positions of the master, boatswain, gunner and carpenter, all of whom were previously warrant officers.

The purpose of their introduction was that at that time of peace there were not enough sea captains; there had previously been no encouragement for gentlemen of worth and ability to go to sea. The state would have had to rely upon the warrant officers to become captains, the objection to which was not on lack of ability, but on social grounds.

LIEUTENANT-COMMANDER. The rank above lieutenant and next below commander, ranking with a major in the Army. Two narrow bands of gold lace with a thin one between ('half stripe') are worn on the uniform cuffs.

This intermediate rank between lieutenant and commander was introduced as a result of lieutenants being placed in command of gunboats during the Victorian era of gunboat diplomacy. In 1864 lieutenants were divided into two classes; those under and over eight years' seniority. The half stripe for lieutenants with over eight years' seniority was instituted in 1877. When introduced the rank was 'lieutenant-in-command', to become known as 'lieutenant-commander' from 1914.

LIEUTENANT-COMMANDER (FLYING). The officer in an aircraft carrier who controls flight deck operations.

LIFEBUOY SENTRY. At sea a rating from the watch on deck is stationed aft, near the two lifebuoys positioned there, in case of a man going overboard. Signal buzzers, near the lifebuoys and activated from the bridge, are sounded in an emergency.

LOCALLY ENTERED PERSONNEL (LEP). Personnel recruited locally, both in the UK and other parts of the world, for duties such as stewards.

LOOKOUT. At sea, lookouts are placed so as to continually scan the horizon through binoculars. The number of them depends on whether a war or peace routine is in force.

LORD HIGH ADMIRAL. Her Majesty The Queen. For centuries the Lord High Admiral was the head of the Board of Admiralty who reported direct to the Sovereign. However, in 1964 the Board was dissolved and the Sovereign is now her own Lord High Admiral.

MARINE ENGINEERING OFFICER (MEO). The officer in a ship responsible for the hull and general structure, the main propulsion, associated systems, power generation, ventilation and controls for all systems, including fuel and water.

MASTER-AT-ARMS (MAA). Once responsible for instructing the men on board a ship in the use of small arms, but in the course of time became the head of the ship's police. He is either of warrant officer rank or is the senior chief petty officer of a ship and often referred to as 'master'.

MASTER-OF-THE-FLEET. The navigating officer appointed to the Commander-in-Chief Fleet responsible for the navigation of the Fleet.

MEDICAL ASSISTANT. A rating of the medical branch who is trained in nursing, first aid and medical administration.

Until comparatively recent times the medical assistant was known as a 'sick berth attendant', a special rating equivalent to that of able seaman which was introduced in 1833 to assist the surgeon. Surgeons were originally assisted by 'surgeons' mates' and men detailed from the ship's company.

MEDICAL OFFICER. Medical officers have the prefix to title 'surgeon' and wear scarlet cloth between the distinctive bands of gold lace on the cuffs. They rank from surgeon-vice-admiral to surgeon-lieutenant.

Surgeons have been carried in nearly all warships since the time of Charles I. Originally there were two classes; the higher being graduates of the College of

Physicians and the lower being recruited from the Company of Barber-Surgeons. Being regarded as civilians, they did not wear uniform until 1843 when the branch was established in its present form.

At one time officers of all branches, except the executive branch, wore various coloured cloths between the bands of gold lace, dependant on branch. This was only one of the many distinctions between officers of the executive branch and those of the civil branches. In 1902 the engineer officers were given executive titles, i.e. 'commander', 'lieutenant', etc., but prefixed by the word 'engineer'. Then in 1918 officers of all other civil branches received executive titles with their respective branch prefixes. Gradually other distinctions were removed and in 1955 coloured cloths were abolished, except those for surgeon and dental surgeon which are still retained. At the same time the prefixes to all civil branch titles, except for surgeon, were removed.

MEDICAL TECHNICIAN. A rating of the medical branch who is specialised as one of the following:

(HP)	Health physicist.
(N)	State registered male nurse.
(R)	Radiographer.
(P)	Physiotherapist.
(HI)	Health inspector.
(L)	Medical laboratory technician.
(M)	Mental nurse.

MESSMAN. A rating detailed to act as an assistant in chief and petty officers' messes.

MIDSHIPMAN. A non-commissioned rank below that of sub-lieutenant. Officers' uniform is worn but no gold lace is worn on the cuffs. A buttonhole of white twist and a corresponding button is worn on each side of the collar of the jacket.

Originally these were young gentlemen who were sent to sea under royal patronage, first to 'learn the ropes' as ordinary and able seamen, eventually to serve for two years afloat as petty officers serving amidships before qualifying for commission as lieutenant. All petty officers had some designate title and these young gentlemen took the title of 'midshipmen'.

NAVAL AIRMAN. Categories of naval airmen are:

(AC)	Aircraft controller.
(AE)	Fitter and mechanic.
(H)	Aircraft handler.
(MET)	Meterological observer.
(P)	Photographer.
(SE)	Survival equipment.

NAVAL SECRETARY. A senior appointment held by a rear-admiral.

NAVIGATING OFFICER. The officer appointed to a ship to take responsibility for all aspects of navigation.

Originally the Master, one of the standing warrant officers in a ship, was responsible for the navigation. In 1863 he was commissioned as Navigating Lieutenant.

NAVIGATOR'S YEOMAN. A rating assisting the navigating officer.

NIGHT GUARD. A guard posted to prevent acts of sabotage and thefts during silent hours.

NIGHT GUARD OFFICER. A warrant officer or an officer of sub-lieutenant rank or above placed in charge of a night guard.

OBSERVER. Following elementary flying training with the RAF, an RN observer is trained in operational skills for helicopters.

OFFICER COMMANDING ROYAL MARINES (OCRM). A Royal Navy officer in charge of a ship's Royal Marines detachment. If a Royal Marines officer is borne for watchkeeping duties, then he naturally commands the detachment.

Originally an RM detachment consisted of an officer and 20 men, but since 1978 this has been reduced to a sergeant, one corporal and eight marines.

OFFICER OF THE GUARD. An officer detailed from the guard ship to visit foreign ships on arrival in a British port, to offer the courtesies and facilities of the port.

OFFICER OF THE DAY (OOD). The officer responsible for the safety of a ship and her company in harbour and also for the running of the daily harbour routine.

OFFICER OF THE WATCH (OOW). The officer responsible for the safety of a ship and company when at sea.

He is responsible to the Captain for maintaining all courses ordered.

ORDINARY SEAMAN (OD). Sometimes also abbreviated as 'ord'. The lowest rating other than juniors under 17½ years.

PARADE TRAINING INSTRUCTOR. A seaman senior rate of the missile sub-branch employed in training establishments for parade training.

PETTY OFFICER (PO). A senior rate, above that of leading seaman and below that of chief petty officer and equivalent to a sergeant in the Army. Fore-and-aft rig is worn, except by acting POs who retain square rig. The rate badge is crossed fouled anchors, worn on the left arm. (From F. 'petit', small.)

Until the introduction of the CPO and leading rate in 1853, the rates of PO first and second classes were the only ones above that of able rate. The rate of PO second class was abolished in 1913.

PETTY OFFICER OF THE DAY (POOD). A PO employed for admin duties such as attending the servery during meal hours and machinery compartment rounds at night.

PHYSICAL TRAINING INSTRUCTOR (PTI). As with the Regulating Branch, PTIs are all volunteers from other branches of the service.

In the days of sail in the navy the sailor was kept in a fit condition, but this was no longer the case when steam came along. And so in 1888 the first 'gymnastic instructors' were trained at Whale Island. The branch in its present form was created in 1903.

PILOT. Following elementary flying training with the RAF, an RN pilot is trained in operational skills for helicopters or the Sea Harrier aircraft.

PORT ADMIRAL. The Flag Officer Plymouth and the Flag Officer Scotland and Northern Ireland also hold the posts of Port Admirals Devonport and Rosyth respectively. Port admirals are responsible for the support of the Fleet.

PORT AND STARBOARD CREWS. The two crews employed in each Polaris submarine. Whilst one crew is aboard at sea on long patrol, the other is either on leave or engaged in training.

POST CAPTAIN. See CAPTAIN.

PRESIDENT OF THE MESS. Usually the senior officer in the wardroom (but not the Captain who is not a member and is only invited as a guest), responsible for the general running of the mess. Also a senior rating voted to that position by members of a chief or petty officers' mess.

PRINCIPLE WARFARE OFFICER (PWO). The officer who takes charge of a ship's operations room.

PROMOTION. Following 'advancement' through the rates to petty officer, a rating's further progression to chief petty officer and above is by promotion.

QUARTERMASTER (QM). The senior helmsman who takes over at the wheel when the ship is entering or leaving harbour. Also, in harbour, the rating responsible to the officer of the day for running the routine, guarding the gangways and keeping watch on the general safety of the ship and her boats.

QUEEN'S HARBOURMASTER. A post, usually filled by a captain, responsible for all of the navigational requirements, including moorings and berths, of a naval base.

RADIO OPERATOR (RO). A rating of the Communications Group, part of the Operations Branch, who is trained in one of the following sub specialisations:

RO(G)	Radio operator (general radio).
RO(SM)	Radio operator (submarines).
RO(T)	Radio operator (tactical).

Radio operators were originally known as 'wireless telegraphists'. In 1958 telegraphists and visual signallers became 'radio communication operators' and 'tactical communication operators' respectively. Those two jobs were merged together to become 'radio operators' in 1963.

RATE. The rating held by a non-commissioned man, i.e. ordinary rate, able rate, leading rate, petty officer rate.

RATED. Advanced or promoted to a higher rate.

RATING. The general term for all non-commissioned men.

REAR ADMIRAL. The rank above that of captain and below that of vice-admiral. One broad band of gold lace with a narrower one above are worn on the uniform cuffs.

During the 17th century the Fleets of the Royal Navy were divided into red, white and blue squardons, with three kinds of admiral commanding; Admiral of the Red, White or Blue. The Admiral of the Red controlled the Fleet with his squadron in the centre, while the Admiral of the White led the Fleet. Considered of less importance, the Admiral of the Blue commanded the squadron in the rear. This order of seniority, depending on whether the squadrons were red, white or blue, led to the introduction of the ranks admiral, vice admiral and rear admiral.

REGULATING STAFF. These are the Royal Navy's police and are borne in all ships and establishments. They are responsible for dealing with requestmen and defaulters, leave, shore patrols, movement of personnel to and from a ship and handling mail. Members of the Regulating Branch are recruited from volunteers from other branches of the Service.

ROYAL MARINES DETACHMENT. Certain ships carry an RM detachment of a sergeant, one corporal and eight marines. Their duties include providing a shore security party and manning small craft. Certain classes of ship are specially prepared for embarked RM detachments, but not all of these carry them because there is a maximum of 19 detachments at sea at any one time.

Originally, because they were considered to be such a trustworthy body of men, the Royal Marines were berthed between the officers and men in a ship to prevent mutiny. In more recent times, when ships carried gun turrets the Royal Marines always manned one of these.

SEABOAT'S CREW. A party detailed from the watch on deck at sea who are ready to man the seaboat.

SEA DUTYMEN. The helmsman and telegraphsman detailed from the watch on deck.

SEAMAN. A rating of the Seaman Group within the Operations Branch, whose job is to work and fight the ship. All seamen are sub-specialists, which is denoted by abbreviation following their rate:

(D)	Diver.	(S)	Sonar.
(M)	Missile.	(SR)	Survey recorder.

(MW)	Mine warfare.	(S(SM))	Sonar submarines.
(R)	Radar.	(TS(SM))	Tactical systems (submarines).
(EW)	Electronic warfare.		

SECOND OFFICER. A WRNS rank equivalent to Lieutenant RN.

SECOND SEA LORD. See CHIEF OF NAVAL PERSONNEL.

SENIOR RATES. Warrant officers and chief and petty officers.

SHIP'S COMPANY RATING. A term to describe a member of the ship's company of a shore establishment as distinct from one of the 'floating' ratings such as new entries or men under training.

SHORE PATROL. A patrol landed to police the conduct of and to protect ratings on shore leave. Each member of the patrol wears a black arm band with the letters 'SP' in red.

SIDE BOYS. Ratings detailed to 'pipe the side' on receiving an important personage on board.

SIDE PARTY. A permanent party of seamen allocated for keeping the general appearance of the ship's side in good condition.

SPECIAL DUTIES LIST OFFICER. An officer with specialist skills who is specially selected for promotion to commissioned rank.

This list was originally created in 1957 from 'branch officers' (formerly warrant officers); the senior commissioned branch officers becoming lieutenants and the commissioned branch officers becoming sub-lieutenants.

SPECIAL SEA DUTYMEN. Special standing ratings who relieve the ordinary sea dutymen in action or on entering or leaving harbour, etc. The chief quartermaster takes charge of the wheel and various other stations are manned by special ratings.

STATE CEREMONIAL INSTRUCTOR. A seaman senior rating of the missile sub-branch employed in training other seaman rates of the missile sub-branch in state ceremonial.

STEWARD. A rating of the Supply and Secretariat Branch, trained in the preparation of food and drink in wardrooms.

STORES ACCOUNTANT (SA). A rating of the Supply and Secretariat Branch trained in store keeping and store management.

SUB-LIEUTENANT. The lowest commissioned rank and the rank below that of lieutenant. One narrow band of gold lace is worn on the uniform cuffs.

The rank was instituted in 1863 when the master's mate was given a commission, formalising the old path from midshipman via mate to lieutenant.

SUBMARINER. An officer or rating of the Submarine Branch.

SUPERINTENDENT. A WRNS rank equivalent to that of Captain RN.

SUPPLEMENTARY LIST OFFICER. An officer entered on a short service engagement in one of the branches which has a special requirement for junior officers.

SUPPLY OFFICER (SO). The 'Pusser', the officer responsible for pay, wardroom staff, stores and catering; an officer of the Supply and Secretariat Branch.

Originally known as the Purser, a long standing warrant rank. In 1808 masters and pursers were granted lieutenant rank, though still retained as wardroom warrant officers. This concession was made in consequence of those who had been taken prisoner during the recent French War, having been treated and exchanged as commom seamen. The purser was eventually commissioned in 1841 and then known by the rank of Purser and Paymaster. In 1851 and 'purser' was dropped and he became Paymaster, later to be changed to Supply Officer.

SURGEON. See MEDICAL OFFICER.

SURGEON GENERAL. The surgeon vice-admiral appointment as head of the medical branch.

SURVEY RECORDER. A rating of the Survey Branch, a small branch whose members are usually employed in survey vessels.

TELEGRAPHSMAN. A hand stationed in the wheelhouse with the helmsman, who transmits the engine orders received from the bridge to the engine room by means of moving pointers. The orders are repeated on telegraph receivers in the engine room.

TELEPHONIST. A WRNS rating operating in a Service telephone exchange.

THIRD OFFICER. A WRNS rank equivalent to that of Sub-Lieutenant RN.

UPPER YARDMAN. A rating under the age of 22 who has been specially selected for promotion to commissioned rank.

In the days of square rigged sailing ships, the yardmen were the picked men of the ship's company who worked on the masts and yards. Among these were the 'upper yardmen' who worked on the topsail and topgallant sail yards; the aristocrats of the lower deck.

VICE-ADMIRAL. The rank above that of rear-admiral and below that of admiral. One broad band of gold lace with two narrower ones above are worn on the uniform cuffs. See also ADMIRAL and REAR-ADMIRAL.

WARRANT OFFICER. An officer, promoted from chief petty officer, who receives his appointment by warrant and not by commission. The uniform is similar to that of chief petty officer, but has a more elaborate cap badge and a cuff insignia incorporating the Royal Arms.

Warrant officer was once an old standing rank in the RN, originally each ship carried four; master, purser, gunner and boatswain. The purser was commissioned in 1841 and the master in 1843, but gradually other branches were formed until there were many different warrant officers. In 1865, higher rank was granted and the title 'chief' given, i.e. 'chief gunner', which was later changed to 'commissioned' in 1918. The name warrant officer was changed to 'branch officer' in 1949, but was eventually to disappear in 1957 when all branch officers became 'special duties list officers', being granted the rank of lieutenant or sub-lieutenant.

The RN had never had an equivalent to the warrant officer grade one (regimental sergeant-major) in the Army and warrant officer in the Royal Air Force. Even the warrant officer rank in the RN, abolished in 1949, had not been an equivalent as it was an officer rank. However, in 1970 the gap was finally filled by the creation of a new senior rating called 'fleet chief petty officer', later to be changed to 'warrant officer' in 1985.

WATCHKEEPERS. Men employed in duties which require a continous watch in harbour, mainly provided by the Seamen Group.

WATCH ON DECK. The seamen watch on duty at sea whose duties include helmsman and telegraphsman, lookouts, lifebuoy sentry and stern lookout, seaboat's crew and lowerers, recovery station party and anchor watch.

WEAPON ANALYST. A WRNS rating trained to serve in weapons trials units.

WEAPONS ENGINEERING OFFICER (WEO). Responsible for the three categories of weapon engineering; radio, control and ordnance.

WELFARE COMMITTEE. A committee formed from officers and ratings of a ship's company to enable discussion to take place between officers and men concerning welfare and amenities within the ship.

WORK PART OF SHIP, TO. For ratings to carry out maintenance or cleaning on their particular part of the upper deck.

WRITER. A rating of the Supply and Secretariat Branch, trained in clerical and office procedures.

YEOMAN. Either navigator's yeoman, a rating assisting the navigating officer; chief communications yeoman, a senior communications rating (once chief yeoman of signals) or boatswain's yeoman, a seaman specialist.

6

DRESS

Uniform for officers of the Royal Navy was introduced in 1748. The colour scheme was selected by George III after having seen and admired the Duchess of Bedford (wife of the First Lord of the Admiralty) dressed in a riding habit of blue and gold.

However no detailed uniform regulations for officers or men were laid down until 1857. Up to that time the sailor had to provide his own clothing, but there was a certain uniformity in dress because all items were either made by the sailor or purchased by him from the limited items available in the ship's stores or outfitters in the main ports. There had never been the same need at sea to distinguish friend from foe as there had been on land. When the need arose, such as when boarding the enemy, coloured scarves or headgear were worn as distinctive emblems.

Even after 1857 the men still made their own uniforms from blue serge material, or white duck for working gear, which they obtained from 'slops' aboard ship, the cost of which was deducted from their wages. It was not until 1907 that ready-made uniforms were issued.

* * *

ACTION COVERALL. A one piece garment made of two layers of flame resistant white cotton material. Worn over the No. 8 working dress, this together with anti-flash hood and gloves is known as the number 11 dress and gives good overall protection against heat, flame and flash.

ACTION DRESS. Officers' No. 11 dress worn in operational or training conditions and similar to the ratings No. 8 action working dress.

ACTION WORKING DRESS. The ratings' No. 8 rig, the blue fire resistant clothing worn for normal working dress aboard ship.

AIGUILLETTES. Ropes of gold lace which are worn hung from the left shoulder by officers serving on the personal staff of flag officers or commodores. Aids-de-camp to the Sovereign, equerries to members of the Royal Family, admirals-of-the-fleet and honorary surgeons to the Sovereign wear aiguillettes on the right shoulder.

ANTI-FLASH GEAR. Special gauntlets to cover the hands and wrists and a hood to protect the head and neck, made from a flame resistant white cotton material and worn to avoid flash burns in action.

BADGES. See BADGES OF RATING, CAP BADGES, LONG SERVICE AND GOOD CONDUCT BADGES and NON-SUBSTANTIVE BADGES.

BADGES OF RATING. These are worn on the left upper arm, above any good conduct badges. Warrant officers wear the Royal coat of arms on both cuffs and chief petty officers wear three buttons on each cuff. The badge of rate for a petty officer (PO) is crossed fouled anchors with a crown above and that for leading seaman is a single fouled anchor. Able and ordinary rates have no badges of rate.

Badges were worn some years before the first official uniform was introduced in 1857. In 1827 badges of white cloth were ordered to be worn by POs on the upper part of the left sleeve in order to distinguish them from the able rates. Many men obtained badges from private sources and so there was a great variety in size and style, there being no uniformity until standard woven designs were introduced in 1879.

POs first class wore a fouled anchor surmounted by a crown and a fouled anchor alone was worn by the second class. When the new rates of chief petty officer (CPO) and leading seaman were introduced in 1853 the badges were changed. The crown and fouled anchor became the PO second class badge and the anchor alone was given to the leading seaman. The PO first class was given a new badge of crossed fouled anchors surmounted by a crown and the new badge for the CPO had a single fouled anchor and crown above surrounded by a laurel.

In 1868, engine room artificers (ERAs) were introduced and to recognise their professional ability they were rated CPO. The uniform for CPOs was changed in 1879 to one with a peaked cap and long jacket. The seamen CPOs retained their rate badge but the ERAs did not. However, in 1890 the seaman CPOs lost their badge also. The rate of second class PO was abolished in 1913.

BALL DRESS. The No. 2 officers' mess wear for official dinners and receptions. Flag officers and captains wear undress tail coats.

BERET. Worn as part of working dress with a metal badge of rank or rate affixed.

BLUE DRESS. The term for the officers' No. 4 dress, which is the normal officers' uniform when worn with sword and medals for such occasions as inspections, minor ceremonial and courts martial.

BUTTONS. The officer's reefer jacket has eight gilt buttons which are domed and have a raised design of a fouled anchor surmounted by a crown with a smooth background and a rim in the form of a rope. Warrant, chief and petty officers' jackets have only six gilt buttons, the design of which is similar to those for officers except that it has a plain rim instead of the rope and the background is of horizontal lines instead of smooth.

When uniform for officers was first introduced in 1748, there were four types of buttons for different groups of officers and for different dress. Over the years that followed there were various changes made to the design of these until, in 1891, a standard button appeared which was very similar to that worn today, with the exception of changes to the crown in 1901 and 1953.

Chief petty officers, on attaining 'fore-and-aft rig' in 1879, were allowed to wear the gilt buttons for officers, but in 1888 a new gilt button for ratings was introduced, similar to that of the officers but without the rope rim. The new officer's button of 1891 had a smooth background instead of a lined one as previously, but the rating's button continued to be described as being similar to that of an officer's button with the exception of the plain rim, implying that the background was now smooth. However, no change was made and to this day ratings' buttons continue to have the lined background.

CAP. The officer's white peaked cap has a black patent leather peak which in the case of a senior officer has an oak leaf design; all round for a flag officer and on the front edge only for a captain or commander. Warrant, chief and petty officers wear a cap of similar design to that worn by officers. Junior ratings wear the round white cap which has a ribbon around bearing the name of the ship.

The officer's peaked cap came into use about 1840 to supplement the cocked hat, the peaks of senior officers becoming embroidered in gold in 1856 and later changed to oak leaf design in 1860. The first peaked cap for ratings was that issued to CPOs in 1879. The rating's round cap was introduced in 1864 to supplement the sennit or straw hat, which itself stayed part of uniform until 1921.

Until 1954, wartime excepted, white caps were only worn in the UK between the months of April and September inclusive; a blue cap being worn during the winter months. Plastic caps replaced the 'blancoed' material ones in 1957.

CAP BADGES. The cap badge worn by officers is woven from gold wire and consists of a fouled anchor surmounted by a crown, the lower part surrounded by oak leaves. Petty officers (POs) wear a fouled anchor, double circled and surmounted by a gold crown. The cap badge for Chief Petty Officer (CPO) consists of a smaller fouled anchor than that for PO and surrounded by a laurel wreath. Warrant officers have cap badges similar to those for CPOs but slightly larger.

When the cap for officers first came into use it had no badge, only a band of gold lace, but during the 1840s some officers wore the crests of their ships on their caps. Officers of *HMS QUEEN* wore crowns on their caps and these were noticed and favourably remarked upon by Queen Victoria during a visit to the ship. As a result of this, an order was issued for crowns to be worn as a cap badge by all officers. With the changes to uniform made in 1856, a new badge was introduced, not unlike the badge of today except that the anchor was surrounded by an oval and the overall size was smaller.

The cap badge given to CPOs in 1879, when they changed uniform to 'fore-and-aft rig', consisted of a fouled anchor within an oval and surmounted by a crown. In 1920 when POs went into fore-and-aft rig on attaining four year's seniority, they were given the CPOs badge, whilst the CPOs received a new badge as it exists today. In 1970 a slightly larger form of this badge was introduced for the new rate of Fleet CPO (now Warrant Officer).

CAP RIBBON. The ribbon worn around the seaman's cap with the name of the ship in guilt letters. It was introduced in the 1860s.

CHIN STAY. A narrow tape sewn inside the seaman's cap to act as a chinstrap and used in windy conditions. Ceremonial Guards are always ordered 'down chin stays' before marching on.

CLEAN, TO. To change clothes, i.e. as an order 'hands to clean into No. 1s'.

COLLAR. The detachable blue jean collar worn by men dressed as seamen. It dates from the time of pigtails, when seamen wore a scarf over their shoulders to protect their clothes from grease. The rows of white tape on the collar were originally a trimming, the number of which varied according to individual taste. When the uniform for seamen was standardised in 1857, three rows were decided upon and they do not, as is sometimes thought, commemorate Nelson's three famous victories.

DAY UNDRESS. Officers' No. 5J dress, where the heavy wool jersey replaces the No. 5 uniform jacket.

DECLARED CLOTHING. All items of kit are marked with the owner's name, to enable anything mislaid to be returned and to avoid theft. Men who have no further use for articles often dispose of them, with permission and also dead men's effects are usually sold by auction for the benefit of their dependants. Anyone acquiring such items are required to take them to the ship's regulating office where the old marking is defaced with a special stamp with the letters 'DC'.

DRESS OF THE DAY. The dress to be worn during the day, as promulgated in daily orders. This may change during the day according to the circumstances of the routine. The various forms of dress are numbered, both for officers and ratings. In the case of officers' dress, besides being numbered the different forms also have a descriptive title. For ratings the dress is known by the number alone as follows:

No. 1	Best blue uniform with gold badges and medals, worn on ceremonial occasions.
No. 2	Best blue uniform with gold badges, worn on duty when best uniform is required and optional on leave.
No. 2J	Senior rates dress when the No. 2 jacket is replaced by the heavy wool jersey.
No. 3	Second best blue uniform with red badges, worn where a blue suit is required on working days.
No. 3J	Senior rates dress when the No. 3 jacket is replaced by the heavy wool jersey.
No. 4	Any old but respectable blue uniform with red badges, worn for night clothing.
No. 6	White drill suit with blue badges and medals, worn in tropical waters in place of No. 1's.
No. 7	White drill with blue badges, worn in tropical waters in place of No. 2's.
No. 8	Blue action working dress with blue badges on a white background, worn for normal working aboard ships and in shore establishments.
No. 8J	No. 8's worn together with the heavy wool jersey.
No. 9	Blue overalls, worn for particularly dirty work.
No. 10	White vest and shorts with blue stockings, worn in place of No. 2's in hot climates.
No. 10A	Blue shorts and sandals, worn as working dress in hot climates.

No. 11 The No. 8 action working dress worn together a flame proof action coverall and anti-flash hood and gloves.

FORE-AND-AFT-RIG. The uniform worn by ratings not dressed as seamen, i.e, double breasted reefer jacket with peaked cap as worn by chief and petty officers. The term comes from the sailing ship days when the sails of fore-and-aft rigged vessels were suspended by stays, gaffs and booms.

FULL DRESS. The No. 1 ceremonial wear for officers. Today only flag officers wear the ceremonial full dress day coat. For all other officers the undress coat pattern doubles for both full dress and undress wear.

GOLD LACE. The lace worn on the cuffs of an officer's uniform jacket as a mark of rank. That for officers of the Royal Naval Reserve (RNR) is the same as that for the RN with the addition of an 'R' in the curl.

Originally introduced by George III to commemorate the battle of the Glorious First of June, bands or 'stripes' of gold lace were used on some of the uniforms for officers after they were adopted in 1748. However, the lace was not the principle means of distinguishing ranks; each rank or group of ranks had a uniform which was different from any other, different grouping of buttons and later in 1795 epaulettes, originally worn in the French Army, were introduced.

It was not until 1856 that the use of gold lace was brought into a definite system. Officers of the executive branch had the top stripe formed into a curl above, while civil branch officers wore straight stripes without the curl and, in 1863, the addition of distinguishing colours between the stripes for the various professions. The curl was authorised for engineer officers in 1915 and for all other branches in 1918. In 1955 all distinguishing colours were abolished with the exception of the scarlet for surgeons and orange for dental surgeons.

In 1919, an Admiralty order was made stating that 'with the King's approval' the flag officer's ⅝″ stripe was to be reduced to ½″. However, the Admiralty had omitted to seek the approval of the King and he, refusing to be told what uniform he should wear, gave instructions that the Royal Family should continue to wear $5/8''$ stripes, a custom which is still continued. In 1931 all stripes were increased in width from $1/2''$ to $9/16''$.

Gold lace for officers of the Royal Naval Volunteer Reserve (RNVR), the reserve formed in 1903, was 'wavy' stripes; thus the old term 'wavy navy'. In 1958 when the former RNR and RNVR were unified as the RNR, the wavy stripes disappeared, except for temporary officers appointed for duty with the Sea Cadet Corps who still wear these today.

HEADGEAR. That worn on the head.

HOUSEWIFE. A mending kit for clothing issued to ratings on entry. (From 'hussif', a case for needles and thread.)

IDENTITY DISC. Not normally worn in the RN, but one is issued to each man and kept in the NBC respirator haversack, to be worn around the neck when ordered. The disc is made of stainless steel and embossed with the man's service number, name and initials, blood group and religion.

JERSEY, WOOL HEAVY. The blue woollen jersey which is worn as part of working dress. Officers and senior rates wear their badges of rank or rate on shoulder straps.

This item of clothing which was introduced during the 1970's revolutionised naval dress, being worn by officers and ratings as part of routine dress.

JUMPER. The top half of the blue square-rig suit worn by men dressed as seamen, which is a slim fitting garment worn outside the trousers. (Earlier 'jump' from the Fr. 'jupe', petticoat.)

When uniform was originally introduced in 1857, the seaman's best rig consisted of a short, round, cloth blue jacket and he soon became known as a 'blue jacket'. He also wore blue serge and white duck 'frocks'; these were loose blouse type garments which tucked into the top of the trousers. The blue jacket was abolished in 1891 and the blue serge frock replaced it as No. 1 rig until that also was replaced in 1906 by the jumper.

The jumper had to be pulled over the head and fashion dictated that it had to be as tight as possible, thereby often necessitating the assistance of one or more messmates for its removal. However, the problem was finally solved in the 1960s when zips in the front were introduced.

IMMERSION SUIT. Worn by aircrew to give protection against exposure in the event of ditching.

KIT. A term which describes all of the items of uniform clothing.

KIT MUSTER. This is an inspection of all of the items of a ratings uniform, required from time to time by Divisional Officers to ensure that kit is complete and in good repair. Leading rates and above are exempt.

KIT UP, TO. To be issued with uniform.

KIT UPKEEP ALLOWANCE (KUA). An allowance included in each man's pay, intended for the purpose of on-going replacement of uniform items.

LIFEJACKET. A personal issue to every man in a ship. These are inflatable and have a face shield and hood which incorporates a battery operated light. Some lifejackets are self inflating on contact with water and are issued to men who are working in hazardous positions.

LOAN CLOTHING. Items of clothing which are issued on loan for specific purposes, such as boots, overalls, etc.

LONG SERVICE AND GOOD CONDUCT BADGES. Chevron badges worn on the upper left arm by all ratings except chief petty officers. Up to a maximum of three badges may be worn, one for each four years service. They are of course subject to temporary forfeiture for misconduct.

The idea of long service was developed by a manning committee in 1835, when boy seamen were to be entered for ten years. When the badges were introduced in 1851, they entitled the wearer to an extra penny a day for each badge. One badge was awarded after five years service, the second after ten years and the third after fifteen. These periods were reduced in 1860 to three, eight and thirteen years and remained in force until 1950 when they were changed to four, eight and twelve years.

Before continuous service was introduced in 1853, service in the Merchant Navy was allowed to count towards badges. The first after seven years of which at least two must have been in the RN, the second after twelve years of which three must have been in the RN and the third after seventeen years with at least four in the RN.

MESS DRESS. Officers' No. 6 evening dress with white waistcoat, worn for dinner with flag officers.

MESS UNDRESS. Officers' No. 7 evening dress, similar to the No. 6 mess dress but with a blue waistcoat or a cummerbund worn instead of the white waistcoat. It is worn for mess dinners and evening wear ashore.

NBC RESPIRATOR. Issued to each man as a protection against nuclear, biological and chemical agents.

NBC SUIT. A suit of non-woven nylon fabric, treated with a liquid repellant and having an inside coating of activated charcoal, worn to counter the effects of nuclear, biological or chemical warfare agents.

NIGHT CLOTHING. See DRESS OF THE DAY.

NON-SUBSTANTIVE BADGES. A non-substantive badge is one which indicates a qualification or duty and not a rank. One of branch or specialisation is worn on each side of the collar by chief petty officers (CPOs) (except artificer CPOs), other ratings wearing it on the right upper arm with a badge for any additional skill worn on the right cuff. Branch badges have letters placed under indicating specialisation within the branch. These also vary according to rate; a crown above and a star below for CPO, a crown above for petty officer, a star above and below for leading rate and a star above for able rate.

Until 1830 there were no special arrangements for the training of men in special duties; then a gunnery school was set up in *HMS EXCELLENT* in Portsmouth Harbour which later moved ashore. The qualified men were rated as seamen gunners and in 1860 were given badges to wear. Other specialised training then followed with the subsequent introduction of badges; for torpedo in 1885; for artisans, gymnast instructors, naval police, signalmen and stokers in 1890; for wireless telegraphy in 1909; for officers cooks and stewards in 1916; for range-takers in 1918; for divers in 1919; for surveying recorders in 1921; for photographers, telegraphist air gunners and anti-submarine in 1930 and for sailmakers in 1932. During the Second World War new specialisations were introduced; air mechanics, electrical (previously the responsibility of the torpedo branch), boom defence and combined operations.

RIG. A term to describe the various uniforms worn, which comes from sailing days when a ship was fitted with a 'suit' of sails. The manner in which these were 'worn', depending on the class of ship, constituted the 'rig' of the vessel.

RIG OF THE DAY. See DRESS OF THE DAY.

SCRAN BAG. A locker or compartment into which all articles of clothing found 'sculling about' are placed. Such items may be redeemed by the owner on the payment of a small sum (originally, by custom, one inch of service issue soap for each article claimed).

SEA BOOTS. Rubber or PVC boots which ashore are called 'wellingtons'.

SEAMAN'S KNIFE. Although not strictly speaking an item of uniform, a clasp knife with one blade and a spike for splicing is issued to each man of the seaman branch.

Once, the Boatswain broke the point off all seamen's knives at the beginning of a voyage to ensure that the crew had no weapons of offence.

SHIRT SLEEVE ORDER. Officers' No. 12 dress, where the No. 5 jacket is removed in warm weather. Distinguishing shoulder straps are worn on the shirt.

SHOULDER STRAPS. These are worn by officers with white uniform, greatcoats, white shirts and jersies, bearing the distinguishing rank stripes. Similar straps are worn by warrant officers and chief and petty officers.

SILK. The black 'silk' around the front opening of the seaman's jumper.

The story of the black silk originally being worn as a token of mourning of the death of Nelson is another incorrect romanticism like that of the white stripes on the collar. Black silk neckcloths were being worn from the 1790s onwards. Later when official uniforms were issued these included a separate square of silk known as a 'silk handkerchief', originally worn knotted but later had to be folded and pressed into a narrow band with the ends stitched together. It was worn under the collar and secured by tapes on the jumper to allow a bight below the bow of the tapes.

In 1934 the black silk handkerchief became a 'neck handkerchief' and was reduced in size to an oblong fifty by twelve inches which was easier to adjust. It was later to become the 'silk scarf' which eventually disappeared as a separate item; the silk is now made up as a permanent part of the jumper.

SLOPS. Articles of uniform clothing which may be purchased from the ship's clothing store.

The term originally referred to the wide baggy breeches once worn by seamen, one of the items of clothing made available to them on repayment out of their wages from the 15th century onwards. When the men were brought on board ship by the press-gangs, their clothes, if not already, soon became rags and they were forced to buy clothing from the purser's 'slop chest' at exhorbitant prices. One of Pepys' reforms in the 17th century was to make good quality slops available to the men at reasonable prices. (OE., breeches.)

SLOP CHIT. A form made out by a supply rating which enables a man to purchase 'slops' from the clothing store.

SQUARE RIG. The uniform worn by 'men dressed as seamen'. A term from the days of sail when square rigged vessels had the principle sails extended by yards and suspended by the middle, not by stays, gaffs and booms.

SUBMARINE ESCAPE SUITS. Special suits to enable personnel to escape from a stricken submarine and ascend to the surface to be rescued.

SURVIVAL SUIT. Designed for personnel abandoning ship and intended for the wearer to be able to remain dry until boarding a liferaft.

TROPICAL RIG. An issue of white uniform which is made to officers and men in ships operating in warm climates (No. 10s).

TYPE. Supplied to a new-entry with his initial kit, this is a wooden 'stamp' bearing the owner's name which is used to mark each item of uniform.

UNDRESS. The term for the officers' No. 5 dress, which is the normal officers' uniform when worn for routine duties afloat and ashore.

UNDRESS COAT. The term for the naval officer's jacket.

WINDPROOF WORKING JACKET. A jacket for use by personnel employed on the upper deck or in boats, which is made from a polyester and cotton fabric material with a water repellent proofing and a quilted lining.

7

GENERAL TERMS AND ORDERS

'Avast' and 'belay there' are the two orders which are usually the limit of the 'landlubber's' general nautical vocabulary. These are very old orders which are indeed very much still in use aboard ship. There are many other orders and terms, of a general nature, which cannot be placed into any particular category.

* * *

ADRIFT. Absent, late.

AHOY.' The usual hail to a ship or boat to attract attention. (ME. 'hoy'.)

AIR DEFENCE TROOP. A Royal Marines Unit equipped with Javelin surface to air missiles attached to HQ 3 Commando Brigade for point defence of Brigade HQ or other important locations.

'ALL HANDS.' An order for the seaman of both watches (all seamen), except those actually on watch, to muster on deck immediately. The full order is 'all hands on deck', but this is usually shortened to 'all hands'.

ALLOTMENT. The method whereby men are able to allot a portion of their pay to their wives or other relatives.

An allotment act was passed as long ago as 1757, but this only provided for men to allot the whole of their net pay and, as can be imagined, few took advantage of it. However, a new act passed in 1795 allowed men to allot half of their full pay.

ALL STANDING. A sudden and unexpected stop.

'ALL THE PORT (OR STARBOARD) WATCH'. A call for the whole of a watch to muster.

AMAIN. Suddenly, at once.

ANTI-FOULING. A general description of the paint used on the underside of a ship below the waterline, applied to resist marine growth.

ARISINGS. Pieces of material left over from a job which are of value and must be collected for sale or re-use.

ARTICLES OF WAR. The disciplinary code for the Royal Navy which applies in peace-time as well as war.

The English version of the ancient sea laws of Oleron was introduced in 1336 and eventually became known as the 'Black Book of the Admiralty'. In subsequent centuries, the laws were supplemented by individual ships' captains and so in order to provide a code of punishment which would apply throughout the whole of the navy, the 'Articles of War' were introduced into the first Naval Discipline Act of 1661. The Articles of War were omitted from the Army Act of 1955 but were retained in the Naval Discipline Act of 1956.

ASHORE. On land.

ATHWART. Across. (From 'thwart', ON. 'thvert'.)

AVAST. The order to stop or cease. (Du. 'vast', fast.)

'AYE-AYE, SIR.' The correct reply when acknowledging an order given by an officer. It means 'yes-yes', indicating that the order has been both heard and understood. Royal Marines reply 'very good, Sir'. (Ice, 'ei', for ever.)

BANYAN. A picnic. This was originally the term given to a meatless day in a ship in the early 19th century. Officially, meatless days were Mondays, Wednesdays and Fridays and although abolished in 1825, continued for many years. They were in fact reintroduced in the First World War. ('Banyan' from a Far East religious sect who could not eat the meat of any living creature.)

BASE PORT. The naval base to which a ship is attached, i.e. Portsmouth, Devonport, Rosyth, Faslane, Gibraltar or Hong Kong.

BATTEN DOWN, TO. To close all openings in the weather decks and superstructure.

'BEAR A HAND.' Give assistance.

BEFORE. In front of. (OE. 'beforan', in front of.)

'BELAY THAT.' Cancel that order.
'BELAY THERE.' A general term to stop or cease. (From 'belay', to make fast.)
'BELOW THERE.' A hail to someone below.
BEND ON, TO. To attach something.
BILLET. A post in a ship or shore establishment, which is filled by 'drafting' a man.
BORNE ON THE BOOKS. To be a member of a ship's company.

The term comes from the old naval practice of entering an infant's name on the crew muster list of a ship to enable him to accrue seniority by the time he reached the age to serve. The custom was abolished early in the 19th century.

BREAK SHIP, TO. To leave a ship without permission, or to desert.
BROACH, TO. To open up a fresh cask, package, etc. (Fr. 'brocher', to pierce.)
CANT, TO. To tilt or slant over, or sometimes to swing around. (Du. 'kant'.)
CHOCK, TO. To secure articles stowed on deck to prevent their moving about in rough weather. (OE. 'ceocian', to choke.)
CLAP ON, TO. To add something temporarily. In sailing days, additional sails were 'clapped on' to take advantage for a fair wind.
CLEAR FOR ACTION, TO. To remove any encumbrance from the upper deck and prepare for action.

In sailing days, the gundecks were cleared of wooden cabin partitions and furniture which was then stowed on the decks below.

'CLEAR LOWER DECK.' The order for men of all branches, except those actually on watch, to muster on the upper deck.
CLENCH. Permanent join. (OE. 'clenchan', to make, to cling.)
CLEW UP, TO. To finish. Originally to draw up the lower ends of the sails to the yards by their clews. (OE. 'cliwen'.)
CLOSED UP. To be at a particular post, for instance; hands are said to be 'closed up' at action stations.

COCOON. The term to describe the sealed envelope placed around a particular piece of armament and from which the air is extracted, which is done to preserve weapons aboard ships of the reserve fleet.

COMMACHIO GROUP RM. A special Royal Marines Unit, based at RM CONDOR, which was formed in 1980 for the protection of the UK's offshore installations and other facilities.

COMMAND. Submarine squadrons and also mine countermeasures (MCM) vessels squadrons are grouped together, each under the command of a flag officer, and known as Submarine Command and MCM Command.

COMMANDO (CDO). A Royal Marines (RM) unit specially trained to overcome every conceivable kind of obstacle in all climatic conditions. It consists of 650 men under the command of a lieutenant-general RM. There are three commandos; 40 Cdo, 42 Cdo and 45 Cdo Group which make up the 3 Cdo Brigade. 42 Cdo and 45 Cdo Gp are specially trained in arctic warfare.

The idea for commandos in Britain evolved during the early part of the Second World War as a means of providing forces to spearhead attacks and secure lodgements for other forces to exploit. The first formed were Army Commandos in 1940. As amphibious landing parties were the natural function of the Royal Marines, these were the obvious choice from which to form commandos. However, there were so many calls on their services, particularly with the RN, that it was not until 1942 that they were able to take commando work. In 1945 the Army commandos were disbanded and commando training passed exclusively to the RM as being most qualified for this role.

The first commandos were Boer farmers who made such formidable light forces in the South African War of 1900–1902. They formed bands of fighting men who relied upon small scale, swift attacks without the burden of supply columns and had much success due to the surprise and capture of arms and equipment from the enemy.

COMMISSIONING CEREMONY. When, on the day after a ship's commissioning pennant has been hoisted, the newly appointed ship's company, together with families, assemble on the quarterdeck or on the jetty alongside. Prayers, led by the Chaplain, then follow.

CONTINUOUS SERVICE. The method by which a man signs on for a period of years and is continuously employed.

Instituted in 1853, prior to which the system was that men signed on for a commission in a ship and were discharged from the service when the ship paid off.

CORPS, THE. The Corps of Royal Marines.

CRAFT. All small vessels. It was once a term to describe fishing gear and then applied to fishing vessels, but now applies to all small vessels, fishing or not. (OE. 'croeft'.)

DD. Notation on a man's service history record for 'discharged dead'.

There is a tradition that regardless of the hour of death of an officer or man aboard ship, the captain must be informed at once. A record of the ship's exact position at the time of death is made in the ship's log.

DEFAULTERS. Ratings who 'default' against the regulations. Those to be charged for misdemeanors are initially mustered before the Officer-of-the-Watch who may warn, dismiss the case, or pass it to higher authority, i.e. Captain's defaulters. In the case of Captain's defaulters, mustered each morning, should punishments be awarded then defaulters become 'men under punishment'.

DEFENCE COUNCIL INSTRUCTIONS (RN) (DCIs). These are published weekly and circulated to all ships and establishments. They provide the means for the rapid circulation of instructions concerning changes to administration and equipment.

Prior to 1964, when the unified Ministry of Defence was formed, they were known as Admiralty Fleet Orders (AFOs).

DETAILED, TO BE. To be given instructions for a particular task.

DETENTION. Confinement in cells or 'detention quarters'.

DETENTION QUARTERS. Naval prison ashore, internment into which is authorised by a Warrant signed by a flag officer.

DHOBI, TO. To wash clothes. (Indian for washerman.)

DISCHARGE. Release from the Service.

DRAFT, TO. To move, or post, men from one ship or shore establishment to another.

DRAFTING PREFERENCE CARD (DPC). A card held by the Naval Drafting Division for each rating. A DPC can be updated by a rating on request, to show his preference for a type of ship or establishment to which he may next be drafted.

'D'YE HEAR THERE.' Routine broadcast messages are 'piped' over a ship's broadcast system by the boatswain's mate, A special broadcast, such as information to the ship's company given personally by the Captain, is preceded by 'd'ye hear there' in order to command special attention.

EASY. Meaning, in general, to take off the pressure and used as an order in a variety of situations.

END FOR END. To turn anything around to reverse its position.

ENGAGE, TO. A target on which fire is opened is 'engaged'.

ENGAGEMENT. The period for which a man serves in the RN.

FAIR. Unobstructed, the opposite of 'foul'. i.e. 'fair wind', 'fair lead' and 'fairway'.

FISHERY PROTECTION SQUADRON. This squadron, the oldest and largest in the RN, was formed in 1586. It is unique in that it is under contract to the Ministry of Agriculture, Fisheries and Food. Some fourteen vessels are employed in the squadron, which operate up to 200 miles from the coast of the UK. The main function of the squadron is to check for fishing vessels operating illegally.

FLEET, TO. To move the position of something. Also the area covered by a stage when painting the ship's side.

FLEET TRAIN. A number of Royal Fleet Auxillary ships supplying the fleet.

FLOTSAM. The wreckage of a ship or cargo which is floating on the surface of the sea. (OFr. 'flotasion', to float).

FOUL. To be obstructed or tangled in some way, e.g. foul anchor.

FULL DUE. Anything finally set up is 'set up for a full due'.

'G'. The note 'G' sounded on the bugle as a preparatory warning call, prior to 'out pipes', 'divisions', etc.

'GANGWAY.' A much heard cry, used when requiring a clearance of bodies through a passageway.

GEAR. A general term for equipment, clothing, etc. (ME. 'gere'.)

HAIL, TO. To shout, or call through a 'loud-hailer', to another ship or boat.

HARD LYING MONEY. An allowance paid to officers and men serving in submarines and minesweepers as compensation where 'living conditions are markedly below those which can be expected in a modern frigate'.

This was instigated by Winston Churchill as First Lord, following a sea trip in a destroyer, just prior to the outbreak of the First World War. The allowance for serving in destroyers was stopped by the time of the Second World War.

HEAD. Used in many instances to mean the top part.

HOG OUT, TO. To scrub out thoroughly. A 'hog' was a stiff brush used for scrubbing the ship's bottom.

HOLIDAY. A gap, for example; an uncovered part when painting.

HOME WATERS. Those waters around the UK.

IN THE REPORT. On the report (or charge) sheet.

JETSAM. Equipment deliberately jettisoned from a ship. (OFr. 'getaison'.)

JOIN A SHIP, TO. When drafted to a ship or establishment, one 'joins'.

JURY. A term for temporary or makeshift, for example; rigging a 'jury' rudder to enable a ship to reach harbour. (OFr. 'juree', temporary substitution.)

KETTLE. A mess pot of any kind.

LAUNCH, TO. To drag or push an object along. (Fr. 'lancer'.)

LAY, TO. To go to an assigned position aboard a ship, e.g., to 'lay aft'.

LIGAN. Sunken gear or cargo which has been cast overboard and buoyed. It is the property of the owners, but if unclaimed becomes the property of the Crown.

LIGHTER. A large, open, flat-bottomed barge like vessel used for loading and unloading ships. (Du. 'lichter'.)

LOCAL FOREIGN SERVICE (LFS). Foreign service where a rating is 'locally' billeted in a shore establishment.

LOCAL OVERSEAS ALLOWANCE (LOA). Paid to personnel serving abroad where the general cost of living overall is more than living costs in the UK.

LOWER DECK. A general term for all ratings which comes from the days when all messes were situated on the lower gun deck, the deck below the orlop deck, in a sailing ship.

LOYAL TOAST. A toast to the Sovereign in the Wardroom Mess. The president of the mess calls upon his vice, usually the most junior officer, to propose 'Gentlemen, the Queen'. All raise their glasses remaining seated, a dispensation granted by William IV because of the low deckhead beams, and repeat 'The Queen, God bless her'.

In 1964 the Queen directed that, to mark their tercentenary, the Royal Marines should in future drink the Loyal Toast seated in RM messes ashore and afloat.

MAKE FAST, TO. To secure something into position.

MAN, TO. To provide hands for a particular function.

MEN UNDER PUNISHMENT. Ratings who have been awarded punishment as a result of being mustered before either the Captain or Commander as defaulters. The degree and length of term of punishment may vary according to the seriousness of the default, but generally consists of stoppage of leave and additional duty out of working hours.

MESS-MATE. A mess companion.

MESSTRAPS. Mess utensils.

MILK ISSUE. A free issue of half of a pint of fresh milk is made to all juniors under the age of 18, whenever fresh milk is available.

MISS-MUSTERS. In order to provide for the payment of men who are unable to attend main payment owing to their having been on watch, a 'miss-muster payment is arranged at a suitable time. The men concerned are referred to as 'miss-musters'.

MUSTER, TO. For a group of men to assemble. (OFr. 'mostre' from L. 'monstrare', to show.)

In the early days of the Royal Navy, a 'muster book' was kept aboard each ship into which was entered the names of all ratings serving aboard. The muster book was the basis on which victuals and payment were made. Often, ficticious names were entered for whom pay and victuals were drawn dishonestely and a periodical muster was held at which men answered to their names.

NAMET. The Naval Mathematics and English Test, the educational qualification for advancement from ordinary rate to able and leading rate.

NAVAL DISCIPLINE ACT. This act embodies the Articles of War and an act of Parliament and is therefore one of the laws of the country. It lays down who shall be subject to it, what acts shall be offences against it, how offences shall be tried and how punishments awarded.

NAUTICAL. Referring to anything which pertains to the sea or seafaring. (L. 'nauticus', from Gk. 'nautikos' from 'nautes', sailor from 'navis', ship.)

NMMIS. Naval Manpower Management Information System. A computer based system providing data on Service personnel and jobs to manpower planners and controllers. It consists of a database supported by a mainframe computer servicing terminals in HMS CENTURION, the RN pay and records office.

NUMBER 10. A punishment of stoppage of leave, awarded by the Captain to certain defaulters.

'OFF CAPS'. The order given for church parades, funerals and at a flag officer's or the Captains inspection of a ship's company. Caps are also removed when entering a senior officer's cabin. Officers when entering messdecks etc., not on business of a particularly official nature, remove their caps as an indication that no marks of respect are required.

Removal of the cap or hat was an early method of saluting in the Royal Navy.

OFFICIAL NUMBER. Each rating on entry to the Service is given an 'official number' which is preceded by letters denoting his base port.

OFFSHORE. Away from the land.

OPEN ENGAGEMENT. Service in the RN up to the age of 18 and then a further 22 years, with the right to give 18 months notice on completion of at least 2 ½ years service.

'OUT PIPES.' The order given to end 'stand easy' (or break period). In wooden ships, pipe smoking was only allowed on the upper deck and the order 'out pipes' was given at the end of the break on deck as a fire precaution.

PAY BOOK. An identity book issued to each rating on joining the Service. Thus named as it is required to be produced when a rating paid by cash receives payment.

PERMISSION TO GROW. A request to the Captain to grow a beard. Anyone requesting 'permission to grow' is allowed to do so during a period of 30 days during which all leave is stopped. (For a compulsive 'shore runner' this is a way of saving money.) After this period, the beard is inspected and a decision made, according to the appearance of the growth, as to whether it may be retained or shaved off.

When Queen Victoria reviewed the requirements of the sailor's face in the RN, she decided that beards were in order, but that it was also equally proper to be clean shaven. However, in spite of her Albert's moustache, she ordained that whilst a whiskered upper lip was alright for the Army, it was not suitable for seafaring.

QUEEN'S REGULATIONS ROYAL NAVY (QRRNs). These regulations supplement the Naval Discipline Act and include all of the various orders and instructions concerning every detail of the government of the Royal Navy.

Prior to 1964, when the unified Ministry of Defence was formed, these were known as the 'Queen's/King's Regulations and Admiralty Instruction (QR & AIs), the origin of which dates back to 1731 when the Admiralty issued its first printed instructions.

'PIPE DOWN'. The call sounded on the boatswain's call last thing at night as the signal for the hands to turn in and for lights to be put out. This is also a term meaning 'be quiet'.

PIPE, TO. The act of making a call using the boatswain's call. Orders given over a ship's 'Tannoy' (broadcast) system are always 'piped', i.e., preceded by a call.

Whistling is forbidden in HM ships because it is likely to be confused with the piping of orders.

Before the advent of broadcast systems, orders were passed on to ship's company by the boatswain's mates piping the orders. The boatswain's call was the whistle used as far back as the 13th century and then later became the badge of the Lord High Admiral until 1562. After that time it reverted to its original use and since 1671 has been referred to as a 'call'. In sailing ships it was used to order different stages of sail drill.

PORT SERVICE. Service in shore establishments or in ships operating on a restricted day running basis from the UK or undergoing long refit or conversion.

PRE-WETTING. A system of spraying the outer surfaces of a ship with salt water to minimise the effects of nuclear fall-out.

RA. Rationed Ashore. Men living ashore with their families are allowed an 'RA' allowance.

RAIDING SQUADRON. Royal Marines operating small craft and trained for all climatic conditions.

RAS. Replenishment at sea, as carried out by jackstay transfer from a supply ship.

RELIEF. One who relieves another of his watch, trick or other duty.

REQUESTMEN. Any ratings who wish to see the Captain or Commander for any reason, i.e. to request advancement, rating, special leave etc. Each request is stated on a Request Form which is passed through a rating's Divisional Officer. Captain's Requestmen are mustered at a suitable time and each rating is seen by the Captain.

RIG, TO. To prepare something for use, such as a boom or an awning, etc.

RUN. Absent without leave from duty. The word 'run' is entered on a man's history sheet.

SCRUB OUT, TO. To clean the deck of a compartment.

SCULLING. Something left lying around not in its proper place is said to be 'sculling around'.

SEAMANLIKE. To function as a skilful seaman.

SEA SERVICE. Generally service in ships in commission, either operating at home or abroard.

SECOND OPEN ENGAGEMENT. Continuing in the Service beyond 22 years for a further 10 years.

SECURE, TO. To finish and tidy away after a job or watch. Also to make something fast.
SEPARATION ALLOWANCE. An allowance paid to a married man whose billet is more than 200 miles from his family.
SERVE, TO. One 'serves' in a ship.
SHAKEDOWN. A trial cruise to determine a ship's fitness and to familiarise the crew with their duties.
SHAKE, TO. To take off fastenings, such as from a packing case.
SHIPBOARD. An activity on board ship, i.e., 'shipboard life'.
SHIPBORNE. Something fitted in a ship, in the context of a type of weapon or piece of equipment which has an equivalent ashore.
SHIPMATE. Said of another serving in the same ship.
SHIPSHAPE. Neat and tidy.
SHIP, TO. To place something into position.
SHIVER, To. To shatter something to pieces.
SHOOT. A gunnery practice.
SHORE BASE. One of the base ports; Portsmouth, Devonport, Roysth or Portland.
SHOREGOING. One going ashore.
SITREP. Situation report.
SLUE, TO. To turn anything around on its axis without removing it.
'SMACK IT ABOUT.' An order to 'get a move on'.
SNUG. Properly secured.
SPECIAL BOAT SERVICE (SBS). A special forces unit of the Royal Marines, formed in the early part of the Second World War, in which all ranks are classed as swimmer canoeists and trained in parachuting and the use of small craft. It is the equivalent of the Army's Special Air Service (SAS) and its main role is to provide the RM with amphibious reconnaissance and intelligence about the enemy.
SPELL. A period of time, either engaged at work or at leisure.
'SPLICE THE MAINBRACE.' Although the rum ration was discontinued in 1970, the traditional order to 'splice the mainbrace' is still made very occasionally to mark a

special event such as a visit to the fleet by the sovereign. On such an occasion, each officer and rating over the age of 18 is issued with one eighth of a pint of rum or, if rum is not available, two cans of beer.

In sailing ships the mainbrace was the stoutest rope of the rigging. If it parted, its repair by splicing was such a difficult and arduous task that it merited an extra ration of rum for the hands completing it.

SQUARE OFF, TO. To make 'shipshape' or tidy, especially caps or clothing.

'STAND BY'. Be prepared to follow orders.

STAND DOWN, TO. For hands to return to normal duties after action stations or a special task.

STANDING. Anything fixed or permanent, e.g. 'standing rigging' and 'standing orders'.

START, TO. To move something from rest.

STAVE, TO. To hole anything or break into it.

STORES. Anything on board a ship which will be used for a specific purpose.

STOW, TO. To put in a suitable place or position. (OE. 'stowigan' from 'stow', place.)

STRIKE, TO. To lower or let down anything. Used emphatically to denote the lowering of colours as a token of surrender.

SULLAGE. Garbage, rubbish.

SWEEP, TO. To drag the bight of a wire or chain along the sea bottom to locate or recover a sunken object.

SWOP DRAFT. A method whereby ratings allocated a 'billet' to a ship or establishment which is not particularly to their liking, may exchange with another rating who is similarly placed.

TAKE UP, TO. To buy from the ship's store, usually in the context of uniform items of clothing, tobacco, etc.

TALLY. A label or name of a person or article.

TAUT. Tight, tense, not slack. Also in good order, trim. (ME. 'togt'.)

TELL OFF, TO. To detail men for work.

TEND, TO. To look after something in operation. (From 'attend'.)

TRICK. To take a turn at something, e.g., the helmsman takes a 'trick' at the wheel.

TURN IN, TO. To go to bed.
TURN TO, TO. To start work.
ULLAGE. A term to describe damaged victuals. (OFr. 'ulhage' from 'ulha', to fill.)
'UNDER BELOW'. A warning for hands to get out of the way of danger from above.
UNDERBORNE. Under strength in personnel.
UNRIG, TO. To dismantle something previously rigged.
UNSHIP, TO. To remove anything from its position.
VERTREP. Vertical replenishment, where a helicopter lifts and transports stores or personnel from a supply ship.
WARRANT. A disciplinary document signed by a flag officer which authorises the sentence of confining a rating to detention quarters ashore. The Warrant is read out by the Captain before the whole of the lower deck. The Captain himself may only authorise a sentence of confinement in cells aboard ship.
WASH UP. A meeting, following an excercise, to discuss events and results.
WATCH BELOW. The hands not on watch.

8

SHIP ORGANISATION

The requirements of a ship at sea are akin to a community ashore. All of the inhabitants, the ship's company, need to be fed, clothed and paid; their work, recreation, leave and welfare have to be organised. Facilities which might be taken for granted ashore all have to be provided on board ship; a church, a laundry, a library, shops, medical care, police, firemen, postmen, etc. At the same time the whole company must be organised into an efficient fighting unit.

* * *

ACTION STATIONS. The fighting positions in a ship. Also the term to describe the first degree of readiness for action which is imminent, with all hands closed up to their quarters.

ACTION STATIONS RELAXED. The second degree of readiness for action with all hands closed up at their quarters except for a small proportion allowed to fall out for meals or relaxation.

AFTERNOON. See WATCHES.

AMMUNITION SHIP. An evolution, a set routine, where a combined effort by a large part of the ship's company is required to embark and strike down armament stores.

CAPTAIN'S OFFICE. The office which deals with the administration of the internal organisation of a ship. It is sometimes combined with the pay office.

CATERING OFFICE. The office which deals with the administration of the victualling of the ship's company, including the cooking and serving of meals and the storage and issue of provisions.

CENTRALISED MESSING. A system of messing in the latest ships, where the dining halls are situated around the galley with serving counters between. Older ships which have no dining halls use a system called 'modified centralised messing', where individuals collect their own food from the servery and take it to their messes to be eaten.

COMMANDER'S OFFICE. The office which deals with the administration of the internal organisation of a ship. Routines and daily orders are issued from there.

COMMUNICATIONS CENTRE. The office which deals with all signals and communications (other than mail).

CONTROL MARKINGS. These are marks painted on doors, hatches and other openings in the way of various letters to denote grades of control of watertight and gastight integrity. Openings are opened or closed according to the conditions required by the 'state of readiness' that a ship has in force at any particular time.

CRUISING STATIONS. The fourth degree of readiness for action which is possible but fairly remote. A proportion of the armament is manned, with the remainder of the ship's company carrying out their normal duties.

DAILY ORDERS. Orders which include the names of officers and men required to carry out routine duties and any instructions for duties of a non-routine nature. These are issued by the Commander's or First Lieutenant's office on the evening before they are to be carried out.

DAMAGE CONTROL. The Nuclear, Biological and Chemical Damage Control (NBCD) organisation for maintaining ship safety, which is ready to deal with any damage a ship may sustain.

DARKEN SHIP. The operation, carried out in wartime and during exercises, of ensuring that no light is emitted from scuttles or apertures during the period from dusk to dawn.

DEGREES OF READINESS. The degrees of readiness of the ship's armament.

DIVISIONS. For general administrative and welfare purposes, a ship's company is divided into a number of 'divisions' of men who normally work and mess together. Seamen, being a large group, may be divided into divisions which correspond with their parts of ship, i.e. forecastle, top and quarterdeck.

The idea of divisions originated from Admiral Kempenfelt who, in the 18th century, divided up his men and appointed officers over each to inspect and control their conduct.

'Divisions' is also a term to describe the mustering of all of ship's company by divisions for inspection, excepting men on watch.

DOG WATCHES. See WATCHES.

EMERGENCY STATIONS. Special stations around a ship which are manned in order to prepare for abandoning ship.

ENTERING AND LEAVING HARBOUR. When a ship enters or leaves harbour, those of the ship's company not required to work the ship are fallen in by divisions on the upper deck, correctly dressed in the 'rig of the day'.

EVOLUTIONS. These are standard routines for carrying out emergencies which it is known from past experience are likely to be encountered. There are many of these, for which orders are included in the ship's Standing Orders. Typical evolutions are replenishment at sea, towing, boarding party and storing ship.

FIRST WATCH. See WATCHES.

FORENOON. See WATCHES.

FREE GANGWAY. In ships lying alongside and in shore establishments, certain times are laid down between which ratings are permitted to use a 'free gangway'. When this is in force, ratings are permitted to pass close by the officer-of-the-watch and salute, instead of reporting or falling in for inspection.

FX. An abbreviation for the Forecastle Division of men in a ship.

GUARD AND STEERAGE. A term applied to watchkeepers, boat's crews, etc., who are allowed to lie in later than the time at which the hands are called.

The 'steerage' was once situated right aft in a ship by the rudder head. Near this flat were berthed the officers who, together with the guard and any passengers, were allowed to lie in later than the rest of the hands. They were roused by the call 'guard and steerage'.

HARBOUR ROUTINE. See ROUTINE.

LEAVE. Granted on a weekend and seasonal basis.

It was not until 1860 that captains were authorised to grant regular leave and not until 1890 was it a right and not a priveledge.

LIBERTY. Daily leave of less than 24 hours duration. (Fr. 'liberte', freedom.)

LIBERTY BOAT. This can mean the boat which carries libertymen from ship to shore, but in a shore establishment the same term is applied to the mustering of libertymen before being allowed 'ashore' through the main gate.

LIBERTYMEN. Men with permission to go ashore for short leave.

MAKE AND MEND. A half day holiday usually granted on every Saturday as circumstances permit. When a ship is in harbour an extra 'make and mend' may occasionally be granted for sports and recreation.

Clothing stocks carried in old-time sailing warships were by necessity limited and clothes had to last for as long as possible. In order to give their men an opportunity to repair their garments or fashion new ones, captains of ships began to set aside one afternoon a week, usually Thursdays, for this purpose. On these days, known as 'rope yarn Sundays', the boatswain's mates would pipe 'hands to make and mend clothes'.

MAIL OFFICE. The office which handles the despatch, receipt, collection and internal distribution of official and private mail. It is usually incorporated in the Regulating Office.

MORNING. See WATCHES.

NAVAL STORE OFFICE. The office which deals with the stowage, issue and return of naval stores, which is usually adjacent to the main naval store.

OFFICERS STATE BOARD. A board situated near the gangway which contains a list of all of the officers. Alongside each name is an indicator which will show either 'onboard' or ashore. The board is kept up to date by the gangway staff.

OPERATION AWKWARD. Measures taken to deal with any threat from underwater attack by swimmers whilst in harbour. These include periodic inspections of the ship's bottom to ensure it is clear.

PAINT SHIP. An evolution, where a large part of the ship's company are required to paint the ship.

PART OF SHIP. For purposes of cleaning and maintenance, a ship is divided into 'parts of ship', the number depending on the size of the ship. Small ships have two; forecastle and quarterdeck, while larger ships have an additional 'top' part of ship. In the largest ships, in addition to the forecastle and quarterdeck parts, there are also the foretop and maintop parts.

PAY OFFICE. The office which deals with all matters concerning pay, allowances and allotments.

PREPARE FOR SEA. The operation of preparing the ship for leaving harbour. This includes testing the main engines, steering gear, compasses and communications systems. If the ship is at anchor, then the cable is shortened. When at a buoy, the slip rope is reeved and the bridle unshackled. If alongside, the berthing hawsers are singled up. In addition, certain watertight doors are closed, all moveable gear is secured and boats covered and secured.

PRIVILEGED LEAVE LIST. There are occasions when only a limited amount of leave can be granted, where leave breaking would cause great inconvenience or misbehaviour ashore might reflect badly on the service. In these cases only men on the 'privileged leave list' are allowed ashore. These are men who have no record of leave breaking and can be trusted ashore. When a ship first commissions, all of the hands are in this category, but those who subsequently misbehave ashore or are late returning from leave have their names removed from the list.

In 1860 new regulations for the first time authorised captains to grant leave of 48 hours or four days. Following this, thousands deserted each year and for this reason in 1866 it became necessary to grant leave in three categories. There was a 'special' class for men of good character, 'privileged' for less reliable men who were given leave when convenient, and 'regular' for anyone else.

QUARTER. Action station. A man's 'quarter' is that part of the armament of a ship to which he is detailed. It may vary according to the degree of readiness.

QUARTER BILL. A list of officers and men in a ship, giving the action station of each.

REGULATING OFFICE. The office on board ship concerned with the discipline, liberty and leave of the ship's company.

RISK MARKINGS. These are coloured markings on doors, hatches and other openings which denote the risk to the water-tight and gas-tight integrity of a ship if they are left open. Red markings denote that compartments will flood immediately if the ship is damaged below the waterline. Orange markings denote a risk to gas-tight integrity.

ROUNDS. A tour of inspection of a ship, carried out by the Officer-of-the-Watch during the first watch. 'Captain's Rounds' are carried out peridiocally.

ROUTINE. The timetable which covers the general activities in a ship. There are different routines depending on whether the ship is in harbour or at sea; these are known as 'daily harbour routine' and 'daily sea routine'.

SEA ROUTINE. See ROUTINE.

SECURING FOR SEA. See PREPARE FOR SEA.

SENIOR RATES' TALLY BOARD. A board situated near the gangway which contains all of the names of the senior rates borne. When going ashore each senior rate places a tick by his name and on returning aboard places a cross tick.

SHIP'S BOOK NUMBER. Each rating is allocated a ship's book number when joining a ship for use as an aid to identification. The number is entered in the 'short leave card' which is issued and also appears in the watchbill.

SHIP'S FUND. A fund used to meet the cost of recreation of a ship's company and also for benevolent purposes within a ship. The main source of income to the fund is a rebate on NAAFI canteen sales.

SHORT LEAVE CARDS. Leading rates and below are issued with these cards on joining a ship. Their cards are surrendered when going ashore and claimed when returning aboard. It is by this method that a check can be made of any ratings 'adrift'.

These were originally called 'station cards' and are often still called this name.

SILENT HOURS. A term which denotes the period of the night watches between the times of 'pipe down' and 'call the hands'. So called from the custom of not marking the time by bells, in the days when the ship's bell was used for that purpose, so as not to disturb those sleeping below.

STAND EASY. A break or rest period, usually at a fixed time during the mid forenoon and also mid afternoon.

STANDING ORDERS. Orders issued by the Commanding Officer which concern all aspects of a ship and her company. These are 'standing' and not subject to change such as daily orders or other temporary instructions.

STATE, THE. The report made daily on a ship's fuel, water and provision levels.

STATION CARDS. See SHORT LEAVE CARDS.

STATES OF READINESS. These are four different states of readiness that are required to ensure that a ship is always ready to combat damage, flooding and fire, no matter how caused. The four states are; 'high' when an attack is imminent, 'war seagoing' when attack possible, 'normal cruising' when attack unlikely and 'normal 'peacetime routine' in harbour. Not to be confused with 'degrees of readiness', which relate to the armament.

STATION. A man's place for a specific duty.

STORE SHIP. This is usually an evolution, a set routine, where a combined working effort by many of the ship's company is required to embark and stroke down stores.

TECHNICAL OFFICE. The office which deals with the administration of the engineering and weapons departments and is concerned with the main, domestic and weapon machinery.

WATCH. A continuous 'watch' must be kept in a ship at sea or in harbour to ensure her safety and to keep her in working 'trim'. A proportion of the complement of officers and men must therefore always be 'on watch'. The number on watch depends on the type of ship, whether at sea or in harbour and the duties on which she is engaged. (OE. 'woeccian', to wake or stay awake.)

A ship's company is divided into 'watches', usually 'port watch' and 'starboard watch', each watch being divided into two parts. A part of a watch is the smallest number that is used to work the ship.

During the first half of the 19th century 'watch stripes' were introduced to be worn, to show at a glance which watch a man belonged to. The stripe was made of red or blue material, depending on the colour of the garment, worn around the top of the sleeve of the left arm by the port watch and the right by the starboard. Where the watches were divided into two parts, the first part wore one stripe and the second two. They were abolished in 1895, though retained for boys in training ships until 1907.

WATCH AND WATCH. A part of a watch working four hours on duty and four hours off duty alternately.

WATCHBILL. A nominal list of all officers and ratings aboard a ship, giving the watches and stations to which each is quartered, i.e., watch, part of ship, station for entering and leaving harbour, station for abandoning ship, etc. Sometimes combined with the quarter bill and then known as the 'watch and quarter bill'.

WATCHES. Divisions of the working day. From midnight to 0400 is the 'middle watch', from 0400 to 0800 the 'morning', from 0800 to noon the 'forenoon', from noon to 1600 the 'afternoon'. The next four hours are divided into two two-hour watches known as the 'dog watches'; they are from 1600 to 1800, the 'first dog' and from 1800 to 2000, the 'last dog'. The purpose of the dog watches is to divide the 24 hour day into an uneven number of watches so that watchkeepers do not keep the same watches every day. The final watch of the day, from 2000 to midnight, is the 'first watch', so called because it is the first watch of the night.

Note that the word 'hours' after the time is not normally used in the Royal Navy.

9

FLAGS, SIGNALS AND SALUTES

Before the days of complex telecommunications the method of conveying messages or instructions at sea was usually by flag. Flag signals have been in use in the Royal Navy since the 16th century. They were first used in the First Dutch War with only five flags; the ensign, jack, red, blue and pendant. From then on flags of different colours and designs appeared, but it was not until the late 18th century that a detailed flag code was introduced with 50 flags conveying some 330 instructions.

Flashing light signals and the sophisticated electronics of today might make communication by flag seem rather primitive. However, the international flag code which is used allows conversation between ships of different nationalities and more than one ship has been grateful for its signal flags when isolated at sea with a faulty power line or technical breakdown.

In the days of sail, one method of making signals was to make use of the sails themselves and another method was to use a combination of ships guns and lanterns. But the real key to the first improvements in signalling was electricity which provided the means for powerful flashing lamps, the siren and the fog signal.

In 1895 experiments in wireless telegraphy were started by Captain H. B. Jackson RN, who by the spring of 1896 had established communications over distances up to 6,000 yards. Although Captain Jackson had worked independently of Senator Marconi and introduced the possibilities of wireless to the navy, the latter's designs were accepted.

* * *

A FOR ALPHA. The letter 'A' in the International Code of Signals. When made on its own it means 'I have a diver down, keep well clear at low speed'.

ALDIS LAMP. A hand lamp fitted with a finger operated shutter for sending morse signals between ships in close company.

Samuel B. Morse, the American inventor, devised his code in 1838. It was in 1867 that Rear-Admiral Philip Colomb adapted the code for use with a heliograph, a device which used sunlight reflected on two adjustable mirrors, and the system was adopted by the Royal Navy. After 1869, when Thomas Edison produced the first practical electric light bulb, it became possible to use electric lamps to flash Morse Code messages.

ALERT, THE. A bugle salute as a mark of respect paid to an occasion or rank. The alert is sounded immediately prior to the hoisting and lowering of Colours, when all hands on the upper deck face aft and salute, remaining at the salute until the 'carry on' is sounded. It is also sounded on the arrival and departure over the gangway of important personages and in harbour or an anchorage when passing or being passed by a flagship or a foreign warship.

Other than for the hoisting and lowering of Colours, when the alert is sounded, all hands on the upper deck stand to attention facing outboard until the 'carry on' is sounded. Where no bugler is borne, the 'still' is sounded on the boatswain's call instead.

ANSWERING PENNANT. A red and white striped pennant used in flag signalling as an acknowledgement of a signal. If the signal is doubtful or flags cannot be distinguished then the answering pennant is hoisted 'at the dip' (two thirds of the way up) and left in this position until the signal is understood.

AT THE DIP. Said of a signal flag when hoisted only two-thirds of the way up the yard instead of 'close up'. Ensigns are dipped as a salute between ships, for instance a British Merchant Navy vessel on passing an RN ship may dip her Red Ensign as a courtesy salute.

RN ships dip their Ensigns to foreign warships only if they dip theirs first. This originated from Cromwell's

Navigation Act of 1651, which made a demand on all foreign vessels to lower their flags to British ships. This sparked off a war with the Dutch which lasted for years until 1673 when they agreed to lower their flag to a British fleet or a single warship.

BATTLE ENSIGN. A White Ensign hoisted at the masthead or other prominent position in the ship for easy identification in battle and in case one is shot away.

BEND ON, TO. To attach a signal flag to a signal halyard for hoisting.

B FOR BRAVO. The letter 'B' in the International Code of Signals. When made on its own it means 'I am taking in, or discharging, or carrying dangerous goods'.

BLUE PETER. See P FOR PAPA.

BREAK OUT, TO. To unfurl a flag which has been hoisted, tied in such a way that a pull of the halyard causes it to open out.

BROAD PENNANT. The distinguishing flag of a commodore, white with a St. George's cross, hoisted instead of a commissioning pennant.

BUNTING. The collective term for an assortment of signal flags.

Bunting was the name for the all wool cloth from which British naval flags were made from the 18th century onwards. In 1955 the Royal Navy abandoned the all-wool formula for one of 75 per cent nylon, 25 per cent worsted. Since then, 100 per cent synthetic material has been adopted, at first nylon, but in 1982 replaced by polyester.

CARRY ON, THE. A bugle call following the 'alert' or a pipe following the 'still'.

C FOR CHARLIE. The letter 'C' in the International Code of Signals. When made on its own it means 'Yes'.

CHRISTMAS DAY. On this day the masthead or other conspicuous position is decorated with sprigs of holly.

CHURCH PENNANT. A special pennant which is hoisted whenever Divine Service is being held on board. It consists of a St. George's cross on a white background with red, white and blue in the fly.

The pennant was first used in 1653, at the time when the English and the Dutch were at war. Neither nation believed in fighting on Sundays and the pennant, combining the flags of St. George for England and the red, white and blue stripes of the Netherlands, was hoisted to indicate a truce.

COLOURS. The ceremony of the hoisting of the 'colours', consisting of the White Ensign and, in harbour, the Union Flag, at 0800 in summer and at 0900 in winter. When at sea, ships hoist colours as soon as there is sufficient light.

This ceremony dates from the year 1800 when Admiral the Earl St. Vincent issued an order for it to be held at 0900 each day, as one of a number of measures to improve discipline. In 1840 the time during the summer was altered to 0800.

COMMISSIONING PENNANT. A long narrow white pennant with a red cross, which is permanently flown at the masthead during the period when a ship is in commission, unless replaced by the command flag of a flag officer or the broad pennant of a commodore. Also known as a 'masthead pennant'.

CLOSE UP. Said of a flag when fully hoisted up to a yard or to the peak of a gaff, as opposed to 'at the dip'.

D FOR DELTA. The letter 'D' in the International Code of Signals. When made on its own it means 'Keep clear of me, I am manoeuvering with difficulty.'

DIAL-A-STAR. A modern alternative to the Very Pistol flare signalling system. It consists of a kit of eight flare cartridges of different colours.

DRESS SHIP. The decoration of a ship on a national occasion or local celebration. A 'dressed ship' flies flags at the mastheads, whilst a ship 'dressed overall' has a continuous array of signal flags from the jackstaff at the stem right aft to the Ensign staff at the stern.

Originally it was the junior captain of a fleet or squadron who drew up the order of flags to be worn when ships dressed with flags overall. However, in 1899 standard instructions were laid down for flags to be worn in a symmetrical and varied manner.

E FOR ECHO. The letter 'E' in the International Code of Signals. When made on its own it means 'I am directing my course to starboard'.

ENSIGN. See WHITE ENSIGN.

ENSIGN STAFF. The staff on which the ensign is flown, situated right aft on the quarterdeck.

F FOR FOXTROT. The letter 'F' in the International Code of Signals. When made on its own it means 'I am disabled. Communicate with me'.

FINIAL. A decorative top to a flagstaff. A jackstaff is surmounted by a naval crown, an Ensign staff by a Royal crown.

FLAG OF COMMAND. The flag of a 'flag officer', i.e. of the rank of rear-admiral or above. It is hoisted instead of a commissioning pennant when the flag officer is aboard his ship.

FLY. The part of a flag farthest from the halyard on which it is hoisted.

FLY, TO. Colours, standards and distinguishing flags are said to be 'worn' by ships and individuals and they may be said to be 'flown' in a ship. Other types of flags are 'flown' and never 'worn'.

GAFF. A short spar which rides on the after side of a mast, used for flying the Ensign when at sea. Originally it was used for hoisting a four-sided, fore-and-aft sail. (F. 'gaffe'.)

GENERAL SALUTE. A bugle salute sounded at 'Colours' and as a salute when receiving a flat officer.

G FOR GOLF. The letter 'G' in the International Code of Signals. When made on its own it means 'I require a pilot'. In the case of fishing vessels it means 'I am hauling nets'.

GIN PENNANT. A green and white pennant flown when a ship wishes to celebrate a special occasion; a welcome for all to come aboard and join the party.

GUN SALUTES. These are fired in honour of a royal or other personage, or of a country. An odd number of rounds is always fired, an even number was once reserved for occasions of mourning.

It was once the custom at sea for the saluting ship to turn head on to the ship being saluted. This originated when ships only had broadside guns and fired salutes with shotted rounds. Heading towards the other ship, the salute could not be mistaken for an act of aggression. However, this is not observed today.

Gun salutes above Gravesend have been prohibited since the 16th century. A shot from a warship firing a salute off Greenwich fell close to Greenwich Palace, where Elizabeth I was residing.

HALF MASTING. Lowering a flag to a point some half way below its normal position, usually as a sign of mourning.

HALYARDS. The ropes used to hoist the Ensign and signal flags. In sailing days halyards were the ropes or tackles used to hoist or lower the sails to and from their yards (haul-yards).

HAND SALUTE. The salute given with the right hand as a mark of respect. All officers are saluted on being approached or passed by ratings, and officers salute each other according to rank. On board ship, everyone is required to salute the quarterdeck as they step on to it. This is a custom which dates back to medieval times when ships used to have a small shrine or crucifix under the break of the poop. Another salute made by everybody is that given when stepping on board a ship, irrespective of the place or means of entry, as a salute to the ship and her company.

The original method of saluting in the RN was the uncovering of the head by the removal of the hat, both when making the salute and acknowledging it. Amongst officers this was accompanied on ceremonial occasions by a bow. On board ship, where often men did not wear hats, the salute was made by going through the motions of removing the hat, or by just touching the forehead.

Queen Victoria was responsible for the modern naval salute and it was introduced in 1890 to conform with the practice of the Army. The salute could be given with either hand; an officer was saluted with the hand further from him, and the boatswain's mates often piped the side holding the call in their right hand whilst saluting with their left. In 1918 the Royal Marines abolished the use of the left hand for saluting and five years later the Navy followed suit.

The original salute of removing the cap is still retained for certain occasions, for instance; at a flag officer's or the Captain's inspection of a ship's company.

H FOR HOTEL. The letter 'H' in the International Code of Signals. When made on its own it means 'I have a pilot on board'.

HOIST. The part of a flag nearest the halyard on which it is hoisted.

HOIST, TO. To put up a flag.

'ICU' An abbreviated flag signal meaning 'Can I come and see you?.

I FOR INDIA. The letter 'I' in the International Code of Signals. When made on its own it means 'I am altering course to port'.

INGLEFIELD CLIPS. Special clips to facilitate the 'bending on' of the Ensign, flags or pennants to signal halyards for hoisting. Indentical clips, spliced both to the halyards and flags, have slots which mate together simply, enabling changes of signal to be made quickly.

Named after the inventor, who was a commissioner of ships in the Royal Navy during the Napoleonic War.

INTERNATIONAL CODE OF SIGNALS. A series of signal flags and pennants, representing letters and numbers, which has been agreed by all maritime nations for communication between ship and ship, and ship and shore.

The International Code was founded in 1817 on a code devised by Captain F. Marryat RN, consisting of fifteen flags and pennants. Some years later it was challenged by other codes developed both here in this country and abroad. As a result of this an international committee was set up to agree on a single code. The committee's recommendation was based almost entirely on Marryat's original code. A revised code, incorporating additional flags and pennants, was introduced in 1902. The code was enlarged again in 1927 and once more in 1948, when the number of flags was brought up to 78.

JACK. See UNION JACK.

JACKSTAFF. The staff on which the Union Flag is flown right forward at the stem.

JAM. To make an enemy radio transmission unintelligible by sending loud transmissions on the same wavelength.

J FOR JULIET. The letter 'J' in the International Code of Signals. When made on its own it means 'I am on fire and have dangerous goods on board. Keep well clear of me'.

K FOR KILO. The letter 'K' in the International Code of Signals. When made on its own it means 'I wish to communicate with you'.

L FOR LIMA. The letter 'L' in the International Code of Signals. When made on its own it means 'You should stop your vessel instantly'.

'MAKE A SIGNAL' The preparatory of the order to send a signal.

MAKE HER NUMBER, TO. For a ship to identify herself by hoisting a group of four alphabetical signal flags in the International Code of Signals, which represent four letters which have been assigned to her for identification purposes. Each country is allocated a group of letters from which they assign individual distinguishing letters to each ship.

MAN SHIP, TO. A form of salute, used on special occasions, such as a fleet review, when all hands line the guardrails at close intervals around the upper deck.

This salute originated in sailing warships, with hands lining the yards by standing on them, supported by lifelines. This showed that a ship's intentions were friendly; with the crew 'manning the ship', they could not be manning the guns at the same time.

MASTHEAD PENNANT. See COMMISSIONING PENNANT.

MAYDAY. The International distress signal made by voice on radio. The Mayday wavelength is 2182 khz and is permanently monitored. (Fr. 'm'aider', help me.)

M FOR MIKE. The letter 'M' in the International Code of Signals. When made on its own it means 'My vessel is stopped and making no way through the water'.

MINUTE GUN. A gun salute which is fired at the funerals of naval members of the Admiralty Board of the Defence Council, flag officers and commodores. So called because it is fired at intervals of one minute whilst the body is being borne to the place of internment. The number fired is dependant upon rank.

'MRU'. An abbreviated flag signal meaning 'Much regret, I am unable to'.

N FOR NOVEMBER. The letter 'N' in the International Code of Signals. When made on its own it means 'No'.

O FOR OSCAR. The letter 'O' in the International Code of Signals. When made on its own it means 'Man overboard'.

PAYING OFF PENNANT. A long white pennant with a St. George's cross in the hoist, flown by a ship when paying off at the end of her commission. By tradition, if a commission exceeds the normal length, then the length of the pennant should indicate this; a ship's length for a normal commission, with one-twelfth added for every two months exceeded.

This pennant is said to have originated from the ship's company knotting together all of their brightwork cleaning rags and flying them from the masthead as a sign that they were no longer required.

PEAK. The outer end of a 'gaff'.

PENNANT. A narrow tapering flag used for the numbers in the International Code of Signals and for other special purposes.

The original RN spelling is 'pendant' (pronounced 'pennant'), but since the Second World War 'pennant' has come to be widely used.

P FOR PAPA. The letter 'P' in the International Code of Signals. When made on its own it means 'All persons should report on board as the vessel is about to proceed to sea'. In the case of fishing vessels at sea it means 'My nets have become fast upon an obstruction'.

The flag is also known as the the 'Blue Peter'. This comes from the days of the former phonetic alphabet used in the RN when RN when 'Peter' was the phonetic word for the signal letter 'P'. Many of the phonetic words were changed to comply with the revised International Code in the 1950s.

PIPING THE SIDE. A ceremonial call made on the boatswain's call as a mark of respect for certain personages when arriving on board or leaving a ship. It is made for members of the Royal Family, admirals and captains of the Royal Navy and foreign dignitaries and naval officers. The same honour is accorded a corpse leaving a ship.

The origin of the call is from the days when visiting officers were hoisted inboard and outboard, to and from a ship, in a 'boatswain's chair' slung from a whip rove from the lower yardarm. The orders for the hoisting and lowering being sounded by the boatswain's call.

PRATIQUE. A certificate of good health. See Q FOR QUEBEC.

PREPARITIVE. A flag, known as the 'prep', used as a preparitive signal preceding a signal proper.

'PSB'. An abbreviated flag signal meaning 'Please send boat'.

Q FOR QUEBEC. The letter 'Q' in the International Code of Signals. When made on its own it means 'My vessel is healthy and I request free pratique'. The quarantine signal.

QUARANTINE FLAG. See Q FOR QUEBEC.

QUEEN'S COLOUR. The Royal Navy 'Queen's' Colour was first presented in 1924 (then the King's Colour). It is a White Ensign charged with the Royal Cypher (EIIR) and surmounted by the garter. It is paraded on board HM ships and on shore on occasions of Royal ceremonial.

R FOR ROMEO. The letter 'R' in the International Code of Signals. The only letter in the code without a specific meaning when made on its own.

'RPC'. Abbreviated flag signal meaning 'Request the pleasure of your company'.

ROYAL STANDARD. Worn at the masthead when the Sovereign is on board.

Throughout the 17th century the Royal Standard, as well as indicating the presence of the King, was used by the Lord High Admiral. After the restoration, the right to wear the Standard was more strictly controlled and in 1702 restricted to ships which actually had the Sovereign on board.

SAMHADS. Submarine Automatic Message Handling System. An automatic signal distribution system for submarines.

SCOT. Satellite Communications On-board Terminal. An SHF via satellite radio system, first developed in *HMS BLAKE*, which allows radio communication between ships at sea and command facilities un-affected by ionspheric interference and jamming.

SENIOR OFFICER'S PENNANT. A special pennant hoisted by the senior officer present in a group of ships.

From 1864 to 1950 in the RN it was a white broad pennant with a St. George's cross, smaller than a commodore's broad pennant. It was hoisted from the starboard upper yard arm and did not displace the masthead pennant. In 1950 the NATO navies adopted the green-white-green 'starboard pennant' as a senior officer's pennant.

S FOR SIERRA. The letter 'S' in the International Code of Signals. When made on its own it means 'My engines are going astern'.

SKYNET. The name of the Royal Navy's satellite communications system.

S-O-S. The International distress signal.

The original distress signal was C-Q-D (Come Quickly Danger) which was superceded by S-O-S in 1908.

SOUND SIGNALS. Signals made on a ship's siren to indicate her movements to other vessels in the vicinity. Sound signals are also for use in fog.

SPEAK, TO. To communicate with another vessel by visual signalling.

SQUADRON COMMAND PENNANT. A white burgee type (swallow tailed) pennant, being fringed at the top and bottom with red, Worn by all Captains (D) and (F) and Commanders of certain other Squadrons. It is worn on the starboard yardarm but does not displace a distinguishing flag or broad pennant.

Until 1984 black bands were painted on the funnels of squadron command ships, but all have been removed in order to improve all-grey camouflage.

STILL, THE. A bugle or pipe call consisting of an eight second note, used to call the hands to attention, either as a mark of respect or any other purpose. It may also be used to stop all work in order to prevent an accident.

STRIKE THE COLOURS, TO. To haul down the Colours as a token of surrender.

SUNSET. The ceremony of the lowering of the Colours, consisting of the White Ensign and, in harbour, the Union Flag.

T FOR TANGO. The letter 'T' in the International Code of Signals. When made on its own it means 'Keep clear of me, I am engaged in pair trawling'.

THROAT. The lower end of a gaff.

TRUCK. A round disc which covers the highest point of a mast and which contains a pulley through which a signal halyard is passed. (L. 'trochlea', a small wheel.)

'UCM'. An abbreviated flag signal meaning 'Can you come and see me?'

U FOR UNIFORM. The letter 'U' in the International Code of Signals. When made on its own it means 'You are running into danger'.

UNION JACK. The small version of the Union Flag worn on the jackstaff on the bows of RN ships in harbour. When flown elsewhere it is called the 'Union Flag'. The Union flag is worn at the masthead of a ship when an admiral-of-the-fleet is embarked. It is also worn at the masthead of a ship in harbour if a court martial is assembled on board.

The use of the Union Flag at sea is confined by law to RN vessels. The reason for this is that in the days when warships and merchant ships looked alike, it was essential that one be distinguished from the other to prevent masquerading under false colours. The Union Flag was therefore ordered to be worn only by HM ships of war.

'Jack' originated as a nickname for the British Flag at sea when the flags of England and Scotland joined under James I in 1603. James usually signed himself 'Jacobus' or 'Jacques'. (Ireland was joined into the Union of 1801.)

V FOR VICTOR. The letter 'V' in the International Code of Signals. When made on its own it means 'I require assistance'.

'VMT'. An abbreviated flag signal meaning 'Very many thanks'.

VERY PISTOL. (Pronounced 'vary'.) A hand held pistol used to fire coloured pyrotechnic signals.

'WMP'. An abbreviated flag signal meaning 'With much pleasure'.

WEAR, TO. See FLY, TO.

WEDDING GARLAND. A garland of evergreen hoisted aloft on the day when a member of the ship's company is married. The custom dates from the 18th and 19th centuries when an evergreen garland was hoisted by a warship entering harbour to indicate that she was out of discipline and that women were allowed on board.

W FOR WHISKY. The letter 'W' in the International Code of Signals. When made on its own it means 'I require medical assistance'.

WHITE ENSIGN. The Ensign flown by all Royal Navy ships and establishments. A red St. George's cross on a white background with the Union Flag in the upper corner nearest the hoist. (Fr. 'enseign'.)

During the 17th century, the fleets of the Royal Navy were divided into Red, White and Blue Squadrons, wearing Red, White and Blue Ensigns as distinguishing colours. These squadrons were abolished in 1864 and the White Ensign was authorised to be worn by all ships. The Red Ensign was allocated to merchant ships and the Blue Ensign to ships of the Royal Fleet Auxillary and certain merchant ships commanded by RNR officers.

X FOR XRAY. The letter 'X' in the International Code of Signals. When made on its own it means 'Stop carrying out your intentions and watch for my signals'.

YARD. A cross member placed across a mast which carries signal halyards. In a sailing ship it was a spar to which a sail was bent. (OE. 'gyrd', stick.)

YARDARMS. The arms of a yard.

Y FOR YANKEE. The letter 'Y' in the International Code of Signals. When made on its own it means 'I am dragging my anchor'.

Z FOR ZULU. The letter 'Z' in the International Code of Signals. When made on its own it means 'I require a tug'. In the case of a fishing vessel it means 'I am shooting nets',

10

SAID OF A SHIP

Many things can be said of a ship, but always she is called 'she'. Even when she is launched, the lady performing the ceremony will say 'God bless this ship and all who sail in her'. This has not always been the case; prior to the middle ages, when the English language had gender, a vessel of any type was masculine.

The word 'ship' originated from 'ship rig'; the rig of a vessel having three or more masts all completely square rigged. Because the ship rig was the standard, the name has almost become a synonym with vessel.

* * *

ACCEPTED. Accepted by the RN from the builders.

ADRIFT. Broken away from moorings and without means of propulsion.

AFLOAT. Clear of the bottom and wholly supported by water. (ME. 'aflot', from OE. 'on flot', deep water, sea.)

AGROUND. Resting on the bottom.

ANCHORED. Held by an anchor.

ATHWART-HAWSE. When driven by the wind or tide across the stem of another vessel.

ATHWART THE TIDE. Swung to her anchor by the force of the wind across the direction of the tide.

AWASH. Lying so low in the water that the seas wash over her.

BEACHED. For her to be run on to a beach.

BENEAPED. When she has gone aground at the top of the spring tides and has to wait for up to two weeks for the next tide high enough to float her off. If a ship is beneaped at the time of the highest spring tides (the equinoxes), she may have to wait for six months to float off.

BERTHED. Having a convenient place for mooring or a place alongside a jetty or wharf.

BILGED. When her bottom has been holed.

BLUFF-BOWED. Having broad, perpendicular bows. (Dut. 'blaf', broad.)

BROACHED. Fallen into the trough of a sea, more or less broadside on.

BROKEN SHEER. When at anchor, forced by the wind or current to swing across her anchor with the danger of fouling it with her cable.

BROKEN UP. The method of her disposal as scrap. This is carried out in a 'breaker's yard'.

BROUGHT UP. Brought to anchor or to a mooring. The term comes from the days of sail when, in order to anchor, it was usual to 'bring to' which was to lay the foresails aback to take off the ship's way.

BUILDING. In the course of construction.

BURDENED. See PRIVELEDGED.

BY THE HEAD. Deeper in the water forward than aft.

BY THE STERN. Deeper in the water aft than forward.

CANTED. The ship's head turned either to port or starboard, depending on the circumstances, when weighing anchor or slipping from a mooring, in order to avoid hazards. (Cant, ME. from L. 'cantus', a turning.)

CAPSIZED. Overturned due to bad weather or instability. (Capsize, Sp. 'capuzar', to sink by the head.)

CARRYING WAY. Continuing to move through the water. (Way, ME. from OE. 'weg', track'.)

CLOSED DOWN. When doors, hatches and ventilation valves are closed for damage control purposes.

COME TO. When her way is stopped and she is riding by her anchor and cable.

COME UP WITH. Overtaking another vessel.

COMPANY. Her company consists of all of her officers and men.

COMPLEMENT. The number of the her complement.

COMPLETED. Her building and fitting out finished.

CONNED. Directed by giving specific orders to the helmsman. (Con, earlier 'cond' from Fr. 'conduire', to guide).

CONSORT. Keeping company with another ship.

CRACKING ON. Increasing her speed.

CRANK. When slow to recover from a roll, sometimes called 'tender'. (OE. 'cranc', upset.)

DECOMMISSIONED. No longer in operational service.

DEEP CONDITION. Her condition when fully loaded with crew, stores, fuel and ammunition.

DEGAUSSED. Having had the magnetic fields around her neutralised or demagnetised. After K. F. Gauss (1777–1855), a German authority on magnetism—Gauss, the unit of flux density in magnetism, being one line per square centimetre.

DEPLOYED. Utilised for a specific purpose.

DERELICT. Abandoned at sea.

DE-STORING. Having her stores disembarked at the end of a commission.

DISPLACEMENT. The weight represented by the weight of water in tons that she displaces.

DOCKED. Placed into dry dock for maintenance or repairs.

DRAGGING. When her anchor is not holding.

DRAWING. Indicating her draught; the depth of water she requires.

DRAWING AHEAD. Advancing ahead of another ship.

DRAWING ASTERN. Dropping astern of another ship.

DRAUGHT. The depth of water that she 'draws'.

DRESSED OVERALL. Decorated with bunting from stem to stern for a national occasion or local celebration.

DRIFTING. Making distance to leeward by the action of the wind or tide. (OE. 'drifan', drive.)

DRIVING. At the mercy of the wind and tide by the anchor failing to hold the ground.

DROPPING ASTERN. Slackening the speed to allow another vessel to overtake.

DUE FOR DISPOSAL. About to be taken out of service and either sold or scrapped.

ENDURANCE. Her range, depending on fuel. Today largely irrevalant because warships are refuelled at sea, thus increasing their range without reliance on shore bases.

FALLING ASTERN. In passing another vessel and making the distance between the two ships greater, the passed ship is said to fall astern.
FALLING OFF. Sagging away from the wind to leeward.
FAST. Secured.
FETCHED. Reached her destination.
FETCHED UP. Run aground.
FITTING OUT. Preparing for sea, following building or re-fit.
FLAGSHIP. Wearing the flag of a flag officer (or the rank of rear-admiral or above) or the broad pennant of a commodore.
FLUSH DECKED. When the uppermost deck runs from stem to stern.
FOUND. To be equipped. If a ship is equipped exceptionally well, she is said to be 'well found'.
FOUNDERED. Sunk by the flooding of her hull through springing a leak or striking a rock. (ME. 'foundren', to send to the bottom, from MFr. 'foundrer', from L. 'fundus', bottom.)
GATHERING WAY. Beginning to move through the water.
GIRT. When she is moored with two anchors, with both cables so taut as to prevent her swinging with the tide or wind. (ON 'gjorth', to secure with a girth.)
GIVING A WIDE BERTH. Steering clear of.
GOING AHEAD. Moving ahead.
GOING ASTERN. Moving astern.
GUARDSHIP. Stationed at a port to act as guard.
HAULING OFF. Altering course.
HAVING A FOUL BERTH. When she has no room to swing at anchor.
HAVING HEADWAY. Having movement ahead.
HAVING LEEWAY. Under way and being blown sideways by the wind.
HAVING STEERAGE WAY. Having sufficient way on to be steered.
HAVING SEAROOM. Having sufficient room to steer clear of hazards.
HAVING STERNWAY. Having movement astern.
HAVING TOO MUCH WAY ON. Moving too fast through the water.

HAVING WAY ON. Moving through the water.
HEADING. The direction in which she is moving.
HEELING. Heel is the angle between the masts and the perpendicular, whatever the cause. (ME. 'heelden' from OE. 'hielden', to incline.)
HIGH AND DRY. Her condition when she is aground and above the watermark.
HOGGING. When her midship portion is supported by a wave crest leaving the bow and stern parts unsupported over the troughs either side of the wave.

Hogging was a problem with wooden ships and this limited the length which they could be built. This problem was eventually countered when Sir Robert Seppings (Surveyor of the Navy between 1813 and 1832) introduced diagonal bracing between the standard rectangular frames of ships. As a result, not only were ships stiffer and stronger but they could be made much longer.

HOVE IN SIGHT. Appeared.
HOVE TO. Deliberately remaining stationary, or almost stationary. (ME. 'hoven', stationary - thus 'hover'.)

Under sail, to heave to was to bring the ship's head into the wind to stop her motion.

HULK. The body of a ship, especially an old one unfit for sea.

In the 16th century the large merchantmen of the northern countries were known as 'hulks'. As they grew obsolete, the name was applied in derision to any crank vessels, until it came to be degraded to its present use.

HULLING. Driving to and fro without rudder or engine.
HULL DOWN. When viewed from a distance below the horizon with only her masts and funnel visible.
HULLED. Her hull penetrated by missile or shell.
IN COMMISSION. A period during which she is in operational service; engaged in a particular duty with a full complement of officers and men.
IN COMPANY. Cruising together one or more other ships.
IN RESERVE. See LAID UP.
IN SOUNDINGS. When she is being navigated in water within the 100 fathom line.

Before the days of sounding machines and echo sounders, the lead line was used to measure depths of up to 100 fathoms, all depths greater than this were 'off soundings'.

IN THE WAKE OF. Following the track of another ship.

KEDGING. Moving her by means of small anchors and hawsers. (A 'kedge' is a small anchor.)

KEEPING STATION. Keeping an accurate station on another ship.

LABOURING. Rolling or pitching excessively in a rough sea.

LAID DOWN. Her building commenced; the keel laid.

LAID UP. Out of commission, in reserve.

The original term for a ship laid up in reserve was that of 'in ordinary'.

LAUNCHED. Slipped into the water from her place of building.

The custom of breaking a bottle of wine over the stem of a ship when being launched originated from the previous practice of toasting prosperity to the ship in a silver goblet of wine, which was then cast into the sea in order to prevent a toast of ill intent being drunk. This practice proved to be too expensive and was replaced in 1690 by the breaking of a bottle of wine over the stem.

In 1811 the Prince Regent introduced the present custom of allowing ladies to perform the launching ceremony. Up to that time it had always been performed either by a royal personage or a Royal Dockyard Commissioner. On one occasion of a launch a lady missed her aim with the bottle, which struck and injured a spectator who sued the Admiralty for damages. An Admiralty order was subsequently issued which directed that in future the bottle was to be secured to the ship by a lanyard.

LEADER. When she is the senior ship of a destroyer or frigate squadron, with the Captain 'D' or Captain 'F' respectively embarked.

Prior to the Falklands War a leader was identified by a broad black band at the funnel top.

LEAD SHIP. The first of a class to be built.

LINES. Her 'lines' refer to the plan or outline of her hull and superstructure.

LISTING. Having a permanent heel to one side or the other.
LIVELY. Rolling quickly from side to side. Sometimes called 'stiff'.
LOLLING. Floating at an angle of heel, caused by flooding or incorrect distribution of weight.
LOST. Sunk.
LURCHING. Suddenly rolling to one side.
LYING ALONGSIDE. Berthed alongside a jetty or wharf.
LYING OFF. Stopping clear of another vessel or the land.
LYING TO. Becoming stopped in the water.
MAKING HEADWAY. Moving ahead.
MAKING HER NUMBER. Identifying herself by hoisting a group of signal flags.
MAKING LEEWAY. Being blown sideways by the wind.
MAKING STERNWAY. Moving astern.
MAKING WATER. Leaking.
MEETING A HEAD SEA. Steaming with her bows meeting the sea end on.
MOORED. Lying with two anchors out, middled between them. (Moor from ME. 'moren' from Dut. 'marren', to retard.)
MOVING BROADSIDE ON. Moving sideways.
NON SEA-GOING. Not fit to put to sea, e.g. an accommodation or harbour training vessel.
NOT UNDER COMMAND. Broken down or otherwise unable to obey the rule of the road.
OFF SOUNDINGS. When she is in waters seaward of the 100 fathom line. See also IN SOUNDINGS.
ON AN EVEN KEEL. With her keel horizontal and drawing the same amount of water forward and aft.
ON PATROL. Deployed for the purpose of maintaining watch.
ON SEA TRIALS. A trial cruise made by the builders before she is handed over.
ON STATION. At her designated place of deployment.
ON THE DISPOSAL LIST. Earmarked for sale or scrap.
OUT OF COMPANY. Not in company with other ships.
OUT OF ROUTINE. Not carrying out normal routine due to re-fit or other cause.
OVERHAULING. Overtaking another ship.

OVER RAKED. Riding to her anchor in bad weather with the sea breaking continuously over her bows.

PAYING OFF. (1) Closing her accounts at the end of a commission.

In the days when men were only paid at the end of a commission or when the ship was laid up, it literally meant a 'paying off' of the ship's company.

(2) Falling to leeward.

PITCHING. Her movement when meeting a head sea or running before a following sea. In each case her bows will alternately rise and fall.

PITCHPOLING. Turning over stern over bows in a heavy sea.

POOPING. When the sea comes inboard over her stern or when she is unmanageable through the action of the sea over the stern. (From 'poop' from L. 'puppis', the stern of a ship.)

POST SHIP. Of sufficient importance to confer the rank of post captain' on her commanding officer. Some ships are commanded by officers of lower rank who might be referred to as 'captain' but do not thereby attain post rank.

Originally, a post ship was one sufficiently important to carry a fully qualified master in addition to her captain. In a smaller non-post ship the captain had to qualify as master and carry out his own navigation.

PRESERVED. Retained as a museum ship instead of scrapping. Major preserved RN ships with their launch dates and current locations are as follows:

MARY ROSE (1536)	Portsmouth
HMS VICTORY (1765)	Portsmouth
FOUDROYANT—Ex *HMS TRINCOMALEE* (1817)	Hartlepool
HMS UNICORN (1822)	Dundee
HMS WARRIOR (1860)	Portsmouth
HMS GANNET (1878)	Chatham
HMS CAROLINE (1914)	Belfast
HMS CHRYSANTHEMUM (1917)	London
HMS PRESIDENT (1918)	London
HMS WELLINGTON (1934)	London

HMS BELFAST (1938)	London
HMS CAVALIER (1944)	Hebburn
HMS ALLIANCE (1945)	Gosport
HMS PLYMOUTH (1959)	Gosport
HMS BRONINGTON (1954)	Manchester

PRESERVED BY OPERATION. When she is decommissioned and placed into the Standby Squadron of the Reserve Ships Unit. A small maintenance crew keep her machinery in full working order with the object of being able to make her operational for service, if required, within about one month.

PRIVATE. Not carrying a flag officer.

PRIVILEGED. When she has the right of way, in the context of the Rule of the Road when two vessels meet. The other vessel is the 'burdened' vessel.

PROCEEDED TO SEA. The official term for sailing from harbour.

RANGING. Sailing in a direction parallel to.

REDEDICATED. The ceremony when she re-enters service following a refit.

REFITTING. Being repaired or reconditioned.

RIDING. She 'rides' to an anchor or to a buoy.

RIDING EASY. Lying at anchor without a great strain on her cable.

RIDING HARD. Pitching violently.

RIDING OUT A GALE. Not driving during a storm.

RIGHT. Set upright.

ROLLING. Alternately heeling from side to side when she has a beam sea.

ROUNDED. To have steered around.

RUN DOWN. Run down by another vessel, either on purpose or by accident.

RUNNING DOWN A COAST. Sailing along a coast.

RUNNING BEFORE A FOLLOWING SEA. Steaming with her stern to the sea.

SAGGING. When her bow and stern are taken on the crests of two successive waves, leaving the midships portion unsupported.

SAILING. Leaving harbour. (Sail, OE. 'segel', the sail of a ship.)

SALVAGED. Saved from shipwreck. (OFr. 'salver', to save.)
SCENDING. When she rises and falls bodily on the crests and in the troughs of heavy seas. This is different from pitching, when the bows and stern are alternatively raised and lowered.
SCUTTLED. Deliberately sunk; normally achieved by opening up seacocks or by using explosive charges to blow holes in her bottom.
SEAGOING. Deemed fit to put to sea.
SEAKEEPING QUALITIES. The way she handles in a rough sea.
SEAWORTHY. Fit for sea service.
SECURED TO A BUOY. Riding to a mooring buoy.
SET SAIL. Begun a voyage. Originally it meant to hoist the sails.
SEWED. When grounded by a falling tide and only refloatable by the rising tide.
SHEARING. Similar to 'sagging', but when poised on three wave crests instead of two.
SHIPPING IT GREEN. When masses of water are coming on board in a heavy sea.
SISTER SHIP. Built to the same design as another.
SLIPPED. Having let go hawsers securing her alongside and proceeded to sea.
SNUBBED. Come to a sudden stop by letting go an anchor with too much way on.
SPRUNG A LEAK. Making water through straining her hull.
STANDING. Sailing in a widely defined direction, e.g. to 'stand southward'.
STANDING INTO DANGER. Approaching another ship or hazard dangerously close.
STANDING ON. Maintaining the same course.

In sailing days to 'stand off and on' was to tack in out along a shore.

STEMMING. Just making headway against a tidal stream.
STIFF. See LIVELY.
STORING. Embarking stores.
STRANDED. Driven aground by the weather. (OE.)
STRUCK. When she hits the bottom.

STRUCK SOUNDINGS. On an ocean voyage approaching land and reaching water sufficiently shallow enough for taking soundings.

SURFACE SHIP. Other than a submarine.

SURGING. Moving ahead, astern or away from a jetty when secured alongside. (Springs and breast ropes are used to prevent this.)

TENDER. See CRANK.

TIDE RODE. Swung to her anchor by the force of the tide.

TRIM. The condition with reference to how she floats on the water, being the inclination to the horizontal in a fore-and-aft sense. (OE. 'trymian', set firm or in order.)

TRAINING SHIP. Taken out of front line service and employed for training personel, either in a seagoing capacity or stationary in harbour.

UNBERTHED. Left a berth.

UNDERGOING TRIALS. Her testing before acceptance.

UNDER WAY. Not at anchor or made fast to the shore or ground.

Sometimes the term is written as 'under weigh', which actually means that her anchor has broken out of the ground but she is still stationary in the water. She is then 'under way' as soon as she begins to move. However, the two terms have today become synonymous.

UNDOCKED. Left a dry dock.

UNSTABLE. Top heavy and so unable to recover when heeled over by wind or sea.

WARPING. Hauling her into position by means of a warp, i.e. a line attached to a buoy, anchor or other fixed warp. (OE. 'weopan', cast, throw.)

WATERBORNE. Afloat.

WATERLOGGED. Full of water, but floating.

WEATHER-BOUND. Unable to put to sea owing to the weather.

WEIGHING. Being set in motion by raising the anchor. (Weigh, OE 'wegan', to carry.)

WELL FOUND. Adequately and fully equipped.

WET. By inadequacy of her design allowing excessive sea water to come on board in heavy weather.

WINDING. Turning her around in her berth end for end.

WIND RODE. Swung to her anchor by the force of the wind.

WORKING UP. Regaining operational efficiency following commissioning after building or after a refit.

WRECK. When her hull has become a total loss, either by sinking or stranding. (ME. 'wrek' from OE. 'wroek', exile.)

YAWING. When, due to the effect of a following wind or sea, she does not steer a straight and steady course. (Ice.

11

RELATIVE TO A SHIP

Is it 'in' or 'on' a ship? Well, one lives 'in' a house and therefore one serves 'in' a ship. However, one does not go 'in' a ship, one goes 'onboard' and having done so one is said to be 'aboard'. To then go 'below' one arrives 'between decks'.

Within the ship one can travel in two main directions; 'fore and aft', relative to the ends of the ship, or 'athwartships', relative to the sides. After moving 'forward' one is 'before' the position one was in before moving. Going 'aft' puts one 'abaft' the position one came from. To move to a position which is neither forward or aft, but in the middle, one is said to be 'amidships'. Following a step from the fore-and-aft midship line towards one of the sides of the ship, one is 'lying' to port or starboard. This also puts one 'outboard' of where one was lying last; one step back puts one lying one step 'inboard' of where one was last.

For a clearer indication of position, one talks of 'port side forward', 'starboard side aft', etc. Anywhere along the fore-and-aft midship line relative to athwartships, equidistant from the sides of the ship, is 'midships'; not to be confused with the aforementioned amidships unless one is in the middle of the fore-and aft-line.

* * *

ABAFT. Nearer the stern, relatively, e.g. abaft the gangway. (OE. 'a', on and 'beoeftan', by aft, behind.)

ABEAM. A direction external to the ship, at a right angle port or starboard to the fore-and-aft line. (OE 'a', on and 'beam'.)

ABOARD. On board; within the ship. (OE, 'a', on and 'bord', ship's side.)
ABREAST. On the same course and level with the ship.
AFORE. Towards the forward part.
AFT. Towards the stern. (OE. 'oeftan', behind.)
AFTERMOST. Furthest aft, nearest the stern. (OE. 'oefternest', hindmost.)
AHEAD. Directly in advance of the ship.
ALOFT. Anywhere in the rigging of, or up, a mast. (Ice. 'a lopt', in the air.)
ALONGSIDE. Side by side and touching the ship.
AMIDSHIPS. In the amidship part of the hull, between the forepart and the afterpart.
ASTERN. In, at or towards the stern, or behind the ship. ('a' and ON. 'stjorn', steering.)
ATHWARTSHIPS. At right angles to the fore-and-aft line. (ON. 'thvert', across.)
AWEATHER. Towards the weather or windward side of the ship.
BEAR, TO. The direction of an object relative to the ship's position.
BEFORE. A position within the ship relative to something further aft.
BELOW. The equivalent of 'downstairs' ashore.
BETWEEN DECKS. Inside the ship. A general term referring to the space between the upper deck and the lowest deck.
DISEMBARK, TO. To quit the ship, to go ashore.
EMBARK, TO. To go on board, or to place on board, the ship. (Fr. 'embarque', 'in' and 'ship'.)
FORE-AND-AFT-MIDSHIP LINE. The term for an imaginary line dividing the ship, running from the stem to the stern, in line with the keel.
FORWARD. Pronounced 'For'ard'. From any point in the ship to the bows. (OE. 'foreweard'.)
IN. One serves 'in' a ship.
INBOARD. Inside the rails round the ship's side (as opposed to outboard) or a position within a ship relative to something outboard.
LEE SIDE. The sheltered side of the ship. (OE. 'hleo', a covering, shelter.)

LINE ABREAST. Her disposition as part of a group of ships all having their keels parallel to one another, and when a line passing through each ship makes, with line of the ships' advance, a right angle.

LINE AHEAD. Her disposition as part of a group of ships all having their keel in one and the same straight line.

LYING. A person is said to 'lie' in a certain position within the ship.

MIDSHIPS. Midway between port and starboard in the ship, in an athwartship line.

ON BOARD. In the ship.

ON DECK. On the upper deck.

ON THE BOW. The bearing of an object outside of the ship, midway between ahead and abeam.

ON THE QUARTER. The bearing of an object outside of the ship, midway between astern and abeam.

OUTBOARD. Projecting beyond and outside the hull, or a position within the ship relative to something further inboard.

OVERBOARD. Over the ship's side and into the water.

OVER THE SIDE. To be suspended over the ship's side for painting, etc.

PORT. The left hand side of the ship looking forward towards the bows.

This side of a ship was originally called 'larboard' from the Middle English 'ladebord', the lading or loading side, as the steering oar projected from the 'steorbord', starboard side making it difficult to lie alongside starboard side to. Sailing warships had entry 'ports' on this side and the term 'port' had been used for some time in order to avoid confusion with the similar sounding 'starboard'. However, the change was officially made by Admiralty order in 1844.

RIGHT FORWARD (OR AFT). A point furthest forward (or aft) in the ship.

STARBOARD. The right hand side of the ship looking forward towards the bows. (OE. 'steorbord', steer-board, the steer side from which a large steering oar was operated and superceded by the rudder.)

STEM TO STERN, FROM. From one end of the ship to the other.

UP TOP. The upper deck when referred to from between decks.

TOPSIDES. On the upper deck.

WEATHER SIDE. The side of the ship which faces the wind.

12

PARTS OF SHIP AND EQUIPMENT

When seafaring began, the men invented names for parts of the vessels in which they sailed, likening them to objects with which they had been familier with ashore. For example, some parts of a ship are named after parts of the human body; 'head', 'eyes', 'waist', 'navel', 'buttock', 'hawse' and 'bows', the latter two being old English for throat and shoulders.

* * *

'A' BRACKET. A bracket shaped like an inverted 'A', fixed under the stern, which supports the propeller shafts.

ACCOMMODATION LADDER. A ladder hung over the side at the gangway.

AFTER-PART. The rear part of the hull, behind the amidship section.

AIRCRAFT LIFT. A power-operated platform fitted in an aircraft carrier and used to convey aircraft up and down between the flight-deck and the hangar below.

ARMAMENT. All of the guided weapons, guns, torpedoes or other weapons carried in a ship.

AWNING. A canvas canopy rigged over a deck to afford protection from the sun. Once the name of that part of a poop deck which continued forward beyond the bulkhead of the cabin.

BADGE. When first commissioned, each ship is allocated a circular badge surmounted by a naval crown and bearing the name of the ship. It is displayed in a prominent position on the superstructure. Shore establishments have square set diamond-wise badges and those of the Royal

Fleet Auxillary are pentagonal. The design of a previous 'name ship' is carried forward where applicable.

Ships have worn badges since the reign of Henry VIII. At that time a lion rampant and open jawed was the badge of all British men of war, except for a few first rates named after the sovereign and his consort which were given royal effigies for figureheads. All these were carved in oak and continued until the middle of George III's reign when ships began to be named after Greek and Roman gods, the figureheads of busts or full length figures replacing that of the lion. Next, around the time of the advent of the ironclad, came a plain shield type of figurehead, bearing the national arms quartered as in the royal standard or as a representation of the Union Flag.

About 1895 all forms of bow decoration disappeared and after that time unofficial badges, devised aboard individual ships, appeared. Official badges were introduced after 1918, some incorporating the designs of the unofficial ones. Badges for battleships were circular, those for cruisers were pentagonal, a shield shape for destroyers and diamond for aircraft carries, submarines and auxillaries.

BALLAST TANKS. Tanks fitted in submarines to allow the vessel to submerge, rise to the surface or be trimmed when submerged. (OE. 'bloest', load).

BARRACKS. The Royal Marine quarters in a ship which carries a marine detachment. By custom, marines are messed between the officers and the ratings. This dates back to 1797, during the naval mutinies, when Admiral, the Earl of St. Vincent ordered that the 'sea soldiers' were to mess between the officers and the men in order to uphold authority.

BATTLE HONOURS. The names of battles or campaigns in which the ship has taken part and those of her predecessors, which are displayed in a prominent position on board.

BEAM. The measurement across a ship at her widest part. The term comes from the transverse piece of timber, the width of a ship, which once supported the deck and stayed the sides. (OE. for tree).

BEEF SCREEN. The meat store. This was the name of the place from which the salt beef was issued in the days when it was general issue to messes.

BELL. The ship's bell bears the name of the ship and her launch date. It remains with the ship until she is broken up or sold, when it is then either presented to some public body or offered for sale.

There is an old custom of Christening the children of officers in their father's ship, using the ship's bell as a font.

Until the 1970s, the ship's bell was struck every half hour of each watch to indicate time. One bell was struck at the end of the first half hour, then two bells after the first hour; and so on, resulting in eight bells being struck at the end of each four hour watch. However, during the four hours of the two dog watches the sequence was 1, 2, 3, 4, – 1, 2, 3, 8. This was not because the dog watches are only two hours each; the custom of striking only one bell at 1830 originated after the naval mutiny at the Nore. Five bells in the dog watch of 12th May 1797 was the signal for the commencement of the mutiny.

The striking of bells ever half hour originated in the 13th century; a bell each time the half hour sand glass was reversed. Although the ships bell is no longer struck in this way, time is still referred to as a number of 'bells'. Also, one custom which is still retained is that of the youngest member of the ship's company striking sixteen bells at midnight on new year's eve; eight for the old year and eight for the new.

BERTH. A place to sleep on board. (From 'bear', in a nautical sense.)

BETWEEN DECKS. Refers to decks inside the hull as opposed to the upper deck.

BILGE. The lowest part inside the hull. It is here that any internal water collects and where bilge pumps are fitted. (From 'bulge'.)

BILGE KEEL. A long projecting fin designed to decrease the rolling of a ship.

BOOT TOPPING. The area of the outside of the hull between the waterline and the start of ship's side grey, painted black.

BOTTOM. When afloat, the sides below the waterline.
BOW. The fore-end. Also 'bows'. (OE. for shoulders.)
BOW THRUSTER. A screw (propeller) fitted to the bow of a ship to give a sideways thrust of power. Fitted to vessels such as MCMs and survey ships where high manoeverability is required.
BREAKWATER. A low barrier on the forecastle which prevents water sweeping along the deck in heavy weather.
BRIDGE. A platform above the upper deck, nowadays usually enclosed, from where a ship is controlled and where navigational instruments and the steering wheel are situated.

In sailing days, ships were controlled and steered from the quarterdeck. When steam populsion came along, the first ships had paddle wheels and the connecting platform between the two paddle boxes was called a 'bridge'. It was discovered that this platform gave a much better view of operations.

BRIDGE FIN. The superstructure projecting above the hull of a submarine, which contains the conning tower, giving access to the bridge, and the supports for the periscopes and radio and radar masts.
BRIDGE WINGS. Projections either side of the bridge in order to provide access to view over the side.
BRIGHTWORK. Brass fittings.
BROADSIDE. The entire side above the waterline.
BROW. A gangway between ship and shore. (Not 'gangplank', which is a gangway laid between ship and ship.) (OE. 'bru', adjoining, eye lid, eye brow, ridge.)
BULKHEAD. The wall of a compartment, except when it is formed by the side of the hull when it is known as the 'ship's side'. (ON. 'balkr', beam.)
BULWARK. Raised plating along the sides of a ship, above the upper deck. Originally as ramparts. (OE. 'bole', tree and 'weorc', work.)
BUNKERS. The stowage space for fuel oil, originally for coal. Refuelling is known as 'bunkering'.
BUTTERFLY CLIPS. The name for the large wingnuts used to secure hatch covers.
BUTTOCK. The term for the breadth of a ship where the hull rounds down to the stern.

CABIN. An officer's accommodation.

CAMBER. The athwartships curve of the surface of a deck which allows for drainage.

CAMEL. A tank secured to a ship to provide it with extra buoyancy.

CANTEEN. All ships have canteens run by the Navy, Army and Air Force Institute (NAAFI) which provide the extra items, such as confectionery, to supplement the normal victuals.

CASING. The light framework fitted externally to the pressure hull of a submarine. This provides a working platform when the submarine is on the surface and also houses the anchor, cable, bollards and sonar equipment.

CELLS. Usually located forward under the forepart where serious offenders may be contained whilst at sea. A sentence of confinement in cells aboard ship can only be authorised by a post captain.

COAMING. The raised lip around a hatchway, fitted to prevent water running to the deck below.

COMMUNICATIONS CENTRE. The signal transmission and reception centre.

COMPARTMENTS. The spaces into which a ship is divided by bulkheads.

CONNING TOWER. A cylindrical extension of the pressure hull through the fin of a submarine, which gives access to the bridge.

CONTROL CENTRE. The space amidships in a submarine which houses the controls for planes and rudder and also the diving and trim tanks. The periscopes are situated here as is the Action Information Organisation (AIO).

COUNTER. The curved part of a ship's stern.

CUT-WATER. The stem of a ship. In sailing vessels with 'bluff' bows it was a false stem.

DAMAGE CONTROL CENTRE (HQ1). The centre from which the damage control organisation is controlled.

DEADLIGHT. A metal plate which hinges down over a scuttle and is secured by butterfly clips. It is normally folded up against the deckhead, but when required it prevents light from showing to seaward at night when a ship needs to be darkened.

DECK APPROACH PROJECTOR SIGHT (DAPS). Fitted in aircraft carriers to facilitate pilots with the correct angle of approach when landing on. It has a series of vertical lights which have to be aligned with horizontal bar lights.

DECKHEAD. The deck overhead.

DECKS. The horizontal floors in a ship. (Du. 'dek', roof, covering.)

DOGS. The metal sealing clips fitted around watertight doors and hatches.

DONKEY ENGINE. A small engine used for providing power when main ship's power is unavailable, e.g. during refit.

DOORWAYS. Openings in bulkheads which are closed by hinged watertight doors.

DOUBLE BOTTOM. The area between the outer plates of the bottom and the plating of the 'floor'.

DRAUGHT MARKS. Marks which show the 'draught' of the ship in feet, which are cut in at the bow and stern and painted. They are usually in Roman numerals.

DYNALEC 1000. A machinery control system aboard ship.

ESCAPE TOWER. Fitted in all RN submarines as a method of escape in case of accident. The tower is flooded and men are shot to the surface wearing escape and immersion suits which are sustained with fresh air.

EYES OF THE SHIP. The extreme foward end. This term comes from the ancient Mediterranean custom of painting eyes on the bows of a ship so that she could see where she was going.

FIN. See BRIDGE FIN.

FLARE. The curve of the bows, designed to throw the water outwards when heading into a sea.

FLATS. Spaces tucked between decks which do not run the length and breadth of a ship.

FLIGHT DECK. The uppermost deck of an aircraft carrier which extends from stem to stern for the purpose of operating aircraft. In a frigate, a part of the upper deck situated aft for operating a helicopter.

FLOOR. A horizontal platform near a ship's bottom.

FLYING CONTROL CENTRE (FLYCO). The position in an aircraft carrier from where operations on the flight deck are controlled. It is situated in the island superstructure aft of, and in line with, the bridge.

FOGHORN. Fitted for giving warning of the ship's presence in fog.

FORECASTLE. (Pronounced 'Foc's'le'.) The fore end of the upper deck between the bows. So named because of the platform built up over the bows of merchant ships of old to turn them into fighting ships, from which archers attacked the enemy.

FORE-PART. The forward part of the hull, in front of the amidship section.

FORE-PEAK. The space between decks in the bows.

FREEBOARD. The height of the upper deck above the waterline.

FUNNEL. An exhaust tube leading from the engine room, terminating well above the upper deck, to take smoke or exhaust gases well clear.

When steam engines were first fitted to sailing ships for auxillary power, the funnels were usually telescopic and were only in the extended position when 'steaming'. Similarly, the screw could be raised or lowered depending on the mode of power employed. The order given when preparing to steam was 'up funnel, down screw'.

FURNITURE. All of the moveable equipment in a ship with which she is fitted out.

GALLEY. A ship's kitchen.

In a ship of Nelson's day, the space between the foremast and the bows on the main deck (the deck below the upper deck) was called the 'galley'. It was here that the kitchens were housed.

GANGWAY. A space made in the guard rails at a ship's side through which the brow is hauled to bridge the gap between ship and jetty or against which an accommodation ladder is rigged. (OE. 'gan', going and 'weg', way.)

GUARD RAIL. A rail, or wires, along outboard edge of the upper deck to prevent men falling overboard.

HANGAR DECK. The storage area for aircraft below the flight deck in an aircraft carrier.

HATCH. An access opening in a deck. (OE. 'haec', gate.)

HATCH COVER. A lid hinged to the coaming of a hatch which may be clamped down to make the hatch waterproof.

HATCHWAY. The vertical space through a series of hatches which are located one above the other.

HEADS. Lavatories.

The name is derived from the original practice of locating the lavatories in the bow, or head, of a sailing ship. They consisted of platforms either side of the 'beakhead' which was forward of the forecastle. They had grating floors to enable the sea to wash them clean and seamen were expected to use the lee side so that deposits fell clear of the ship.

HOLD. The lowest space in a ship, the interior cavity where stores or cargo is stowed. (Earlier 'hole'.)

HULL. The main body of a ship. (OE. 'hulu', husk.)

HYDROPLANES. Horizontal rudders at each end of a submarine which control the depth when submerged.

HYDROSEARCH. A hull-mounted stabilised high definition sonar fitted in survey ships which is capable of detecting wrecks and other seabed obstructions.

ISIS. Decca machinery plant monitor system, fitted in the machinery control rooms of the latest ships.

ISLAND SUPERSTRUCTURE. The superstructure of an aircraft carrier, which includes the bridge, funnel and masts, etc., situated on the starboard side of the ship.

JUMPING LADDER. A portable ladder which is hung over the ship's side in order to embark personnel from boats whilst under way. It is constructed of chain ropes with wooden treads and is telescoped by a lanyard which passes through the centre of the treads.

KEEL. The lowest longitudinal steel member on which a ship is built up. (MDu. 'kiel' akin to OE. 'ceol', ship.)

KEELSON. A stringer bolted to the inside of the ship's keel to provide additional strength and to support the floor (the lower section of the transverse frames). (Sw. 'kolsvin'.)

LADDER. That which ashore would be called a staircase.

LIFEBUOY. A lifesaving device made of buoyant material such as expanded polystyrene and fitted with a lifeline secured to it in four places to form four easily grasped beckets. Attached to the lifebuoy by a line is a smoke marker which is ignited by a sea cell and supported by a small float. Also attached to the float are two electric lamps powered by sea cells. In the event of an alarm being given for man overboard, one or more lifebuoys are released.

LIFERAFTS. 25-man inflatable liferafts are carried in ships, the number dependant on the complement with ten per cent extra as spare. These are packed in GRP containers and are self inflating on launch. Each raft has an air inflated floor and a double fabric Nylon canopy to give protection from cold. Equipment carried includes a survival pack containing provisions for three days, solar stills and water bags, water collection apparatus, interior and exterior lights and a SOLAS survival transceiver.

LIFTS. Elevators for transporting aircraft to and from the flight deck from the hangar deck in an aircraft carrier.

LOBBY. A platform between decks which does not run the length and breadth of a ship and which gives access to one or more compartments.

LOCATION MARKINGS. In order to identify one's position, each compartment bears a location marking according to a standard system. This divides the ship up and down by decks, numbered in sequence from the upper deck downwards (1, 2, 3, etc.) and in the superstructure upwards (01, 02, 03, etc.). Sections are lettered A, B, C, etc. in sequence from forward. Thus a figure is combined with a letter as the marking, e.g. 4F.

MAGAZINE. A storeroom for explosives, embedded deep in the ship where enemy fire should not easily penetrate.

MAIN BALLAST TANKS. Tanks running alongside the pressure hull of a submarine which can be filled with water for the submarine to dive or pumped full of air to surface.

MAIN NAVAL STORE. The store where all naval stores are held with the exception of departmental stores such as armament stores.

MANHOLES. Small escape 'hatches' fitted in some large hatch covers which are fitted with double clips to enable them to be opened from either side.

MAST. Once the long upright spar set in a ship for supporting yards and sails, but nowadays to carry aerials etc. (OE. 'moest', the stem of a tree.)

MASTHEAD. The top of a mast.

MESS. A space allocated to a number of men for the purpose of eating and sleeping. Senior rates' messes are separate from those of junior rates. The name comes from the 16th century when the hands sat down in groups to 'mess from the common pot.' (OFr. 'mes', a dish.)

MESSDECK. A deck space containing a number of separate messes.

NAME. The name of a warship is displayed in permanent raised letters or on a nameboard on either side of the superstructure, or sometimes on either side of the hull. Submarines sometimes display a nameboard when entering or leaving harbour. RFA and RMAS ships have their names painted on either sides of the bow and on the counter at the stern.

OPERATIONS ROOM. The control centre of a ship in action where the Action Information Organisation (AIO) is situated.

PENNANT NUMBER. Each ship is allocated a pendant number, for identification purposes, which is preceded by a type letter as follows:

A	RFA and RMAS ships
D	Destroyers
F	Frigates
K	Specialist RN ships
L	Assault ships and landing craft
M	Mine countermeasures vessels
P	Patrol boats
R	Aircraft carriers
S	Submarines
Y	Certain of the water carriers, coastal tankers and fleet tenders.

With the exception of *HMS BRITANNIA* and all submarines, each ship has her pennant number painted on both of the ship's sides and sometimes also on the stern.

PERISCOPE. An instrument fitted in submarines for giving a view above the surface all around the horizon whilst the 'boat' is submerged. In addition to the normal main 'scope an 'attack' periscope is also carried which gives a smaller profile. (G. 'peri', round and 'scopien', to look.)

POOP. Any raised deck right aft, above the upper deck.

In large square-rigged sailing ships this deck formed the roof of the 'coach' or 'roundhouse' where the master had his cabin. (ME. 'pupe' from L. 'puppis'.)

PORT. See SCUTTLE.

PRESSURE HULL. The inner hull of a submarine, constructed to withstand the pressure of water at the greatest depth for which the submarine is designed.

PUNKA-LOUVRES. Adjustable nozzles set into fresh air trunkings to allow the flow to be directed as desired. (Hindu 'punka', a large fan hanging from the ceiling, swung by a rope or other mechanical device.)

Until the advent of electrically driven ventilators, foul air, damp and condensation below decks had always been a problem. Admiral Boscowan was noted for introducing a type of ventilator in his flagship in 1747 and these were tried in a few other ships. In the 1850s various methods were tried, but none were very successful as most employed a canvas wind funnel which was required to be turned into the wind for air to be directed to the decks below. In the tropics, where these devices might have been useful, there was often no wind anyway.

Q-TANK. The quick diving tank in the bow of a submarine.

QUARTERS. The two after parts, port and starboard quarters, which are between amidships and astern.

QUARTERDECK. The after end of the upper deck between the quarters. On arrival on the quarterdeck a salute is always given as a mark of respect paid to the authority of the Royal Navy, as symbolised by the white ensign which is hoisted on the ensign staff at the after end of this deck.

QUARTERMASTER'S LOBBY. A lobby, situated near the gangway when a ship is in harbour, provided for the use of the quartermaster.

RADOME. An external blister or housing fitted on either the hull or superstructure of a ship which houses radar antennae.

RAKE. The projection of the upper parts of the hull at the stem and stern beoynd the keel.

RIGOL. A curved strip of metal above a scuttle which prevents any water running down the ship's side from entering. (It. 'rigolo', small circle.)

RUDDER. The device by which a ship is turned, hung on a rudder stock which enters the hull at the stern through a rudder post. At the top of the stock is a quadrant called a rudder stock, to which force is applied by a steering engine to turn the rudder. (ME. 'rother', steering oar, from OE. 'rother', paddle.)

SALT WATER MAIN. A system of piping within a ship which is painted bright red and which carried sea water under pressure for fire-fighting purposes.

SCREW. The screw propeller of a ship, which may have fixed or variable pitch blades. The latest Voith-Schneider cycloidal propellers have a specialised form of variable pitch which rotate on a vertical instead of horizontal axis and blades can be adjusted to impart thrust in any direction. They are fitted in survey vessels and the seabed operations vessel *CHALLENGER* giving the ability for dynamic positioning. A ship fitted with a cycloidal propeller does not need a rudder and can even move sideways.

In 1843 the sailing sloop *ARDENT* was lengthened, fitted with a screw and relaunched with the new name *RATTLER*. Shortly afterwards the Admiralty conducted an experiment by engaging her in a tug of war with the paddle steamer *ALECTO*, to see which of the two kinds of propulsion was the most effective. The *RATTLER* proved the stronger.

SCUTTLE. A circular port in the ship's side to admit light and air. It has a metal frame and a thick glass hinged window designed to be secured by butterfly clips or folded back sideways against the bulkhead. Now only found in older ships. (ME. 'skottell', a small opening in a wall or roof, from OFr. 'escoutille'.)

The first ships to have gun ports cut in their sides were the *HENRY GRANCE A DEU* (Great Harry) and the *MARY ROSE* around the year 1513. Previously guns were sited in the fore and after castles, but the size of gun required by Henry VIII precluded this. And so the naval constructor James Baker adapted the French cargo loading watertight door called a 'porte'.

SEA CABIN. A cabin for use by the Captain when at sea which is located nearby to the bridge and which may be used instead of the normal cabin aft, if required.

SEACOCK. A valve on a pipe connected to the sea. (All valves or taps are known as 'cocks'.)

SEATUBE. A tube which passes through the double bottom of a ship to which the salt water main is connected.

SENIOR RATES' MESS. In a small ship or establishment, the mess where all of the warrant officers and chief and petty officers mess together. In a very large ship or establishment, the petty officers are allocated a separate mess.

SHEER. The rise of the deck at the head and stern above the midship part.

SHIP CONTROL CENTRE (SCC). The position where all of the electrical and mechanical services are monitored.

SHIP'S SIDE. The sides round the hull above the waterline.

SHOT MAT. A heavy rope mat used to protect the deck from heavy weights. Originally to protect the deck from cannon shot being dropped on it.

SKI JUMP. An aircraft take-of ramp fitted at the forward end of the flight deck in the *INVINCIBLE* class aircraft carriers. It is the invention of an ex RN engineer officer, Lt. Cdr. D Taylor, and allows a Sea Harrier aircraft to make a 'rolling take-off' (as against a vertical take-off) with up to 1500 lbs more fuel or ordnance on board.

SICK BERTH. Also known as 'sick bay'.

In 1798, Admiral the Earl St. Vincent, when C-in-C Mediterranean, ordered that 'a sick berth was to be provided in each ship of the line, to be situated under the forecastle with a roundhouse enclosed for the use of the sick'. The rounded forepart of a ship between decks was known as a bay as it resembled the bay of a room.

SIDELIGHTS. Fixed circular windows fitted in compartments situated in the superstructure.

SPITKID. A receptacle for cigarette ends placed in a convenient position on a deck.

In the days when men chewed tobacco, 'spitkids' were placed on deck to receive spit. As a punishment for splitting on the deck, an offender was required to hang a spitkid around his neck, a practice which continued until 1905. A 'kid' was an old nautical term for a small wooden tub or vessel.

SPONSON. A projection from the ship's side or superstructure which houses armament or other equipment.

SPURNWATER. A breakwater on a ship's forecastle, also a low coaming around the edges of decks to prevent water spilling over the ship's side.

STANCHION. A supporting deck pillar or any supporting post. (OFr. 'estanson'.)

STEM. The foremost near vertical part to which the sides are joined. (OE. 'stemn'.)

STERN. The afterpart. (ME. 'steorne' from Ice. 'stjorn', steering.)

TILLER. A large steel bar fitted to the head of the rudder, which is worked by hydraulics and linked to the ship's wheel.

TOP HAMPER. Weight carried on deck or aloft which is an encumbrance.

TRIMMING TANKS. Tanks spaced throughout the hull in order to correct the trim of the ship. Sea water may be admitted or pumped out as required.

TUMBLE HOME. The amount by which the two sides of a ship are curved in towards the fore-and-aft line above the point of the widest beam.

UPPER DECK. The highest continuous watertight deck.

WAIST. The midship part of the upper deck between the forecastle and the quarterdeck.

WARDROOM. Officers' Mess.

In sailing days the gunner was responsible for the training of the junior officers, the midshipmen, who slung their hammocks in his quarters, known as the 'gunroom' and situated in the after part of the lower deck. Strangely, the more senior officers, the lieutenants, marine officers, chaplain, surgeon and purser, had no mess of their own and generally took their meals in their own cabins.

In larger ships, situated beneath the 'great cabin', which was for the use of the captain or admiral, there was a store room for valuables known as the 'wardrobe'. During the middle part of the 18th century, the lieutenants began to use this compartment for meals in preference to eating in their own cabins and it soon became known as the 'lieutenants' mess'.

The position as regularised by the Admiralty in 1856 when the lieutenants' mess officially became the 'wardroom' and the junior officers' and midshipmens' mess the 'gunroom'. In 1956 the gunroom mess was done away with and today all junior officers now join ships and establishments as full members of the wardroom mess.

WASHDOWN. Equipment which facilitates the spraying of salt water over all of the upper deck surfaces to clear contamination after nuclear, chemical or biological attack.

WATERLINE. The line made by the water's edge when a ship has received her full complement of stores.

WATERTIGHT DOORS AND HATCHES. Each compartment contains one or more watertight doors and hatches which are secured by clips and bear the location markings of the compartment to which they give access.

WEAPON STORAGE COMPARTMENT. Situated at the foward end of a submarine. This is what was previously known as the 'forward torpedo room'; the torpedo has been supplemented by other tube launched weapons such as missiles and mines.

WEATHER DECKS. Decks which are exposed to the weather.

WHEELHOUSE. A housing on deck containing the steering position, usually nowadays forming part of the bridge.

WHIP AERIALS. Transmitting and receiving aerials for short range radio communication.

13

NAVIGATING AND STEERING

Towards the end of the 13th century, two fundamental navigational discoveries were made; the compass and the rudder. No one knows who invented them, but the Arabs, who were very active on the seas at that time, adapted both and spread their use in Europe. The early compass was simply a magnetic needle placed through the centre of a piece of wood which floated in a bowl of water. Although this floating needle was not very accurate, nor the early rudder very practical, sailing ships were no longer compelled to follow the direction in which the wind was blowing. By using a rudder, a ship could make progress in a zig-zag fashion against the wind. When this happened, man was thus launched upon the discovery of the world.

The compass and the rudder were not the only inventions which enabled navigation to make progress. In 1569, the Flemish geographer Kromer, perhaps better known as Mercator, conceived the idea of covering the globe with imaginary lines; longitude meridians and parallel lines of latitude. By dividing the globe in this way, it became possible to accurately fix the position of a ship on the ocean, even though the vessel was out of sight of land. However, two instruments were essential to this operation. Firstly, the astrolabe, which has today become the sextant, with which to measure the height of the sun above the horizon, and secondly the watch, today the chronometer. By determining the time of the sun's maximum height at mid day and comparing that time with that of noon at Greenwich it was possible to calculate longitude. Each difference in time of four minutes is equal to one degree of longitude, east or west of Greenwich. Latitude is calculated in a similar fashion, but the procedure is more complicated.

Today the sextant is all but obsolete as ships are able to make use of satellite and inertial navigation systems.

* * *

ALTER COURSE. To change the direction of the ship's head.

ALTERNATING LIGHT. A navigational light with two colours shown alternately, with or without a period of darkness separating them.

AZIMUTH RING. Each bridge compass has an azimuth ring, which includes an azimuth mirror, fitted on the top of the compass bowl. In order to obtain a bearing, the ring is trained round until the object appears over the mirror. The compass card is reflected in the mirror and the bearing may be read off. (Azimuth from Arabic 'as sumat', the way.)

BAR. A bank of sand, gravel or earth forming a shoal at the mouth of a river or estuary.

BEACONS. Posts or erections on shore to guide ships past dangers. (OE. 'beacn'.)

News of the Spanish Armada's arrival off Plymouth was signalled by means of lighting beacons and the news went from Plymouth to York via London in 12 hours.

BEARING. The position of an object relative to the ship.

BINNACLE. The wooden housing for the compass which also contains corrector magnets and bars. Prior to the 18th century it was known as a 'bittacle'. (ME. 'bitakle' from OSp. 'bitacula' from L. 'habitaculum', dwelling place.)

BLUFF. A headland with a broad, perpendicular face. (Dut. 'blaf', broad.)

BOWLIGHTS. Navigation lights carried by a ship, in addition to the steaming and overtaking lights. One, being a red light, is carried on the port side and the other, a green light, is carried on the starboard side. The lights are placed at a lower height than the steaming light and show from right ahead to 22.5 degrees abaft the beam on their respective sides. They are sometimes called sidelights. See also NAVIGATION LIGHTS.

BUOY. A floating mark, mainly used for navigation and attached to the sea bed by anchors and cable. (OE. 'boei' from L. 'boia', a fetter.)

Buoys first came into use in European waters in the 16th century. The first were laid in the Thames in 1538.

CAN BUOY. A flat topped (can shaped) buoy, painted red or red and white, used to indicate the port hand side of a channel when entering it with the flood tide.

CANE. Computer Assisted Navigation Equipment. A computerised navigation system fitted in small warships which also gives limited Action Information Organisation (AIO) for weapon control.

CARDINAL MARK. A mark indicating navigable water on the named side.

CHANNEL. The deeper part of a strait, bay or harbour.

CHART. A map of a sea area, showing details of any coastlines, positions of buoys, lights, etc. and depths of water. (F. 'charte' from L. 'charta' from Gk. 'charte', a sheet of papyrus).

The first Admiralty chart was issued in 1801 by Alexander Dalyrmple, Admiralty Hydrographer since 1795 when the department was first established. In 1819 permission was given by the Admiralty to sell charts to the Merchant Marine and since then the world has navigated almost entirely on British Admiralty charts.

CHART DATUM. The level above which the heights of the tide are shown in tide tables and below which the depth of water shown on a chart is measured.

CHRONOMETER. A clock or watch which measures the time with consistent accuracy, used as an aid for accurate navigation.

CLEARING MARKS. Shown on a chart to indicate clearance of a hidden danger by keeping the marks 'open'.

COCKED HAT. A term used in chartwork when determining a ship's position by the plotting of three bearings. If perfect bearings are obtained and correctly plotted, the three lines drawn on the chart should intersect at the same point. When they do not, then a triangular space, known as a 'cocked hat', is formed, indicating an error.

COMPE UP WITH A VESSEL, TO. To overtake her.
COMPASS BOWL. The container in which the compass rests.
COMPASS CARD. The card over which the needle of a compass rests, marked with the directional points of the instrument.
COMPASS PLATFORM. The position from which a ship is conned, the bridge.
COMPASS REPEATER. The principal bridge gyro compass repeater, which is 'repeating' the position of true north from the main gyro compass. Also known as 'pelorus'.
COMPASS ROSE. A circle printed in a convenient position on a chart which shows the points of the compass marked in degrees, together with the annual rate of increase or decrease of variation.

The compass of the ancient mariners was a 'wind rose' which was a circular device and eight points for the prevailing winds which blew from the various countries around the Mediterranean.

CONICAL BUOY. A cone shaped buoy, usually painted black, used to indicate the starboard side of a channel when entering it with the flood tide.
CONTOUR LINES. Lines on a chart which connect similar points of the same depth.
COURSE. The direction, by compass, in which a ship is being steered. (OF. 'cours' from L. 'cursum', a running, from 'currere', to run.)
DAN BUOY. A small buoy used for temporarily marking a position. It consists of a cylindrical can with a sloping top and a tube through the centre through which a stave is passed. A flag is attached to the stave and the buoy is laid by means of special moorings.
DEAD RECKONING. The method of obtaining a ship's position by applying to the chart courses steered and speed made through the water from the last known observed position.
DEEP. A depression on the sea-bed.
DEPARTURE. The navigator's last professional sight of land.
DEVIATION. The error of a magnetic compass caused by a ship's own magnetism.

DISTANCE RUN. An estimation of the distance the ship has run over the water in each hour or on each course, as entered in the ship's log.

DIVIDERS. A charting device used to mark off distances.

EASE, TO. This is a general nautical term meaning to take off pressure. In a steering context, a helmsman ordered 'Port 15' may subsequently be ordered to 'Ease to 10'.

ECHO SOUNDER. A machine by which soundings are taken which sends out sound impulses from the bottom of the ship. The impulses travel to the sea bottom and are reflected back to the ship. An instrument on the bridge or in the charthouse automatically calculates the time taken for the sound to travel and provides a continuous record of the depth on a paper roll.

EMERGENCY STEERING POSITION. A steering position situated aft in a ship, usually near the engine room, for use should the forward steering position be out of action.

ENGINE AND REVOLUTION TELEGRAPHS. Engine and revolution orders are passed to the engine room by these instruments.

ENGINE ORDER REPEATERS. Engine and revolution orders from the wheelhouse, passed by means of engine and revolution telegraphs, are received in the engine room on these repeaters and are applied to the engines by the MEAs on watch.

ENGINE REVOLUTIONS. A certain number of revolutions are required to drive a ship at a certain speed and a table of these is displayed on the bridge. Changes in revolutions are passed to the helmsman in the steering position for transmission to the engine room by way of the engine and revolution telegraphs.

ESTIMATED POSITION. A position which is the most accurate that may be obtained from a dead reckoning position adjusted for the estimated effects of 'wind across', currents and tidal streams.

FAIRWAY. A navigable channel in a harbour.

FATHOM. A unit of measurement equal to six feet, used for the depth of the sea and the length of rope, which is rapidly now becoming obsolete due to metrification. The word comes from the old English 'faedm', which meant embrace and is a measurement across the body between the outstretched arms - approximately six feet. (100 fathoms = 1 cable length and 1000 fathoms = 1 nautical mile.)

FIX. The process of obtaining a ship's position from observations of land or sea marks, or heavenly bodies and by radio or other electronic methods of navigation.

FIXED AND FLASHING LIGHT. A navigational light which has a steady beam, varied at intervals by a flash of brighter intensity.

FIXED LIGHT. A navigational light which has a steady beam with no interval of darkness.

FLASHING LIGHT. A navigational light, either on land, lighthouse or fixed to a buoy, with the period of light less than the period of darkness.

FLAT. A flat surface shoal or bank close inshore, which may or may not uncover at low water.

FLINDERS BAR. Permanently magnetised soft iron bars situated on a ship's magnetic compass binnacle in order to compensate for the ship's magnetic condition. Named after Captain Matthew Flinders, RN in recognition of his work in the field of investigating problems of ship magnetism.

FORWARD STEERING POSITION. The normal steering position in the wheelhouse; an emergency steering position is situated aft in a ship.

GIMBALS. Two metal rings which move within each other and form the mounting for a compass or chronometer to allow the instruments to remain level despite the pitching and rolling of a ship. (OFr. 'gemel', twin.)

GRAIN. The line of water ahead of a vessel along which she will pass. The opposite to 'wake'.

GREENWICH MEAN TIME (GMT). The basis of all navigational measurement of time by which the results of observations of heavenly bodies are worked out in order to fix the position of a ship at sea.

In 1880 international agreement was reached to accept the longitude of Greenwich, the home of the Royal Observatory, as the prime meridian from which all time at sea should be measured.

GYRO COMPASS. A mechanically and electrically operated master gyro which accurately indicates the direction of true north. The master gyro drives a number of repeaters on the bridge and elsewhere in a ship.

The first Sperry gyro compasses were fitted in RN submarines just prior to the First World War. These were based on the work done for the United States Navy by Elmer A Sperry.

'HARD-A-PORT' (OR STARBOARD). A helm order given in an emergency for 35 degrees of rudder. The normal order would be 'Port (or Starboard) 30'.

HARD OVER. Said of the wheel and rudder when the maximum of 35 degrees of rudder angle is put on.

HAUL OFF, TO. To alter a ship's course.

HEADING. The direction in which a ship is moving.

HELM. The term connected with orders for steering a ship. Also another name for a tiller in a boat. (OE. 'helma'.)

HELM INDICATOR. An electrical instrument connected to the rudder which may be on the bridge. It consists of a pointer moving over an arc graduated in degrees, either to port or starboard and gives the angle of the rudder at any moment.

HELM ORDER. An order given to the helmsman which bears direct relation to the helm indicator which is situated on the top of the steering pedestal. Not to be confused with 'steering order' which relates to a particular course.

HELMSMAN. The rating responsible for steering the ship.

HF/DF. High Frequency Direction Finding. A method of obtaining the bearings of high frequency radio beacons, enabling the position of a ship to be plotted. A loop aerial is employed which can be turned to find the weakest signal strength. The bearing of the beacon thus lies at right angles to the plane of the loop aerial.

HIFIX 6. An advanced navigation radar used for minesweeping and surveying.

HORIZON. The apparent intersection of sea and sky. (Gr. 'horos', boundary.)

'HOW IS THE SHIP'S HEAD?' Meaning in what direction are the bows pointing.

HYPERFIX. An accurate position fixing system.

INCLINATION. The angle between the line of sight from an observer and another ship's course. Expressed in degrees, from 0 to 180, right or left.

INSHORE. Towards the shore.

INTERNATIONAL REGULATIONS FOR PREVENTING COLLISIONS AT SEA. The internationally agreed rules by which ships at sea keep clear of each other; more commonly known as the RULE OF THE ROAD.

ISOPHASE. A navigational light which flashes with equal periods of light and darkness.

KNOT. The measurement of speed at sea in nautical miles per hour which has been in use since the 15th century. At that time the speed of a ship was found by the use of a half minute sand glass and a 'log'. The sandglass, which consisted of two globes connected by a narrow neck, was a means of measuring the passage of time. The 'log' was originally a wooden plank, thrown overboard from the stern of the ship, attached to which was a line marked with knots spaced at intervals representing the speed of one nautical mile per hour. As the plank remained floating on the sea in a near stationary position, the number of knots which ran out during the period of the sand glass emptying gave the speed of the ship.

LANBY. Large Automatic Navigation Buoys. Some Trinity House light vessels are being replaced by this type of buoy. A LANBY is a discus shaped steel buoy 12 metres in diameter, 2 metres deep and fitted with a central tubular mast superstructure 12 metres high which houses a high power light. These buoys are also fitted with electric fog signals and can also be fitted with radio beacons and racons if required. The equipment is controlled by radio from a shore station.

LANDFALL. The first sight of land when at sea. A ship is said to 'make a good landfall' when the land is sighted at the point calculated.

LANDMARK. Any distinctive feature ashore which can serve as an aid to navigation.

LATERAL MARK. A navigation buoy marking port or starboard of a well defined channel.

LATITUDE. Angular measurement of position north or south of the equator.

LEADING MARKS/LIGHTS. Marks or lights which, when brought into line, indicate a channel or best water.

LEAD LINE. A method of obtaining soundings in shallow water, by the use of a weighted line which is marked along its length by a series of knots, leather and bunting. It was once the only method of sounding, but today, with the provision of electronic sounding devices, it is rarely used.

LIST OF LIGHTS. Issued by the Hydrographic Department of the RN and gives more complete particulars of shore lights, light vessels and fog signals than given on charts.

LOG. Any device for measuring the speed of a ship through the water. The word comes from the old primitive method of obtaining a ship's speed by throwing a line with a log of wood attached overboard at the bows and timing its arrival at the stern.

LOG BOOK. The book containing the official record of the daily events of a ship's voyage, referred to as the 'log'. The information recorded includes courses steered, speed, details of the weather, visibility, state of the sea, work done, etc. The log is written up from a 'rough log' which in former days was a slate. Prior to the slate a 'logboard' was used which consisted of two boards shutting like a book and containing the hours of the day and night. See also KNOT.

LONGITUDE. Angular measurement east or west of Greenwich meridian.

LUBBER'S LINE. A line drawn on the inside of the bowl of a compass representing the ship's head. When ordered to steer a compass course, the helmsman keeps the lubber's line constantly opposite the desired point on the compass card.

MAGNETIC COMPASS. A compass which obtains its directive force from the Earth's magnetic field and therefore seeks magnetic north.

MARINER'S HANDBOOK. This is issued by the Hydrographic Department of the RN and contains all information on charts and navigational publications, general meteorology and ice.

'MEET HER'. A helm order. When the rudder has been put over in altering course, it is necessary to 'meet her' with opposite rudder to prevent 'her' swinging too far.

MIDDLE GROUND. A sand or mud bank in a fairway, marked by middle ground buoys, which ships can pass on either side.

NAUTICAL MILE. Also known as a sea mile and longer than a mile on land, being equal to 6080 feet (approx 2000 yards) or 1852 metres.

NAVSAT. Navigation Satellite System. The satellite system providing data by means of which the position of RN ships and submarines anywhere in the world can be accurately fixed. Four satellites are used, continually orbiting the Earth.

NAVIGATION. The art of directing a ship's passage from place to place. (L. 'navigatus', p.p. of 'navigare' from 'navis', ship and 'agare', to drive.)

NAVIGATIONAL LIGHTS. Lights displayed on shore or by lighthouses, lightships, buoys, etc., as an aid to navigation.

NAVIGATION LIGHTS. Lights carried by vessels under way as laid down by the International Regulations for Prevention of Collisions at Sea. They are designed to show approximately in which direction vessels are heading. See also STEAMING LIGHT, BOWLIGHTS and OVERTAKING LIGHT.

NAVIGATION RECORD BOOK. A book in which a complete account of the ship's movements are recorded; all courses, speeds, bearings, depths and the ship's position in more detail than that recorded in the ship's log.

NOTICES TO MARINERS. These are issued weekly by the Hydrographic Department of the RN and contain the latest information on all navigational subjects including corrections to charts.

OBSERVED POSITION. The ship's position found from reliable sextant observations of heavenly bodies.

OCCULTING. A navigational light with the period of light greater than the period of darkness.

OFFING. The distance a ship keeps away from the shore to avoid hazards.

OVERTAKING LIGHT. A single white light mounted on the stern of a ship which must be visible for at least three miles and showing 22.5 degrees abaft the beam through the stern on both sides. Also known as a stern light.

PASSAGE. A ship's journey from starting point to destination.

PELORUS. See COMPASS REPEATER.

PILOT. A qualified coastal navigator, licenced by Trinity House, taken on board ship to conduct her along a coast or into a harbour where navigation is difficult and requires special knowledge.

PILOTAGE. The precise navigation required in the restricted waters of a port, channel or inland waterway. (Du. 'peillood', sounding lead.)

PILOTS. The name for 'Sailing Directions', which are issued by the Hydrographic Department of the Royal Navy. They give worldwide information about coasts to supplement that shown on charts and each covers a particular area of coast such as the 'Channel Pilot', 'Mediterranean Pilot', etc.

A 'Coasting Pilot' covering the sea coast of the UK was first produced in 1693, following a survey carried out by Greenville Collins who was appointed Hydrographer to the King. Up to that time the British had depended upon Dutch charts.

POSITION LINE. A line drawn on a chart as a result of a bearing or sight.

PRICK A CHART, TO. To plot, to trace a ship's course on a chart.

QUICK FLASHING LIGHT. A navigational light which rapidly flashes, with the period of light less than the period of darkness.

RACON. A beacon which responds to a radar set's transmission and shows up on the display.

RADAR. An abbreviation of Radio Direction and Range. It is a method of detecting objects by transmitting radio waves and then receiving the waves bounced back from an object. Distance of objects is calculated by measuring the time taken for a wave to be sent out and return; the results being displayed visually on a cathode ray tube. Navigation types 978 and 1006 are common in the RN.

The Hunt class minesweeper HMS SALTBURN was the first RN ship to be fitted with radar in 1939.

RADIO BEACON. A radio transmitter of known frequency and position from which a position line may be obtained.

REEF. A ridge of rock, coral, sand, etc., in the sea, at or near the surface of the water. (Dut. 'rif'.)

RELATIVE BEARINGS. The bearings of outside objects relative to the ship, expressed in degrees from ahead on each side.

RHUMB LINE. A course which cuts all meridians at the same angle. (A straight line on a Mercator chart). (OFr. 'rumb', a compass point.)

ROAD. See ROADSTEAD.

ROADSTEAD. A bay or place of anchorage at some distance from the shore and therefore 'open', or exposed, to wind and gales.

RULE OF THE ROAD. The 31 rules which make up the International Regulations for Preventing Collisions at Sea which covers shapes or lights by which ships may be identified by day or by night, steering and sailing rules, sound signals and distress signals.

RUNNING FIX. A method of obtaining the ship's position when only one object can be seen and therefore only one position line obtained. The line is used later to obtain a fix when another bearing of the same object, or another object, can be taken.

SAILING DIRECTIONS. See PILOTS.

SEA ANCHOR. Any device used in order to hold a ship's head to the sea in heavy weather.

SEA MARK. Any floating navigational mark such as a buoy or lightship.

Once, marks set up ashore by Trinity House where necessary as aids to navigation (now known as landmarks) were known as sea marks. A fine of £100 was imposed upon any person found destroying a sea mark.

SEA ROOM. Sufficient distance from the shore or a hazard.

SEAWARD. Away from the shore or towards the sea.

SECONDARY PORTS. See STANDARD PORTS.

SEXTANT. A navigation instrument, developed in 1757 by Captain John Campbell RN from its predecessor the quadrant, with a graduated arc of a sixth of a circle for the measurement of horizontal and vertical angles at sea. (L. 'sextans', a sixth part.)

SHALLOW. See SHOAL.

SHAPE A COURSE, TO. To select a course.

SHIP'S HEAD. The direction in which a ship's bows are pointing at any given moment.

SHOAL. A sandbank or bar. (ME. 'shold', shallow from OE. 'sceald'.)

SHOOT THE SUN, TO. To take an altitude of the sun with a sextant.

In the 16th century John Davis invented the quadrant, the forerunner of the sextant, which did the job of the old astrolabe and cross staff but did it more exactly. Old captains who had spent their lives at sea laughed at the new invention; they joked that the users were 'shooting at the sun', asking if they had struck it.

SIDELIGHTS. See BOWLIGHTS.

SIGHT. An observation of the sun, moon or stars by means of which a ship's position may be determined.

SINS. Ship's Inertial Navigation System. A system originally developed for use in nuclear submarines which, because of the need to remain submerged for long periods, require a method of navigation to make it unnecessary to come to periscope depth to fix their position. At the start of a voyage, the ship's position is accurately plotted and all subsequent alterations to course and speed are detected by sensitive measuring equipment to give an accurate position at any time. Certain surface ships are also fitted with the system which is expensive because of the high electronic and engineering precision required.

The first system was fitted for trials in the experimental vessel *STEADY* in 1961. A year later the system was installed in *HMS DREADNOUGHT*, Britain's first nuclear powered submarine.

SIPS. Survey Information Processing System. Currently being developed for fitting into coastal survey vessels with the intention of improving the speed and efficiency of the survey of the ocean bed.

SNAPS. Ships Navigation Processing System. An integrated navigation system where all navigational data from various sensors is fed into a central computer which analyses the information and provides a positional fix with the highest accuracy.

SOUND. A channel or strait. (OE. 'sund'.)

SOUNDING. A measurement of the depth of water. See ECHO SOUNDER.

SOUND SIGNALS. As laid down in the International Regulations for Preventing Collisions at Sea, in order that a ship may indicate her intentions. They may be used in fog or in normal visibility in a harbour or restricted waterway and are as follows:

One short blast.	I am turning to starboard.
Two short blasts.	I am turning to port.
Three short blasts.	My engines are going astern.
Four short blasts.	Pilot vessel underway, stopped or at anchor. (In addition to normal signals.)
Five short blasts.	I do not understand your intentions.
Two long blasts and one short blast.	I intend to overtake you on starboard side.
Two long blasts and two short blasts.	I intend to overtake you on port side.

SPHERICAL BUOY. Used to indicate a channel to either side, but usually have a predominant colour, red or black, to indicate on which side is the main channel.

SPIT. A point of land or narrow shoal extending into the sea.

SPOIL GROUND. An area of the seabed, marked by buoys, where sewage, spoil from dredging, etc. is dumped.

STANDARD PORTS. Those ports for which the times and heights of high and low water have been predicted for every day of the year in Tide Tables. Each standard port is allocated a number of secondary ports, the tidal features of which are related to those of their parent standard port. Part II of the Tide Tables includes the differences between the times and heights of high and low water at the secondary ports and those at their parent standard port.

STAND, TO. To sail in a widely defined direction, e.g. to 'stand southward'.

STAND OFF, TO. To direct the course away from the land.

STATION KEEPING. For a ship to keep accurate station on another.

'STEADY'. A helm order which cancels any previously given and requires the helmsman to use whatever wheel is necessary to keep the ship to the compass course ordered, e.g. 'Steady on 180'.

STEAMING LIGHT. A navigation light carried by a ship in addition to the bow and overtaking lights. It is a white light showing from right ahead to 22.5 degrees abaft either beam. A ship over 150 metres in length carries a second steaming light aft, fixed at a lower height than the first light.

STEER, TO. The operation of directing a vessel's course by means of a tiller or steering wheel. (OE. 'steoran' akin to 'steor', rudder.)

STEERING ENGINE. The power applied to the rudder head in order to turn the rudder.

About 1880 RN warships were given steam steering engines so that the rudder could be operated by one helmsman in place of up to 40 men at four-fold wheels. Hand steering conventions were not completely abandoned, even though power steering did away with the need to have many turns of the tiller ropes round the wheel drum, because the Admiralty insisted that there must always be three turns of the wheel to move the rudder from midships to full helm.

STEERING ORDER. An order given to the helmsman to steer on a particular course and to keep the ship steady on that course. It is always prefixed by the word 'steer', such as 'Steer 210' or 'Steer on the lighthouse'.

STEERING POSITION. The wheelhouse.

STERNBOARD. A method of manoeuvre carried out by a ship needing to turn in a narrow waterway and unable to do so whilst going ahead. The helm is reversed when going astern, enabling the bows to swing in the original direction of her turn.

STERN LIGHT. See OVERTAKING LIGHT.

STRAIT. A channel of water connecting two larger areas. (OFr. 'estroict' from L. 'strictum', narrow, restricted.)

STRAND. The sea beach.

SWING SHIP, TO. To swing a ship around a buoy on a succession of compass headings in order to carry out compass corrections.

TIDE TABLES. A publication of the Hydrographic Department of the Royal Navy, which was first produced in 1833, in which the time and height of tides is predicted for every day of the year at every standard port in the world.

TOP MARKS. Particular shapes placed on the tops of buoys as an aid to identification.

TRANSIT. A means of obtaining a position line by sighting two known objects in line with each other.

TRICK. A spell on watch. The helmsman takes a 'trick at the wheel'.

TRUE. An exact geographical position as opposed to a reading of magnetic north, as in the expression 'true north'.

VARIATION. The difference in angle between magnetic north and true north, which varies in different parts of the world.

VOYAGE. A ship's journey from starting place to destination and back again. (OFr. 'voiaje' from L. 'viaticum', a journey by water.)

WATCH, TO. A navigational buoy is said to be 'watching' when it is in its correct position as indicated on a chart with its signal, if fitted, in working order.

WHEEL. The wheel by which the helmsman steers the ship and thus activates the steering engine to work the tiller bar and rudder.

It was not until the start of the 18th century that a method was devised for joining the tiller cables to a windlass so as to avoid the problem of the differential lengths of the two ropes, once the tiller had been moved from amidships. However, once the mechanical problem had been overcome, the wheel replaced the tiller in nearly all medium and large vessels.

WHEELHOUSE. The steering position from which the helmsman applies to the wheel and the telegraphs the orders passed down from the compass platform.

WHEEL INDICATOR. An indicator marked in degrees to show the helmsman how much wheel is 'on' (how much has been turned).

WRECK BUOY. Wrecks are marked with green buoys and usually have 'wreck' written on them. They may be can, cone or conical in shape to indicate a safe channel.

14

WIND AND SEA

For the captains of sailing ships embarking on voyages to and from various parts of the world, the shortest routes were of no consideration. The all important factor in those days was to seek out the most favourable winds to catch astern. For instance, a voyage from Europe to North America and back meant plying an almost circular course. Outward a ship would have sailed south to the tropics off North Africa to catch the trade winds and thence up to America. She would have returned in a north-easterly direction with the aid of the Westerlies.

Thus it was that sailors observed the prevailing winds throughout the world and used them to their advantage. The scientific explanation for the various winds lies at the equator where hot air rises causing the doldrums (calms). Consequently air rushes in from the north and south which is deflected westward by the earth's rotation, causing the steady north-east and south-east trade winds. Air that rose at the equator cools; part of it replenishing the trade winds and part rolling towards the poles to feed the Westerlies.

Wind is no longer a requirement for propulsion, but its effects, together with those of the sea, have to constantly be taken into consideration.

* * *

BACK. Said of the wind when its direction shifts in opposition to the direction in which the sun goes round.
BACK WATER. An area of water unaffected by the tide.
BEAM SEA. With the wind abeam.

BEAUFORT SCALE. A numerical scale of wind strength, developed by Sir Francis Beaufort, Hydrographer of the Navy in the early 19th century. When originally introduced in 1805, the scale ranged from 0 (calm) to 12 (hurricane force). Additional strengths, 13 to 17 (72 to 118 knots), have been subsequently added.

BORE. Tidal flood. (ME. for wave, from ON. 'bara', a billow.)

BROKEN WATER. Surf caused by breaking waves.

CALM. Description of the condition where the wind speed is less than 1 knot, 0 on the Beaufort Scale.

CALM SEA. There are two states of calm sea; one where the surface is glassy with no waves (sea state 0) and the other where the surface is rippled and the mean maximum height of waves is up to one foot (sea state 1).

CHOPPY SEA. A short, steep and usually confused sea.

CREST. The highest part of a wave.

CROSS SEA. A rough or irregular sea caused by waves and wind that are running in opposite directions.

CYCLONES. Tropical storms of hurricane strength which occur in the Arabian Sea, the Bay of Bengal, the South Indian Ocean and the vicinity of North-west Australia.

CURRENT. The flow of the sea in one direction.

DEAD WATER. The eddy water which closes in on a ship's stern as she passes through the water; where there is no water.

DIURNAL TIDES. When there is only one high water and one low water in each lunar day. This occurs around the area of the tropics and the range of tide is not normally large.

DURATION. The time between low water and high water, normally slightly more than six hours.

EBB. The return of the tide to the sea. (OE. 'ebba'.)

EBB STREAM. The stream that accompanies a falling tide in harbour.

EDDY. A current of water circling back, or in the direction contrary to the main stream. (OE. 'ed', back and 'ea', water.)

EYE OF THE STORM. The relatively calm weather in the centre of a severe tropical cyclone.

EYE OF THE WIND. The exact point from which the wind blows.

FAIR. Favourable of wind or weather.

FLOOD STREAM. The stream that accompanies a rising tide in harbour.

FLOOD TIDE. The tide when rising.

FLOW. The rise of the tide. (OE. 'flowan'.)

FRESH BREEZE. A wind of force 5 on the Beaufort Scale (17-20 knots). (Sp. 'brisa', the north east wind.)

FRESHEN, TO. For the wind to gain strength.

FRESHET. An exceptionally strong outgoing tidal stream, due to a river current meeting tidal water, especially after recent heavy rains.

GALE. A wind of force 8 on the Beaufort Scale (34-40 knots). (Dan. 'gal', furious.)

GENTLE BREEZE. A wind of force 3 on the Beaufort Scale (7-10 knots).

GREEN SEA. When masses of water are coming on board in a heavy sea. Also called 'shipping it green'.

GROUND SWELL. A broad, deep, heavy swell of the sea, due to a spent or distant storm.

GUST. A brief burst of wind. (Ice. 'gustr'.)

HIGH SEA. Where the mean maximum height of the waves is 20-30 feet (see state 7).

HIGH WATER. The greatest elevation of the tide.

HORSE LATITUDES. A belt of light, variable winds, between the Westerlies and the Trade Winds in the northern and southern hemispheres. The name originated in the middle of the 19th century when numerous horses were transported from Europe to America and the West Indies. In these belts sailing vessels were often becalmed and the belt in the North Atlantic was often studded with dead horses having been jettisoned to save water.

HURRICANE. A wind of force 12 on the Beaufort Scale (64 knots and over). These chiefly occur in the western North Atlantic, the eastern North Pacific and the western South Pacific; similar tropical storms occuring in other parts of the world are known by different names (see CYCLONES and TYPHOON). (Sp. Huracan.)

LAND BREEZE. Air flowing offshore by night due to the cooling of the land and consequently the air in contact with it, to take the place of the warmer air rising from the sea.

LEE SHORE. A shore on to which the wind is blowing. (Lee ME. from OE. 'hleo', protection, shelter.)

LEE TIDE. A tidal stream running in the same direction as the wind.

LEEWARD. Down wind, the direction towards which the wind blows.

LIGHT AIR. A description of a wind speed of from 1-3 knots, force 1 on the Beaufort Scale.

LIGHT BREEZE. A wind of force 2 on the Beaufort Scale (4-6 knots).

LOW WATER. The lowest level reached by the sea during a tidal oscillation.

MAKING. The tide is said to be 'making' as the range increases from neaps to springs.

MEAN SEA LEVEL. The average level of the surface of the sea.

MIXED TIDES. These prevail in certain parts of the world; Australia, the Pacific coast of North America and eastern Asia. There are two high waters and two low waters in each lunar day, but there is inequality in the heights of successive high waters and successive low waters.

MODERATE BREEZE. A wind force of 4 on the Beaufort Scale (11-17 knots).

MODERATE SEA. Where the mean maximum height of the waves is 4-8 feet (sea state 4).

MONSOONS. Winds found in the Indian Ocean, blowing from south-west half the year then reversing.

MUZZLER. A gale blowing from right ahead.

NEAP TIDES. Tides, which twice in a lunar month, rise least and fall least from the mean level, which happens when the sun and the moon act at right angles to each other.

NEAR GALE. A wind of force 7 on the Beaufort Scale (28-33 knots).

OFFING. A vaguely defined part of the sea which lies between the entrance to a harbour, or the shoal water of a coast, and the horizon.

OFFSHORE WIND. A wind which blows from the land towards the sea.

PHENOMENAL SEA. Description of a sea where the mean maximum height of the waves is over 45 feet and as might exist at the centre of a hurricane (sea state 9).

RANGE OF TIDE. The difference in height between successive high and low waters.

ROUGH SEA. Where the mean maximum height of the waves is 8–13 feet (sea state 5).

SCEND. The 'scend' of the sea is the vertical movement of its waves.

SEA BREEZE. An onshore wind which occurs during the day due to the heated air over the land rising and the cooler air over the sea flowing in to take its place.

SEA STATE. A standard method of identifying the state of the sea, using a scale from 0 (calm) to 9 (phenominal).

SEAWAY. Part of the sea which is rough.

SLACK WATER. The condition of the tide 20 minutes each side of high and low water when the rate of flow slackens.

SLIGHT SEA. Where the mean maximum height of the waves is 2–4 feet (sea state 3).

SMOOTH SEA. Where there are wavelets of 1 to 2 feet (sea state 2).

SPINDRIFT. The spray blown from the tops of waves when the sea is exceptionally rough. The surface of the sea becomes covered with this spray. (Variation of 'spoon-drift', 'spoomdrift' from L. 'spuma', loom.)

SPRAY. The water which is blown from the tops of waves.

SPRING TIDES. Tides which, twice in a lunar month, rise highest and fall lowest from the mean level. This is the result of the attractive force of the sun and the moon when they act in a straight line, either in conjunction or in opposition.

SQUALL. A violent blast of wind or a sudden storm. (Ice. 'skuala'.)

STAND OF TIDE. The period at high or low water during which no rise or fall can be detected.

STORM. A wind of force 10 on the Beaufort Scale (48–55 knots). (OE.).

STREAM. See TIDEWAY.

STRONG GALE. A wind of force 9 on the Beaufort Scale (41–47 knots).

SURF. The sea as it breaks at the shoreline. (Formerly 'suffe').

SWASH WAY. A channel across or between shoals or spits.

SWELL. A wave formation on a large scale giving the effect of large areas of sea rising and falling slowly. It is caused by a wind blowing from the same quarter for some time. (OE. 'swellan'.)

TAKING OFF. Said of the tide as the range increases from springs to neaps.

TIDAL STREAM. The horizontal movement of water caused by the rise and fall of the tide.

TIDE. The rise and fall of the sea caused by the effect of the pull by the sun and the moon. (OE. 'tid', time.)

TIDE RACE. The flow of a tide accelerated by a sudden rise or fall in the depth of water caused by rocks or a fault in the bottom formation. (ME. 'ras'.)

TIDE RIP. Ripples or short waves caused by two currents meeting or eddies made by a tide flowing over an uneven bottom.

TIDEWAY. The water in a channel caused by the ebb and flow of a tidal stream. Also known as a 'stream'.

TRADE WINDS. Regular steady winds which blow in a belt around the equator; north-easterly to the north of it and south-easterly to the south of it. They are known as Trade Winds because they assisted the sailing ships which once carried the trade around the world.

TROUGH. The lowest part between two successive waves.

TURBULENCE. The disturbance of the even flow of a current or tidal stream, due to the meeting of opposing currents, a sudden change in the depth of water or an obstruction such as a pier, jetty, promontory or island.

TYPHOON. A tropical storm of up to hurricane strength which occurs in the western North Pacific.

VEER. Wind is said to veer when its direction changes and that direction is the same as that in which the sun goes round.

VERY HIGH SEA. Where the mean maximum height of the waves is 30-40 feet (sea state 8).

VERY ROUGH SEA. Where the mean maximum height of the waves is 13-20 feet (sea state 6).

VIOLENT STORM. A wind of force 11 on the Beaufort Scale (56-63 knots).

WAKE. The track which a ship leaves in the water, formed by the meeting of the water behind. (Ice, 'vokr', a track through the ice.)

WASH. The waves caused by a vessels progress through the water.

WAVE. A moving swell of the surface of the sea. (OE. 'wafian'.)

WEATHER TIDE. A tide which carries a vessel to windward.

WESTERLIES. West winds found north and south of the tropics.

WIND'S EYE. See EYE OF THE WIND.

WINDWARD. The direction from which the wind is blowing.

15

ANCHORING

The earliest form of anchor was simply a rock attached to a rope, sometimes with a hole bored through it. Such a method served to hold a small ship in sheltered waters, but when man ventured out into the open sea in larger ships, something more substantial and reliable was required. Thus wooden anchors with flukes evolved and were certainly in use by the Romans in the 2nd century AD. The most important advance since anchors changed from weighted devices to those having flukes with a stock was made in the last century, when in 1821 the stockless anchor was patented in England.

As well as developing a variety of shapes, the modern anchor has added to its role of keeping a ship firmly moored. Ships today carry a variety of anchors to deal with special conditions.

* * *

A-COCKBILL. Said of an anchor when it has been eased out of the hawsepipe and is hanging vertically by its ring.
In the days of sail this was also said of yards when tipped at an angle to the deck—a symbol of mourning.

ANCHOR. A heavy implement dropped from a ship, and so constructed as to grapple the sea bottom, to hold her fast in the water. (OE. 'ancor' from L 'ancora' from Gk. 'agkura'.)

ANCHORAGE. Ground suitable for anchoring.

ANCHOR BUOY. A buoy used to mark the position of a ship's anchor on the sea bottom.

ANCHOR COMING HOME. A term to describe an anchor which is dragging towards the ship as the cable is hove in. This should not happen; the ship should always move up to the anchor until the cable is 'up-and-down'.

ANCHOR LIGHT. See RIDING LIGHT.

ANCHOR SHACKLE. The means by which an anchor is secured to the outboard end of the anchor cable.

ANCHOR STROP. A wire rope rove through the ring of the anchor and shackled to an eyeplate on each side of the hawsepipe. It is used when securing the anchor for sea as an additional preventer.

A-PEAK. The position of the anchor when the bows of the ship have been drawn directly over it whilst weighing, but before it has broken out of the ground.

ARM. The section of an anchor from the fluke to the crown.

AT LONG STAY. Said of an anchor cable when it is taut and leads out to the anchor well away from the bows.

A-TRIP. See A-WEIGH.

A-WEIGH. Said of an anchor at the moment when it is broken of the ground. Also known as 'a-trip'. (OE. 'wegan', carry, lift.)

BACK AN ANCHOR, TO. To provide additional holding power for an anchor by laying out a smaller anchor ahead of it.

BILL. The pointed end of the fluke of an anchor; also called a 'pea'.

BITE, TO. For the flukes of the anchor to hold fast in the sea bed without dragging.

BITTER END. The inboard end of a ship's cable. From the centre-line bollards called 'bitts' to which cables of ships were once attached.

BLAKE SLIP. A general purpose anchor cable slip which has a tongue which passes over the cable. It is situated between the cable holder and the hawsehole and is mainly used as a preventer when a ship rides to her anchor.

BONNET. The covering over a navel pipe, to prevent water entering from the deck down to the cable locker.

BOWER ANCHORS. The two anchors carried in a ship, one on either bow, which are permanently attached to their cables ready for letting go.

BREAK GROUND, TO. The moment when the anchor cable lifts the anchor off the bottom and the flukes break out of the ground.

BREAK SHEER, TO. For a ship at anchor to be forced by the wind or tide to swing across her anchor with the danger of fouling it with her cable.

BRIDLE. The length of cable securing a ship, between the hawsepipe and a buoy.

BRING TO, TO. To pass a cable round a capstan, cable holder or windlass, ready for working.

BUOY JUMPERS. Hands who man a mooring buoy from a boat in order to secure the bridle.

BUOY ROPE. The rope which is used to attach an anchor buoy to the anchor.

BUOY SHACKLE. The ring of a mooring buoy to which a ship attaches her cable.

BUOY THE CABLE, TO. When the cable has been slipped, to mark the position by a buoy attached to it, so that it may subsequently be recovered. (See SLIP THE CABLE, TO.)

CABLE. See CHAIN CABLE.

CABLE CLENCH. A lug in the bottom of a cable locker to which the inboard end of the anchor cable is secured.

CABLE DECK. The part of a ship's forecastle upon which the exposed cables are situated.

CABLE HOLDERS. These are capstan-like devices mounted on the forecastle of large ships, linked to a capstan engine, which heave in or veer out the bower anchors. When an anchor is let go, the cable holder is unclutched from the capstan engine so that the cable can run free.

CABLE JACK. A hand lever device which is used to lift up heavy cable in order to fit a slip.

CABLE LOCKERS. Compartments situated some decks below the forecastle into which a ship's anchor cables are fed through the navel pipes from the upper deck above and stowed.

CABLE SLIPS. Fittings which are shackled to the deck, which in operation are able to hold the anchor cable to the deck for various cable handling purposes.

CAT, TO. The operation of hoisting an anchor to a clump cathead so that the cable may be removed when requiring to secure to a mooring buoy.

CATENARY. The curve of the anchor cable from the anchor on the sea bed to the ship. The greater the catenary the better, in order to effect a horizontal pull on the anchor to dig the flukes in deeper.

CHAIN CABLE. The chain cable by which an anchor is attached to a ship. It is supplied in lengths of a 'shackle', which is 15 fathoms long or a 'half shackle', which is 7½ fathoms long. Shackles of cable are joined together by 'joining shackles'. (L. 'capulum' from 'capere', to take hold of.)

Anchor 'cable' was originally a large hemp rope and chain cable was adopted in the early 19th century.

CHAIN HOOK. An iron hook with a long handle used for hauling detached lengths of chain cable when ranging it.

'CLEAR ANCHOR'. A report given when the anchor is being weighed and is seen to be hanging fairly by the ring and not fouled.

CLEAR AWAY ANCHORS AND CABLES, TO. To prepare the anchors for letting go.

CLUMP CATHEAD. A fitting on the bow of a large ship to which the anchor is secured when requiring to remove the cable in order to secure to a mooring buoy.

COME HOME, TO. Said of an anchor which is not holding in the ground and dragging.

COME TO, TO. A ship is said to have come to anchor.

COMPRESSOR. Some ships with fixed bonnets over the naval pipes have compressors fitted in the bonnets to take the place of riding slips. A compressor is operated by a handwheel which moves a steel wedge down until it nips a link of cable.

CROWN. The part of an anchor where the arms join the shank.

DECK CLENCH. A deck fitment to which cable slips are shackled.

DRAG, TO. A ship is said to drag when her anchor is not holding.

DROP ANCHOR, TO. The correct sea term for to anchor.

DROPPING MOOR. When a ship stops to drop the first anchor, then drops back on it to let go the second.

FLAKE, TO. To lay out the anchor cable on the forecastle for maintenance inspection.

FLUKE. The end of each arm of an anchor, below the 'pea' or 'bill' (point), which gives the holding power when dug into the ground.

FOUL ANCHOR. When the anchor cable is round the anchor or foul of any obstruction such as a bight of rope or chain picked up from the seabed.

FOUL BERTH. When a ship has no room to swing at anchor.

FOUL HAWSE. When the two cables of a ship lying to two anchors cross.

GIRT. The situation of both cables of a moored ship being so taut as to prevent her swinging with the tide or wind.

GROUND TACKLE. All of the equipment carried by a ship to enable her to anchor or moor.

GROW, TO. An anchor cable is said to grow in the direction in which it is lying. When the captain asks 'how does the cable grow'? the cable officer indicates the direction with his arm.

GYPSY. An attachment to a windlass shaped to take the links of chain cable.

HANG CABLE, TO. To temporarily hold the cable with a rope stopper.

HAWSE. The distance between the ship's head and her anchor on the bottom. (Ice. 'halse', neck.)

HAWSEHOLE. The hole in the forecastle deck through which the anchor cable passes.

HAWSEPIPE. The tube which leads from the hawsehole to the outside of the ship through which the anchor cable is led and into which the shank of the anchor is housed.

HAWSEPIPE COVERS. Metal covers which are secured over hawsepipes as a safety precaution to prevent personnel falling down the hawsepipes.

HOLDING GROUND. The type of bottom with respect to anchoring.

HOOK ROPE. A wire or cordage rope with a hook fitted to the end, used for manhandling chain cable.

JOINING SHACKLE. A shackle by which shackles (lengths) of anchor cable are joined together.

JOGGLE SHACKLE. A long and slightly curved shackle, shaped to fit across a link of cable. It is used to attach a wire rope to a bight of cable.

KEDGE. A small anchor used for kedging.

KEDGE, TO. To move a ship by means of warping using small anchors and hawsers.

KILLICK. A light anchor carried by small ships for general purposes.

'LET GO.' The order given by the Captain for the blake slip to be knocked off the anchor cable, allowing the anchor to fall.

MESSENGER. A small rope attached to the eye of a hawser which is used to haul it out to the ring of a mooring buoy.

MOOR, TO. For a ship to lie with two anchors out, middled between them. (ME. 'moren' from Du. 'marren', to retard.)

MOORING BUOY. A buoy permanently in position, connected by chain cable to several large anchors, to which a ship may secure her bridle.

MOORING SHIP. To secure a ship between two anchors which are let go at some distance from each other.

MOORING SWIVEL. When a ship is moored between two anchors, the two cables are usually brought to a swivel below the hawsepipe to allow the ship to swing to the tide and thus avoiding a foul hawse.

MONKEY PLATE. A three eyed plate attached one each end of a mooring swivel to which are attached short lengths of cable. Also known as a shamrock plate.

NAVEL PIPE. The pipe which leads from the forecastle deck down to the cable locker through which the anchor cable passes.

OPEN HAWSE. When a ship is lying to two anchors and the cables not becoming crossed.

PALM. The flat part of an anchor's fluke.

PARTING STROP. A strop which is passed through a link of cable and then both bights secured to an eyeplate. Thus, by veering the cable slowly, part of its weight is transferred to the strop and parts of cable may then be separated.

PEA. See BILL.

PICKING UP ROPE. A wire hawser with a strop and a spring hook shackled to an eye in the end, used in the operation of securing a ship to a buoy. The loop is passed through the ring of the buoy and then looped over the hook, allowing the ship to then be hauled close to. The anchor cable is then shackled to the ring of the buoy, hove taut, and then the picking up rope cast off.

RANGE CABLE, TO. To heave the anchor cable up from the cable lockers and lay it out along the deck for inspection and maintenance.

REDUCING LINKS. Links attached to the buoy shackle of a mooring buoy for use by small ships whose securing-to-buoy shackles are too small for the buoy shackle.

RIDE, TO. A ship 'rides' to her anchor or to a buoy.

RIDE EASY, TO. For a ship to lie at anchor without a great strain on her cable.

RIDING LIGHT. A white light, visible all around the horizon, shown forward in a ship at anchor or made fast to a buoy. A ship over 150 metres in length shows a second similar light near the stern at a lower height than the first light.

RIDING SLIP. A blake slip situated above the cable locker which is put on the cable as a preventer when the ship is riding at anchor.

RING. The upper part of an anchor to which the cable is fastened.

ROAD. (Also 'roadstead'.) A place where ships may ride at anchor.

ROUSE IN, TO. To haul in any slack anchor cable when lying at single anchor, to prevent the anchor becoming fouled.

RUNNING MOOR. When a ship lets go the first anchor, then continues ahead on her course to let go the second.

SCOTCHMAN. A piece of metal or wood to prevent chafe on the deck by the anchor cable.

SCOPE. The amount of anchor cable run out by a ship lying to a single anchor.

SCREW SLIP. A blake slip with a bottle screw incorporated in the chain securing the slip to the deck. It is used to haul the anchor close up into the hawsepipe when securing it for sea.

SEA LASHINGS. Wire or rope strops placed around a ship's cables, which are drawn together to remove any slack in the cables. This prevents the cables from 'chattering' on the cable deck.

SENHOUSE SLIP. A slip used to secure the end of a cable. The tongue of this slip passes through the end link of a cable instead of over the cable as with other slips.

SHACKLE. The name for a length of anchor cable which is 15 fathoms. A 'half shackle' is 7½ fathoms in length. A ship's bower cable is usually made up of four half shackles of cable and a number of shackles of cable.

SHAMROCK PLATE. See MONKEY PLATE.

SHEET ANCHOR. An anchor carried in reserve by a ship, ready for use in an emergency. (Originally 'shoot anchor', one to be shot out.)

SHANK. The main structure of an anchor with the arms joined at the bottom and the ring at the top.

SHORTEN IN CABLE, TO. To heave in only part of the anchor cable.

SHORT STAY, AT. Said of an anchor cable when hove close in at a steep angle, but not 'up and down'.

SLIP ROPE. A wire hawser which is passed through the ring of a buoy and back to the ship before unshackling a cable. The cable is then veered to give enough slack to unshackle, leaving the ship riding by the slip rope.

SLIP THE CABLE, TO. To allow the cable to run out when there is not time to weigh the anchor.

SNUB, TO. To arrest an anchor cable by applying the brake on the cable holder.

SNUGS. Projections on the sprocket of a cable holder which fit and grip the links of chain cable.

STOCK. The crosspiece of an Admiralty pattern anchor which on hitting the seabed turns the arms vertical to enable the flukes to dig in. (ME. from OE 'stocc', tree trunk.)

STOCKED ANCHOR. An anchor, of a type usually known as Admiralty pattern (though it was in use long before the Admiralty existed), fitted with a horizontal stock. This type is not used for ships' bower anchors.

STOCKLESS ANCHOR. A type of anchor which can vary in pattern and shape, which is used for all bower anchors. A 'tripping palm' is fitted to enable the flukes to swing

45 degrees away from the shank and dig into the ground. Types include 'Admiralty', 'Danforth' and 'CQR'.

The first RN ships to be fitted with stockless anchors were the battleships *HMS QUEEN* and *HMS PRINCE OF WALES*, completed in 1908. Stockless anchors did away with the laborious task of housing the anchor by cat pendant and cat davit.

STREAM ANCHOR. An anchor, which is about one quarter the weight of the usual bower anchor, used astern to prevent a ship swinging at anchor.

SURGE, TO. To allow a cable to run out by its own weight or strain on the outboard end.

SWIVEL PIECE. A swivel with a few links of cable each side of it which is fitted one at each end of a complete cable.

TRIP AN ANCHOR, TO. See A-TRIP.

TRIPPING PALM. A flat section forming the crown of a stockless anchor, which enables the flukes to swing 45 degrees away from the shank and dig into the ground.

UP AND DOWN. Said of an anchor cable just prior to the anchor being aweigh.

VEER, TO. To pay or ease out cable.

WEIGH, TO. To heave in the anchor cable until the anchor is broken out of the ground and hove up clear of the water. (OE. 'wegan', to carry.)

WINDLASS. A power driven device with a horizontal shaft; used in smaller ships in place of cable holders and capstan. With the turning mechanism on deck, it serves a dual purpose for handling chain cable and hawsers. (ME 'wydlas' alteration of 'wyndass' from ON. 'vindass' from 'vinda', to wind and 'ass', pole.)

16

BERTHING AND DOCKING

In the middle ages the small vessels of the time, operating from the Cinque Ports, required little by way of support facilities, other than might be found adjacent to the local hard or strand. As the need for bases within striking distance of the French coast grew and ships became larger, the site for a south coast base was sought. As a result the great naval basin at Portsmouth was built in 1496.

The expansion of the fleet under Henry VIII and the threat from the Dutch led to the building of Dockyards at Deptford and Woolwich on the Thames and also at Gillingham (Chatham). Under Elizabeth the main threat to England was posed by Spain which led to the growth of Plymouth as a naval base, although it was not until 1693 that a dockyard was completed. Sheerness, a forward base for Chatham, was also developed during the 17th century.

The four Royal Dockyards at Plymouth, Portsmouth, Chatham and Sheerness served the needs of the early Royal Navy throughout the French Wars of the 18th century. However, there was a need for a dockyard in Ireland and a small yard was built at Milford Haven in 1809, to be superceded by a larger dockyard at Pembroke Dock in 1814.

During the latter part of the 19th century the overseas dockyards were developed, the first at Malta with its first large dry dock being built in 1871. The others to be constructed were Port Royal (Jamaica), English Harbour (Antigua), Halifax (Nova Scotia), Jamacia, Trincomalee (Ceylon), Hong Kong, Esquimalt (Vancouver Island), Simonstown (Cape of Good Hope) and Gibraltar. Those in the now independent dominion territories are administered by their respective governments. Only Gibraltar remains under the operational control of MOD(N).

With the emergence of Germany as a naval power at the beginning of this century and with no RN base north of the Thames, it was decided to build a dockyard at Rosyth near Invertheithing. The work started in 1905 but it was not operational until 1916.

Today only two Royal Dockyards remain, those at Plymouth (Devonport) and Rosyth, since 1987 both under commercial management. The Royal Dockyards at Chatham and Portsmouth closed in 1984, but Portsmouth is still a major base and operating port with a Fleet Group Maintenance facility.

* * *

APRON. The area around the shore's edge of a pier or wharf.

BACKSPRING. A hawser led forward form the stern of a ship and made fast to a bollard ashore, to prevent any surging backward when secured alongside.

BASIN. See WET DOCK.

BERTH. A place in harbour either where a ship is secured alongside or anchored.

BERTH, TO. The act of securing alongside to a berth. (From 'bear' in a nautical sense of direction.)

BOLLARD. A vertical wood or iron post fixed to the jetty to which a ship's berthing lines are made fast when alongside. They are usually placed in pairs.

BOLLARD EYE. A large eye, spliced in the end of a berthing hawser, for the purpose of placing over a bollard.

BREAST ROPES. Hawsers secured inboard abreast the positions where they are made fast ashore. They are used, in addition to other securing hawsers, to prevent a ship surging away from a jetty.

BREAST SHORES. The means by which a ship is kept in an upright position when in dry dock.

BULLRING. A single circular fairlead type of fitting in the bow of small ships through which a berthing hawser may be led.

CAISSON. (Pronounced 'casoon'.) A floating vessel used as a dock gate. (Fr. 'caisse' from L. 'caspa' - 'capere', to hold.)

CAST OFF, TO. The action of letting go a rope or hawser securing a ship alongside. (Ice. 'kasta', to throw.)

CATAMARAN. Long rafts of timber moored alongside a jetty for the purpose of protecting a ship from damage. (Tamil word meaning bound up wood.)

DOCK. See WET DOCK.

DOCKING. The operation of placing a ship into dry-dock for the purpose of hull inspection, propellor change or cleaning the bottom.

DOCKYARD. A yard containing a dock in which ships may be refitted or repaired.

DOLPHIN. A large wooden pile used as a mooring post for ships.

DOUBLE UP, TO. A berthing hawser may be 'doubled up' by a second hawser between ship and shore.

DRY DOCK. An artificial basin fitted with a gate or caisson into which a ship may be floated and from which the water may be pumped out to expose the bottom of the vessel. It is used for repairing, building and painting ships. Sometimes referred to as a 'graving' dock, which is derived from the old method of removing weed from a ship's bottom by burning which was 'to grave'.

FAIRLEAD. Metal fittings, located in convenient positions on the upper deck of a ship with guides for ropes to 'lead' through.

FENDER. Used to place between the ship's side and another ship or wharf to prevent chafing or to take the shock when going alongside. Fenders are made from a variety of materials.

FLOATING DOCK. A floating structure which is able to partially submerge, by the flooding of 'pontoon tanks', in order to dock a ship.

GRAVING DOCK. See DRY DOCK.

HARBOUR. A port, shelter for ships. (ME. 'hereberge' from OE. 'here', army and 'beorg', shelter.)

HARD. An area for beaching boats.

HAWSER. A large rope of over five inches in circumference. (ME. from OFr. 'haucier' to hoist.)

HEADROPE. The hawser by which a ship is secured alongside by the bow.

HEADSPRING. A hawser led aft from the bow of a ship and made fast to a bollard ashore, to prevent any surging forward when secured alongside.

HEAVING LINE. A light line with a weighted end which is used to make initial contact with a jetty or another ship when going alongside. A berthing hawser is made fast to the inboard end for passing asore.

HURRICANE HAWSER. A special berthing hawser for use in heavy weather.

KEEL BLOCKS. Blocks on which a ship's keel rests when in dry-dock.

JETTY. A solid structure in a harbour, alongside which ships can lie. (ME. 'jette' from OFr. 'jettee', projection.)

LOCK. The approach to a wet dock through which ships are moved to or from tidal waters, without appreciably altering the level of water in the dock.

MOLE. A long pier or breakwater forming part of the sea defences of a port. (Fr. from L. 'moles', a heap.)

OFF-FAST MOORINGS. Moorings laid in harbours with exposed berths for the purpose of providing the means for ships to haul themselves clear of jetties in bad weather. Each mooring consists of an anchor, cable and a wire which is secured to the jetty bollards. On taking up a berth, a ship takes the ends of the wires and adjusts the tension according to the state of the weather.

ON-FAST MOORINGS. Moorings laid in a harbour where the bollards or dolphin may not be strong enough to hold a ship in a high wind. Each mooring consists of an anchor, cable and wire which is picked up and secured by a ship when berthing.

PANAMA PLATE. A plate fitted over the top of a fairlead to prevent the berthing hawser from jumping out when berthed on a high jetty. The term originated in the Panama Canal where ships are hauled through the locks at varying heights.

PATENT SLIP. A sloping runway extending to below the water, on which rails are laid. A cradle with a wheeled carriage is run out to receive the ship and it is then hauled up clear of the water by capstan or winch.

PENS. Bays formed by a series of jetties or piers for accommodating a number of small ships alongside.

PIER. A structure which extends into the water from the shore and functions like a dock. It is supported by pilings and is usually longer than a wharf. (OFr. 'piere', from L. 'petra', stone.)

PONTOON. A floating metal structure used alongside quays, which rises and falls with the tide; thus providing ease of access. (Fr. 'ponton' from L. 'pontis', bridge.)

PORT. A sheltered piece of water into which vessels can enter and remain in safety. (OE. from L. 'portus', a harbour.)

QUAY. A stone or concrete projection along the boundaries of a harbour, provided for ships to lie alongside. (ME. 'key' from OFr. 'kay'.)

RAT GUARDS. Metal discs which are clamped on each berthing hawser of a ship berthed alongside, to prevent rats from climbing aboard.

ROVE DOUBLED. Said of a berthing hawser when passed around a bollard ashore with both ends made fast inboard. This is done when there is no-one on shore to cast off when a ship unberths.

SINGLE UP, TO. As a preparation for leaving a jetty; to leave only those hawsers which are required to actually hold a ship in position.

STAGHORN. A metal bollard, having three arms in the shape of a cross, to which hawsers are belayed.

STERN ROPE. The hawser by which a ship is secured alongside by the stern.

SURGE, TO. The act of a ship moving ahead or astern when berthed alongside, prevented by the use of head and back springs.

SYNCHROLIFT. An alternative to dry-docking for small vessels, the synchrolift actually lifts a vessel up out of the water and facilities movement to a covered area.

TIDAL BASIN. A small dock which has an open entrance.

TROT. A line of moored buoys between which a number of small ships can be secured head and stern.

UNBERTH, TO. The act of a ship casting off her berthing hawsers and leaving a berth.

UNDOCK, TO. The operation of removing a ship from a dry-dock.

WARP, TO. To haul a vessel into position by means of a warp, i.e. a hawsers secured to an anchor, buoy or other fixed object. (OE. 'weorpan', cast, throw.)

WET DOCK. Also known as a 'basin'. An area of water, which, except at its entrance, is enclosed by walls and having sufficient depth to take floating ships. The entrance is usually through a 'lock'. (M Dut. 'docke', ditch.)

WHARF. A wood or stone projection built in a harbour, provided for ships to lie alongside. Virtually the same as a quay but this is usually thought of as a stone construction. (OE. 'hwerf', bank, dam.)

'WHICH SIDE TO?' Asked to ascertain which side of the ship is to be secured to a jetty. When known, hawsers, heaving lines and fenders are prepared for going alongside.

WIND, TO. To turn a ship around in her berth end for end.

17

BOATS

Some 'landlubbers' find it difficult to differentiate between ships and boats. British Rail add to the confusion by calling the trains which service the cross-channel ships 'boat trains'. Possibly the best way of thinking about it is that ships carry boats. However, as far as warships are concerned this is becoming less of a fact these days. Since the Falklands War of 1982, increased close-in armament has been fitted to most RN ships and, in order to compensate for the increased top-weight, many ships' boats have been replaced with lighter inflatable liferafts. Of course, boat-handling is still one of the important skills of the seaman.

Many foreign navies are fortunate enough to have sail training vessels, but the RN does not (The Sea Cadet Corps does have its small training brig *TS ROYALIST*), though sailing is an important recreational and training activity. Sailing terms are therefore very much still in use.

* * *

ADMIRAL'S BARGE. A special motor boat carried in a flagship for the use of the admiral. The hull is painted dark blue, except in the case of a commander-in-chief's barge which is painted dark green. A small admiral's flag is painted on each bow instead of the ship's badge.

'AWAY LIFE-BOAT'S CREW.' The order for the sea-boat to be lowered in an emergency for lifesaving, such as man overboard. The boat is manned by the nearest hands on deck, not necessarily being the duty crew.

'AWAY SEA-BOAT'S CREW.' The order for the sea-boat to be manned by the duty crew and to be lowered.

'AYE AYE.' The reply from the coxswain of a boat, which has an officer on board below the rank of captain, when hailed from a ship. Boats are hailed in this way so that is known what form of salute is required when officers arrive on board. If the reply is 'Flag', this indicates to the officer-of-the-watch that a flag officer is about to come aboard. If the reply is 'No no', then this indicates that no officers are about to board.

'BACK.' An order given in a pulling boat when wishing to go astern; 'back together', 'back port' or 'back starboard'.

BACKBOARD. A rectangular board which is fitted across the after side of the stern benches in a boat.

BADGE BLOCK. A circular wooden block secured outboard on each bow of a boat to take the ship's badge.

BAILER. A bucket used to bail a boat.

BAIL, TO. To empty water from a boat by means of a bailer. (Fr. 'baile'.)

BANKS. The number of oarsmen to each thwart in a pulling boat, either 'single banked' or 'double banked'.

BARGE. The name of the boat of a flag officer. See ADMIRAL'S BARGE.

BEAR AWAY, TO. To steer a sailing boat away from the wind.

'BEAR OFF'. An order given in a boat for the bowman and sternsheets man to shove off.

BEATING. To sail as close to the wind as efficiently as possible.

BELAYING PINS. Metal pins fitted through a sailing boat's thwarts to which the halyards are belayed.

BENCHES. The seats fitted around the sides and after end of the 'stern sheets' of a boat.

BILGE RAILS. Lengths of wood which run along the outside of a boat at the turn of the bilge. They are fitted to reduce rolling and have hand slots cut in them for the use of the crew in the event of the boat capsizing.

BLADE. The broad flat section of an oar; the part which enters the water.

BOATHOOK. A large hook with a point at the back, fitted to a staff, used for holding a boat from a ship or jetty, a ship or jetty from a boat, or for bearing off.

'BOAT OARS.' An order for the oars in a pulling boat to be unshipped from the crutches and laid fore-and-aft in the boat.

BOATROPE. A rope, always provided for a seaboat, which is led from the bows of the boat to a position well forward in the ship. It's purpose is that when the boat is lowered and slipped with the ship moving ahead, it will give steerage way to the boat, enabling her to be steered away from the ship's side.

BOAT'S BAG. A bag carried in a ship's boat containing tallow, tingles, etc. for emergency repairs and also hand signalling equipment.

BOAT'S COMPASS. A magnetic compass housed in a special portable binnacle for use in boats.

'BOAT'S CREW.' The order given by a boat's coxswain for the crew to come to attention - when sitting, an upright position with the arms folded.

BOAT'S DISTRESS BOX. A box carried by a ship's boat which contains distress signals.

BOLTROPE. The roping on the edge of a sail.

BOOM. A horizontal spar, pivoted to the ship's side, for securing boats alongside. Also the spar to which the foot of any sail is bent. (Du., a tree.)

BOTTOM BOARDS. Boards which form the floor of a boat and which are usually removable for baling or repairs.

BOW LINE. A line which is led through the bow for the purpose of securing the boat to a mooring, etc.

BOWMAN. The member of a boat's crew responsible for the securing and fending off of the forward end of the boat when alongside and for shoving off when leaving the ship's side or jetty.

BOW OAR. The oarsman nearest the bow in a pulling boat.

'BOWS.' A pulling boat order for the bowman (bow oar) to boat his oar and stand by to hold on or fend off with the boathook, or to jump ashore with the painter.

BREASTHOOK. A strengthening piece of wood fitted right in the bows of a boat where the two parts of the gunwhale meet.

BROAD REACH. Reaching with the wind abeam.

BROUGHT BY THE LEE. Said of a sailing boat when the wind suddenly changes from one quarter to the other.

BUOYANCY TANKS. Tanks of plastic or copper fitted in the bow and stern of some boats for buoyancy.

CAREEN, TO. To intentionally turn a boat on to her side in order to work beneath the waterline. (Fr. 'cariner' from L. 'carina', keel.)

CARPENTERS BAG. A bag containing tools for emergency repairs carried in a seaboat.

CARVEL. A method of wooden boat construction, with planks edge to edge and giving a smooth finish. (From 'caravel', an early Portugese ship.)

CAST OFF, TO. To release a boat's painter or other lines in order to get under way.

CENTRE PLATE. A metal plate which can be lowered through a slot in the keel of a boat in order ro reduce leeway when under sail. It is also known as a 'drop Keel'.

CHEVERTON. A motor boat carried abroad larger warships.

CHINE. The angle between the bottom and the waterline in a boat.

CLEW. The bottom inboard corner of a sail, the corner to which the 'sheets' are bent. (OE. 'cliwen'.)

CLINKER. A method of wooden boat construction with the planks overlapping. (From the method of construction with clinched nails.)

CLOSE HAULED. A sailing term; sailing as close to the wind as possible with all sails drawing when beating to windward. The sheets are hauled taut to flatten the sails.

CLOSE REACH. When nearly closed hauled, also known as 'fetching'.

COXSWAIN. The rating in charge of a boat.

CRINGLES. Eyes at the corners or sides of a sail to which the halyards and sheets are bent. (LG. 'kringel', dim. of 'kring', a circle or ring.)

CRUTCHES. Metal U-shaped fittings to take the shafts of oars in a pulling boat.

CRUTCH PLATES. Metal fittings in the gunwhale of a boat into which crutches fit.

DAVITS. Steel supports in pairs for hoisting, carrying and launching a ship's boats. (Formerly 'david', probably from the Christian name.)

DINGHY. A small boat. (Hindu 'dingi'.)

DISENGAGING GEAR. Equipment fitted in ships boats to allow release from the falls following lowering from davits. The falls are shackled to hooks on the gear. A releasing slip on the gear parts the fore-and-after chain, tension is thereby slackened and the two hooks attaching the gear to the falls are released. Also known as 'Robinson's Disengaging gear, from the inventor.

DISTRESS BOX. A box carried in a seaboat containing pyrotechnics for use in an emergency in order to attract attention.

DORY. A small utility motor boat found in great numbers.

DOUBLE BANKED. A pulling boat having two men pulling on each thwart.

DROP KEEL. See CENTRE PLATE.

DROWN, TO. To fill a boat with water by removing the plug.

EAR-RING. The lashing which secures the throat, peak, tack or foot of a sail to a spar.

EYELETS. The eyes in the head or foot of a sail for lacing it to a spar.

FALLS. The tackles used to hoist or lower a ship's boat to or from the davits.

FEATHER, TO. To position a boat's oars so that the blades are parallel with the water. When the blade is in the air, the action reduces wind resistance and makes water run off in a feather like spray.

FEND OFF, TO. To prevent a boat, which is going alongside, from making violent contact by the use of a boathook or fender. (Abbreviation of 'defend'.)

FETCHING. See CLOSE REACH.

'FLAG.' See AYE AYE.

FOOT. The bottom edge of a sail.

FORESAIL. The foremost sail, set before a foremast, or before a mainmast if there is no foremast.

FORESHEETS. The forward part of a boat, right up in the bows.

FULL AND BYE. In a sailing boat, to bear away from the wind by a small amount from close hauled, so that the sails are full.

GAFF. A spar with jaws at the throat which fit around a mast, to which the head of a four-sided sail is bent.

GAFF SAIL. A four-sided sail, the head of which is bent to a gaff.

GEMINI. An inflatable boat which has been in service with the RN for 25 years and is carried in many ships for general purpose use. A 'jumbo gemini' capable of carrying a Landrover or 38 armed men is also in service in the RN.

'GIVE WAY TOGETHER.' The order given in a pulling boat for the crew to commence pulling.

GLASS-REINFORCED PLASTIC (GRP) BOATS. Boats made of layers of glass fibre impregnated with polyester resin.

GO ABOUT, TO. A sailing term; to tack and bring the wind on the other side of the sails.

GOOSENECK. A fitting by which a boat boom is attached to the ship's side. When not in use, a boom may be stowed by pivoting in the gooseneck and swung back against the ship's side.

GOOSEWING, TO. To have alternate sails set to port and starboard when running before the wind.

GRIPES. Bands of canvas or plaited rope used to secure a boat against the davits or to the deck at sea. (Gripe from OE. 'gripan', to seize and hold firmly.)

GUARD BOAT. A boat which goes around the fleet or squadron at night to ensure that a proper watch is kept in all ships. On approaching each ship, it is hailed by the watch on deck.

GUDGEONS. Metal rings fitted to a boat's stern for the purpose of locating metal pins called 'pintles' attached to the boat's rudder.

GUNWHALE. Pronounced 'gunnel'. The top stringer at the edge of a boat's side. ('Gun' and OE. 'whale', plank.)

GYBING. A sailing term; the action of putting the stern through the wind in a controlled manner. (Dut. 'gijben'.)

HALYARD. A rope by which a sail is hoisted and lowered. The name comes from 'haul-yards'.

HARD CHINE. A type of power boat which has a flat bottom and shallow draught, designed to plane on the surface at high speed.

HEAD. The top corner of a three-sided sail and the top edge of a four-sided sail.

HEAD SHEETS. The space in the bows of a boat between the stem and the bow thwart.

'HOLD WATER'. A pulling boat order; to stop the boat by putting the oars into the water and holding them steady at right angles to the boat.

HORSE. A metal bar, fitted along the top of the transom in a sailing boat, to which the after block of the mainsail sheet is shackled. The block is thus able to travel from side to side of the horse as the boat is put about.

HUNTRESS. A fast motor boat (FMB) carried in several classes of ship.

IN IRONS. When a sailing boat has failed to go about from one tack to another and remains head to wind with no way on.

JACOB'S LADDER. A ladder made from rope or wire with wooden bars for steps, which hangs from a ship's lower boom, to which boats may be secured and the crew may ascend. (From the ladder seen in a dream by Jacob in Gen. 28.12.)

Also once used in sailing ships abaft the topgallant masts, where no ratlines were provided.

JIB. A sail set before the foresail.

KEEL. The 'backbone' of a boat which runs from the stem to the sternpost.

KEELSON. A length of wood bolted to and above the keel, inboard in a boat, which runs from the bows for about two-thirds of the length of the boat.

KNEES. The fittings which secure the thwarts to the sides of a boat.

LAUNCH. A large ship's boat carried for harbour duties. (Sp. and Pg. 'launcha'.)

Since 1800 the largest of a ship's boats has been known as a launch. Before that time it was known as a 'long boat'.

LAZY PAINTER. A line by which a boat may be hauled under the Jacob's ladder when made fast to a boom. One end is secured to the stem ringbolt and the line is passed through the eye in the bottom of the ladder.

LEACH. The side of a sail nearest to the mast.

'LET DRAW.' The order to let go the weather sheet after tacking and to haul the lee sheet.

'LET FLY.' The order to let a sheet run out so that the sail flaps and the wind is spilled out of it.

LIE OFF, TO. For a boat to wait for some reason before approaching a ship or jetty to secure.

LIFEBOAT. The name given to a ship's sea boat when it is used for life-saving.

LIFELINES. Lines, one to each thwart, which are secured to the span between davits. These are held on to by the crew as a boat is lowered.

LIZARD. A wire rope, which hangs from a ship's lower boom, to which boats may be secured.

LOOM. The inboard end of an oar which is grasped by the hands. (OE. 'geloma', originally a tool or implement.)

LOOSE FOOTED SAIL. A sail which has no boom at its foot.

LUFF. The side of a sail outboard from the mast, the opposite side to the 'leach'.

LUFF, TO. To steer a sailing boat nearer to the wind.

LUGSAIL. A four-sided sail, the head of which is bent to a yard.

MAKE FAST, TO. To secure a boat to a boom or jetty, etc.

MAST STEP. A slot in the keelson of a boat into which a mast may be fitted.

'MARRY THE FALLS'. When hoisting a boat at the davits by hand, the falls are 'married' together for an even pull.

MISS STAYS, TO. For a sailing boat to fail to go about from one tack another and pay off on her original course.

MIZEN. A sail set on a mizen mast (aft in a boat). (Fr. 'misaine'.)

'NO-NO.' See 'AYE-AYE'.

OAR. The wooden lever worked by the hands to propel a boat. (OE. 'ar'.)

'OARS.' A pulling boat order for the crew to stop pulling and to sit up straight with their oars horizontal.

PACIFIC. A motor boat now only found aboard older warships or for training purposes.

PAINTER. A length of rope attached to the stem of a boat, a bow rope, used for securing to a boom or alongside. (OFr. 'pentoir' from L. 'pendere', to hang.)

PEAK. The top inboard corner of a four-sided sail.

PINTLES. Metal pins attached to a boat's rudder for the purpose of locating into rings, called gudgeons, which are fitted to a boat's stern. (OE. 'pintel', penis.)

PLANE, TO. For a boat of light construction and particular shape, such as hard chine, to run along the surface of the water at high speed.

PLUG. A bung which fits into a hole in the bottom of a boat for draining when hoisted.

PORT TACK. Said of a sailing boat when she is close hauled with the wind on her port side.

PUDDING. A small round fender for use with small boats. Also the name of fenders used on the bows of tugs and harbour launches.

PULL, TO. To row with an oar in a boat; the oar is pulled towards the body.

PULLING BOAT. A boat propelled by oars.

RANDAN. A method of pulling in a boat with an equal number of oars on each side with only three men. The stroke and bowmen each pull one oar, whilst the man in the centre pulls a pair of oars.

REACHING. Sailing with the wind free, i.e. not close hauled or running.

'READY ABOUT'. The warning given to the crew of a sailing boat to stand by to tack.

REEFING. A method of reducing sail area by rolling part of it and securing at the reef points with reef knots. (Ice. 'rif'.)

RIFFLES. Holes drilled at the ends of a boat's keel, fitted with bushes to take shackless and used for various purposes such as towing.

ROBINSON'S DISENGAGING GEAT. See DISENGAGING GEAR.

ROUND BILGE. A type of power boat which has a rounded bottom, deep draught and slow or medium speed.

RUNNING. Sailing efficiently with the wind abaft the beam.

RUNNING BY THE LEE. A sailing boat running with her mainsail set on the windward side.

SAIL. (OE. 'segl'.)

SAILING FREE. Sailing with the sails filled and not close hauled; free to manoevre without having to go about.

SCULLING. The method of rowing where each member of a boat's crew mans a pair of oars. In the RN it is more commonly known as propelling a boat by a single oar over the stern; the loom is worked in a figure-of-eight motion and the blade does not leave the water.

SEA BOAT. A ship's boat which, when a ship is at sea, is ready for use at the davits. When used for lifesaving it is called a 'lifeboat'.

SEARIDER. A rigid hull inflatable boat carried in most ships for purposes where a high speed in a heavy sea is necessary. It is particularly useful as a boarding craft.

SHAKE DOWN A REEF, TO. To take a reef out of a sail.

SHAFT. The main body of an oar; between the loom and the blade.

SHEET. A rope bent to the clew of a sail by means of which the sail is trimmed.

'SHIP OARS.' An order given in a pulling boat for the crew to place their oars into the crutches ready for pulling.

SHORTEN SAIL, TO. To reduce sail, either by reducing the number or by reefing.

'SHOVE OFF.' The order given for the bowman to shove a boat off from the jetty, using the wooden end of his boathook.

SHROUD PLATES. Plates fitted into the gunwhale of a sailing boat, either side of the mast, to which the lower ends of the shrouds are attached.

SINGLE BANKED. A pulling boat having one man pulling on each thwart.

SLINGS. The wire rope or chain assemblies by which a boat is hoisted.

SOLDIER'S WIND. When a sailing boat can sail to a destination on one reach and return from it on the other.
SPINNAKER. A large balloon like sail with a luff and leach of equal length, used in place of a foresail when the wind is abaft the beam.
SPRING AHEAD, TO. To haul a boat ahead on a guest-warp or the boatrope.
SPRING OFF, TO. Casting off in a boat which has been secured by springs.
STARBOARD TACK. Said of a sailing boat when she is close hauled with the wind on her starboard side.
'START THE FALLS.' An order given when lowering a boat from davits, upon which the falls are eased until they begin to render around the staghorn and the boat to lower slowly.
STAYSAIL. Any three-sided sail whose luff is supported by a stay.
STEM. The foremost member of a boat, formed upwards from the keel.
STEP, TO. To put a mast in its place.
STERNFAST. The rope securing the stern of a boat.
STERNPOST. The aftermost member of a boat, formed upwards from the keel.
STERN-SHEETMAN. The member of a boat's crew responsible for the securing and fendering of the after end of the boat.
STERN-SHEETS. The space right aft in a boat.
STRIKE, TO. To lower a mast or sails.
STROKE. The cadence of pulling.
STROKE OAR. The oarsman nearest the sternsheets in a pulling boat by whom the rest of the pulling crew follow for the stroke.
STRETCHER. A length of wood fitted in the bottom of a pulling boat, used for bracing the feet when pulling.
TABERNACLE. A wooden frame, incorporating the mast step, which forms the housing of the mast.
TACK. The bottom outboard corner of a sail on the luff.
TACK, TO. A sailing term; the action of putting the bows through the wind, thus 'going about' from one tack to the other.
TAKE DOWN A REEF, TO. To put a reef in a sail.

THROAT. The outboard top corner of a four-sided sail.

THWART. Wooden benches placed athwart a boat serving as seats for the crew. (OE. 'thweorth', transverse.)

TINGLE. A copper sheet for temporarily repairing a hole in a boat.

TORNADO. A rigid inflatable boat used as a seaboat.

TOWING BOLLARD. A post in the headsheets of a boat around which a towing rope may be belayed.

TRANSOM. The square stern end of a boat. (ME. 'traunson' from L. 'transtrum' from 'trans', across.)

TRYSAIL. Any three-sided sail (except the mizzen) set immediately abaft the foremast, or the mainmast if there is no foremast.

'TURNS FOR LOWERING.' An order given when lowering a boat from davits, upon which the lowerers take surplus turns off the staghorn.

'WAY ENOUGH.' The order given in a pulling boat for the crew to stop pulling and allow the way of the boat to carry the oar blades so that the looms pass over their heads. The oars are then 'boated'.

WEAR, TO. To alter course in a sailing boat by carrying the wind over the stern; as opposed to tacking, in which the bow is brought around by the wind. (From 'veer'.)

WEATHER, TO. For a boat to pass an object to windward.

WHALER. A ship's boat, nowadays known as a three-in-one whaler because it may be rigged for power, sail or pulling. The design of previous types of whaler was taken from the original whaleboats.

YARD. A spar which crosses a mast, to which the head of a four-sided sail may be bent and supported. (OE, 'gyrd', stick.)

18

ROPEWORK AND RIGGING VERBS

It is interesting that there are no less than 72 verbs associated with ropework and rigging.

* * *

BACK UP, TO. To haul taut on the free end of a rope after taking a turn.

BELAY, TO. To make fast a rope to a cleat or bollard. (Du. 'beleggen', to lay over.)

BEND ON, TO. To join one rope to another or an object. (OE 'benden'.)

BOWSE, TO. To tighten something such as a rope or lashing.

BREAK IN A ROPE, TO. To force a wire rope around a thimble prior to making an eye splice.

BRING TO, TO. To pass a rope or hawser around a capstan ready for working.

CARRY AWAY, TO. For a rope or spar to break.

CAST OFF, TO. To let go a rope securing a ship to a buoy, ship or quay.

CATCH A TURN, TO. To take a holding turn on bollards.

CHECK, TO. To ease away a rope, slowly. (Fr. 'echec'.)

CHEESE DOWN, TO. To coil a rope in neat, tight, concentric circles on the deck, finishing with the end in the centre. Also known as a 'flemish coil'.

CHOKE, TO. To trap a rope intentionally to prevent it from slipping.

CHOKE THE LUFF, TO. A method of temporarily holding a small tackle. The hauling part of the rope is trapped against the shell of the upper block behind the rope leading from the adjacent sheave.

CLAP ON, TO. To attach one tackle to another or to a rope.

CLINCH, TO. A method of fastening large ropes to heavy objects by a half hitch with the end stopped back on its own part by seizing. (See to seize.)

COIL, TO. The method of stowage of rope. (Fr. 'coillir', gather.)

CRIPPLE, TO. To force a wire rope into sharp bends or 'nips'.

DOG, TO. To halve the rope strands left after completing a splice and whipping one half to one half of the strand next to it.

FAG OUT, TO. For the strands of an unwhipped rope's end to unlay and fray out.

FAKE DOWN, TO. To coil a rope down on the deck so that it clear for running.

FISH, TO. If a spar requires to be strengthened or repaired it can be 'fished'. This consists of lashing lengths of wood, known as 'fishing spars', equidistantly around the spar.

FLAKE, TO. To lay out hawsers in large coils on deck ready for free running.

FLEET, TO. To overhaul a tackle which is 'block and block' to its full scope.

FRAP, TO. To bind together with rope. (OFr. 'fraper', strike.)

FRESHEN THE NIP, TO. To shift the position at which a rope is being chafed by paying it out or hauling it in slightly.

GLUT, TO. To prevent something from slipping, for instance, a tackle is glutted by choking the fall across the sheave of a block to prevent it slipping through.

GRAFT, TO. To cover an eye splice in a rope with nettle for decoration.

HAUL, TO. To pull a rope by hand, with force. (Fr. 'haler', to pull a boat.)

HAUL TAUT, TO. To take the strain on a rope.

HEAVE, TO. To throw, or to pull on, a rope. (OE. 'hebban'.)

HOIST, TO. To haul on a rope when a weight is to be lifted.

LASH, TO. To secure two crossed spars together with a rope. (ME. 'lasschen' from MFr. 'lacier' from OFr. 'lachier', to lace.)

LET RUN, TO. To let go a rope or chain, etc. so that it runs out of its own accord.

MAKE FAST, TO. To secure something with a ring or an eye. (OE. 'foest'.)

MARL, TO. To put a serving on a rope in order to secure worming and parcelling (see TO WORM, TO PARCEL and TO SERVE'.) Each turn of the serving is secured by a marline hitch.

MARRY, TO. To bring two ropes together, such as boat's falls, for a combined haul.

MOUSE A HOOK, TO. (Pronounced 'mowze'.) To take a few turns of spunyarn over the bill of a hook to prevent it slipping out of whatever it has been hooked into.

OVERHAUL, TO. To separate the blocks of a purchase further apart by easing out the fall.

PARCEL, TO. To wind strips of canvas around a rope as part of the operation of worming, parcelling and serving in order to provide a watertight covering.

PART, TO. The breaking of a rope.

PAY AWAY, TO. To slacken a rope.

PAY OUT, TO. To ease a rope out by hand.

POINT, TO. To taper the end of a rope to make it easier for reeving through a block. Done by gradually thinning down the strands and holding them down with a west country whipping. (OFr.)

RACK, TO. To hold two ropes together temporarily by binding them together with marline or some other small stuff.

RANGE, TO. To lay out rope along the deck.

REEVE, TO. To pass a rope through something. After passing through, it is said to be 'rove' through the object. (It. 'refare', to thread.)

RENDER, TO. To ease away a rope gently. (Fr. 'rendre'.)

ROUND UP, TO. To haul in on a tackle before taking the strain.

SECURE, TO. To make fast.

SEIZE, TO. To bind one rope to another. (Fr. 'saisir'.)
SERVE, TO. To wind spunyarn around a rope as the final part of a three part operation to waterproof it. (See also TO WORM, and TO PARCEL).
SLIP, TO. To let go of a rope.
SPLICE, TO. To join two ropes permanently together by interlocking the strands, to form an eye by the same method or to prevent the strands from unlaying at the end of a rope. (Du. 'splissen'.)
SNUB, TO. To suddenly restrain a rope that is being checked. (Dan. 'snibbe', to nip.)
START, TO. To ease away a rope by rendering it around a bollard.
STOP, TO. To secure a rope with another. For instance, to take the strain of a large rope whilst it is being belayed.
STRAND, TO. Said of a rope when one of its strands is broken.
STRIKE DOWN, TO. To lower equipment by crane or tackle.
SURGE, TO. To check a rope by letting the turns slip around a bollard or capstan.
SWEAT UP, TO. To give an extra hard pull on a rope to take down every vestige of slack in it.
SWIG OFF, TO. To haul out on the bight of a taut rope at a right angle to its lead in order to take up the slack in its span.
TAIL ON, TO. To clap something on to a rope.
TAKE A TURN, TO. To pass a rope around a fixture in order to take the strain.
TAKE CHARGE, TO. Said of an item of equipment under restraint which breaks loose.
TAKE UP THE SLACK, TO. To tauten a rope.
THOROUGHFOOT, TO. A method of joining two ropes together when each has an eye spliced in the end. The ropes are rove through each other's eyes so that when applied taut the eyes are interlocked.
TRICE UP, TO. To hoist something up and secure with a small line. Washing lines are 'triced up'. (Du. 'tryssen', to hoist.)
TURN UP, TO. To make a rope fast to a cleat.

UNDER RUN, TO. To separate all the moving parts of a tackle so that all is clear and ready for use.

UNLAY, TO. To open up the laid strands of a rope.

WHIP, TO. To bind a rope's end to prevent the strands from unlaying.

WORM, TO. To pass a small line spirally between the layed strands of a rope as a preparation for parcelling and serving. (See TO PARCEL and TO SERVE.)

19

ROPEWORK

In sailing days a seaman spent much of his time handling ropes and canvas. He had to be able to make knots, bends and splices, often under difficult circumstances and often with a great deal of urgency, as the safety of the ship might well have depended on his skill. Today's seaman does not have to work aloft, but one of the skills of his trade is still ropework. However, synthetic cordage has revolutionised ropework at sea and there is less knotting and splicing required. Also an advantage is that ends can be sealed by heating to prevent them unlaying and so it is not always necessary to whip them with light line.

* * *

AMERICAN WHIPPING. A whipping for a rope's end to prevent the strands from unlaying. It is similar to the simple common whipping, but finished off differently.

BACK SPLICE. An alternative to whipping a rope's end to prevent it from fraying by unlaying the rope, forming a crown knot, then tucking the strands back a few times. The end however will not reeve through a block.

BECKET. A short length of rope with the ends spliced together to form a ring.

BEND. The name for any knot used to join two ropes or to attach a rope to something semi-permanently. (OE. 'bendan', Ice. 'benda'.)

BIGHT. A loop of rope. (OE. 'byht', corner.)

BLACKWALL HITCH. A quick means of attaching a rope's end to a hook. The end is passed around the shank of the hook and then trapped under the standing part.

BOWLINE. A knot tied in a rope to form a temporary eye which will not slip or jam. 'Bowline' was once the name of a rope used to steady the weather edge of a sail forward when the ship was sailing close to the wind. The bowline 'knot' was originally used for fastening the bowline bridles to the cringles.

BOWLINE ON THE BIGHT. A bowline made on the bight of a rope, consequently forming two bights which are adjustable in size. It is used for lowering a man over the side when there is no boatswain's chair available; he sits in one bight and the other goes under his arms.

BUNTLINE HITCH. Used to secure a rope's end to a cringle or small eye. The rope is passed through the eye and a clove hitch is made on the standing part.

CABLE LAID ROPE. A rope made by laying up together three ordinary three stranded ropes. It is used for the heaviest work on board ship and for towing cables for tugs.

CARRICK BEND. Used for bending two hawsers together when required to go around a capstan.

CATS PAW. Used for temporarily shortening a rope strop, effected by taking a bight in both hands and twisting and then placing both twisted ends over the hook.

CHAIN SHORTENING. A series of hitches made by forming a loop, pulling the bight through the loop and repeating the process until the rope is shortened sufficently. The last loop is secured by passing the end through.

CHAIN SPLICE. Used for splicing the end of a rope to a chain which is required to lead through a block or fairlead.

CLOVE HITCH. Used to secure a rope to a spar or to a larger rope. Commonly used, but it will slip if subjected to a sideways pull. It is made with a jamming form of two half-hitches around the object securing to. (From 'cloven', divided into two parts, as a hoof.)

COACHWHIPPING. An ornamental covering of rope used on stanchions, boathooks, etc.

COCKSCOMBING. A covering of rope on a metal eye or ring.

CODLINE. A small line, originally used for cod fishing, which is used for many purposes where the smallest of ropes are too clumsy.

COIR. Rope manufactured from the husks of coconut which floats, but only has half the strength of manila rope. (Malay 'kayar', cord.)

COMMON WHIPPING. As the name suggests, a whipping commonly used to prevent the strands at the end of a rope from unlaying.

CONSTRICTOR KNOT. A variation of the clove hitch, which is used where a firm grip is required.

CORDAGE. A collective term for ropes and lines.

CROWN KNOT. A knot formed in the end of a rope by tucking the strands over and under each other to interlock them. It is the preliminary knot formed when back splicing a rope's end.

CROWS FOOT. Made by untwisting the strands in the bight of a rope and laying the three parts up in their natural lay. It is used when requiring to splice an eye in the bight of a rope.

CUT SPLICE. An eye formed by splicing two ropes together end to end, each as an eye splice and overlapping by the required amount.

DIAGONAL LASHING. See LASHING.

DIAMOND KNOT. A decorative knot usually made on the bight of a rope. It may be single or double.

DOUBLE BLACKWALL HITCH. A blackwall hitch with an extra turn around the shank of the hook. (See BLACKWALL HITCH.)

DOUBLE SHEET BEND. A sheet bend doubled to make a more secure bend. (See SHEET BEND.)

EYE SPLICE. A loop spliced into the end of a rope, usually around a 'thimble'.

FAG END. A rope's end where the strands have become unlayed and fagged out (frayed). A condition which is prevented by whipping.

FAKE. A complete turn of a rope which has been 'faked' down in a coil, clear for running. Each fake must be able to run out within fouling those below it.

FID. A wooden spike used to open up a rope for tucking a strand through when splicing.

FIGURE OF EIGHT KNOT. Put in the end of a rope to prevent it unreeving through a block.

FISHERMAN'S BEND. Used for bending a rope to a boat's anchor. It is similar to a round turn and two half hitches, but the first of the half hitches is passed through the round turn.

FLEMISH COIL. When a rope is coiled on the deck in neat, tight, concentric circles. More popularly known as 'cheesed down'.

FLEMISH EYE. An eye formed in the end of a rope, made by unlaying the strands and yarns, dividing them and then knotting in pairs over a circular piece of wood equal in diameter to the inside of the required eye. The eye is finished off by cockscombing or ringbolt hitching.

FOX. See NETTLE.

FRENCH BOWLINE. A variation of the Bowline on the bight.

GASKET HITCH. Spare lengths of rope are frequently used for an assortment of jobs around a ship and it is important that they are ready for instant use at the time they are required. The rope is made up into a coil, leaving a few feet spare. This spare end is turned around the coil twice, in such a way as to draw the top of the coil together to form an eye. A bight of the end is passed through the eye of the coil and then brought over the top to meet the remaining spare end. The end is passed through the bight and pulled taut.

GRANNY KNOT. See ROGUE KNOT.

GRASS ROPE. Rope made from sisal which floats, but is not particularly strong.

GROMMET. A rope ring made by laying up a single strand around upon itself three times.

HALF HITCH. The basis of many knots or bends, effected by a single turn of rope around an object with the end of the rope led back through the bight.

HANK. A skein of twine or small line used for whippings or seizings.

HAWSER BEND. The common method of joining two hawsers together, by a round turn through each other and two half hitches on their own parts with the ends stopped down.

HAWSER EYE. A method of making a thimble eye so that if damaged the thimble may be removed and replaced. The eye is first spliced larger than the thimble, then the thimble is secured in place by a strong seizing.

HAWSER-LAID ROPE. Rope made up of three strands laid up together; the normal form of rope used for most purposes on board ship.

HEAVING LINE KNOT. An alternative to the monkey's fist, which is more quickly and easily made.

HEAVING MALLET. A wooden mallet used when seizing heavy ropes, to ensure that the turns are taut.

HEMP. Rope made from the plant cannabis sativa which is the best natural rope. (OE. 'henep'.)

HITCH. A series of knots joining a rope to another or to an object very temporarily so that they may be quickly cast off. (ME. 'hichen'.)

JAW. The distance between adjacent strands of a rope. Where the lay is slack in an old rope, the rope is said to be 'slack jawed'.

JUNK. Condemned rope. This was once also the name given to the salt beef supplied to ships, from its being as tough as old rope.

KILLICK BEND. Used for improvising an anchor from a stone. It is made by placing a timber hitch around the stone and then a half-hitch beside it. (Killick is the name for a small anchor.)

LANYARD. A short line or cord used for securing small articles such as a knife.

LASHING. Used to secure two crossed spars together. A 'square lashing' for securing the spars at right angles and a 'diagonal lashing' for securing them at an acute angle.

LAY. The direction in which the strands of a rope are twisted.

LINE. Any light rope used aboard a ship.

LONG SPLICE. A method of joining two ropes permanently by interlocking the strands, with the splice finishing up the same size as the rope in order to be rove through a block.

MACKEREL LINE. A small light line, about half the size of codline, used for a variety of purposes.

MANILA. Rope made from the fibre of the wild banana plant which is grown in the Philippines. It is the strongest of the natural fibre ropes used in the RN.

MAN MADE FIBRE ROPES. Ropes made from Nylon, Terelene, and polypropelene. In many cases these ropes have advantages over vegetable fibre ropes, such as strength and long life, and are gradually taking their place. See POLYAMIDE, POLYESTER, POLYTHENE AND POLYPROPOLENE.

MANROPE KNOT. A decorative knot made at the end of gangway manropes to prevent them unreeving.

MARLINE. A two stranded light line used for a variety of purposes. (Du. 'marren', to tie and 'line'.)

MARLINE HITCH. A hitch used when lashing up sails, awning, etc. It is made by a series of round turns, passing the end over the standing part and under the bight, hauling taut on each turn.

MARLINE SPIKE. A steel spike used for opening up the strands of rope when splicing.

MARLINE SPIKE HITCH. A hitch, made in the bight of a rope, for securing a marline spike or to secure a sling or the bight of a rope to a hook.

MATHEW WALKER KNOT. The only knot given the name of a person, yet no-one knows who Mathew Walker was. It is a stopper placed in the end of a rope to prevent it unreeving; a neater development of the wall knot.

MIDSHIPMAN'S HITCH. Used instead of a blackwall hitch when a rope is slippery or greasy. It is made by forming a blackwall hitch and then placing the trapped part over the bill of the hook. (See BLACKWALL HITCH.)

MONKEY'S FIST. A knot very similar to a turk's head, used to weight the end of a heaving line.

NETTLE. Two yarns laid up together for use in pointing or grafting a rope. Also known as 'fox'.

OAKUM. Loose fibre from old rope, once used for caulking seams between planks. (ME. 'okum' from OE. 'acumbe', off combings.)

Picking oakum was once a task employed for cell punishment.

POLYAMIDE ROPE. Rope made from Nylon which is two and a half times stronger than Manila (the strongest of the natural fibre ropes). It stretches about 50% before parting, but loses 10% of its strength when wet. It is used for anti-shock strops and towing lines and can be identified by a green yarn in one of the strands.

POLYESTER ROPE. Rope made from Terelene which is twice as strong as Manila. It stretches 36% before parting and retains its strength when wet. It is used for safety nets and can be identified by a blue yarn in one of the strands.

POLYTHENE ROPE. Rope made from Courlene which is one and a half times as strong as Manila. It stretches 33% before parting, retains its strength when wet and it also floats. Identifiable by an orange yarn in one of the strands or all orange in colour rope.

POLYPROPOLENE ROPE. Almost twice as strong as Manila, this rope stretches 44% before parting, retains its strength when wet and also floats.

REEF KNOT. A method of joining two ropes of equal size, formed by crossing against the lay and then with the lay so that the ends fall in line with the outer parts.

It is commonly used by seamen as it holds firmly and can be undone easily. Originally it was used for tying the reef points when rolling up sails to reduce sail area. (ON 'rif'.)

RINGBOLT HITCHING. A method of covering curved fittings and frequently used on circular fenders.

ROGUE KNOT. A reef knot tied incorrectly, with the ends finishing on opposite sides of, instead of in line with, the outer parts. Sometimes known as a 'granny'.

ROGUES YARN. A single coloured yarn laid up in a strand so that the materials from which it is made may be identified as follows:

	Naval	Commercial
Manilla	Red in two strands	Black
Sisal	Yellow in two strands	Red
Hemp	Red in three strands	None

Coir	Yellow in one strand	Yellow

Originally, the colours indicated in which ropeyard the ropes were made and were introduced to stop thieving. Naval rope was considered better than any other and it was often smuggled out of the dockyards and sold to captains of merchant ships.

ROLLING HITCH. Used for bending a rope to a spar. Similar to a clove hitch, but will not slip when subjected to a pull in one direction.

ROPE. A cord usually more than one inch in thickness.

ROUNDING. Condemned rope under four inches in size. Also a serving on a rope or spar.

ROUND TURN AND TWO HALF HITCHES. A knot commonly used for securing a rope to a large ring or a spar.

RUMBO. Old condemned rope.

RUNNING BOWLINE. A noose made by pulling the bight of a rope through the eye of a bowline.

SAILMAKER'S NEEDLE. A large needle used for sewing canvas.

SAILMAKER'S PALM. A leather device which fits over the hand to enable one to drive a needle with the palm of the hand when sewing canvas.

SAILMAKER'S WHIPPING. A method of whipping a rope's end to ensure that the whipping will not slip or come off. The end of the rope is unlaid and the bight of the twine laid over the middle strand, leaving a short end. After laying up the end of the rope again, the whipping is commenced towards the end. When enough turns have been made, the bight of twine is taken outside the whipping followng the lay of the strand over which it was placed and passed over the end of the same strand. Next, the short end is pulled, tightening the bight, and brought outside the whipping following the lay of the rope. Finally, the two ends are joined in the middle of the rope between the strands with a reef knot.

SEIZING. The name given to the cord or twine used to seize ropes together. Also the name given to the finished product. (Fr. 'saizir'.)

SENNIT. A braid which is made by plaiting or weaving rope together in a pattern.

SERVING MALLET. A wooden mallet with a groove in the bottom which is used to keep the spunyarn taut when serving a rope.

SHEEPSHANK. Used for shortening a rope which requires lengthening again.

SHEET BEND. Used for joining two ropes of unequal thickness or for securing a rope's end through an eye, such as a boat's lazy painter to the jacob's ladder on a boom. Also called a 'swab hitch'.

A 'sheet' is a rope fastened to the corner of a sail. (OE. 'sceata', lower corner of a sail.)

SHORT SPLICE. A method of joining two ropes end to end permanently by interlocking the strands. The splice finishes thicker than the rope and will not therefore reeve through a block.

SISAL. Rope made from the hard fibre of the leaves of agave sisalana which is grown in Cuba, East Africa and Indonesia.

SLIP KNOTS. Certain bend and hitches can be made into 'slip knots', in order to be released quickly, by using a bight instead of the end in the last phase of making them. The three main ones are the sheet bend, the bowline and the clove hitch.

SLIPPERY HITCH. A bend or hitch used to secure a rope to a ring or spar, made in such a way that by pulling the free end of the rope it becomes free.

SMALL STUFF. Any light line or twine.

SPUNYARN. A small line made up of a few yarns, used for seizing and serving.

SOFT EYE. A small eye spliced into the end of a rope without a thimble.

SQUARE LASHING. See LASHING.

STOPPER KNOT. The name of any knot used to form a knob at the end of a rope for the purpose of providing a stop. Usually seen in the ends of handropes rove through rings.

STRAND. A number of yarns twisted together. Three strands laid up right handed form a hawser-laid rope, which is the type commonly used. (ME, 'stron' from OFr. 'estran', rope.)

SWAB HITCH. See SHEET BEND.

THIMBLE EYE. An eye spliced around a thimble in a ropes end.

TIMBER HITCH. Used to secure a rope to a spar. It is simply made by passing the rope around the spar and then twisting the end around its own part which will jam when hauled taut. For towing a spar astern, a half hitch is placed alongside the timber hitch, the two parts being lengthened out for the half-hitch to direct the pull.

TURK'S HEAD. An ornamental knot resembling a turban. It can be made in the end of a rope to provide a stopper knot, on the bight of a rope, or running as on the lanyard once worn as part of uniform by men dressed as seamen.

TWINE. Used for whipping rope's ends and for sewing canvas, it is made up of a number of yarns made from flax or Italian hemp.

WALL KNOT. A stopper knot formed at the end of a rope by unlaying the strands and interweaving them. (From wale knot.)

WEST COUNTRY WHIPPING. A method of whipping a rope's end by centering the twine around the rope and tying it with an overhand knot at every half turn so that each consecutive knot is on the opposite side of the rope. Useful when required to whip the bight of a rope.

YARNS. A number of fibres twisted together, which are themselves twisted to form strands of a rope. (OE. 'gearn'.)

20

RIGGING

The end of sail resulted in the loss of a multitude of rigging and sail names together with their operative jargon. In the modern warship there is little rigging left in the true sense, the term rigging itself nowadays being associated with such operations as replenishment at sea and lifting and moving items within the ship.

* * *

ANCHOR SHACKLE. Used for joining together two wire hawsers which each have a hawser eye. It is a long shackle with a flush ended bolt, secured by a tapered pin and lead pellet.

BAGGYWRINKLE. A serving placed on standing or running rigging to prevent chafing where one rope crosses another.

BALE SLING STROP. An endless sling.

BECKET. The eye sometimes fitted at the tail of a block.

BRACES. The standing rigging by which a yard is held square athwartships.

BLOCK. The wooden or metal pulley assembly as used in a purchase. Originally this was a block of wood with a hole in it for a rope to reeve through.

BLOCK AND BLOCK. See CHOCK-A-BLOCK.

BOATSWAIN'S CHAIR. A short board, having two holes in each end through which strops are rove, used for lowering a man over the side or hoisting him aloft for painting, etc.

BOLLARD STROP. A wire strop with a thimble spliced in one end, used for securing a hawser which has a hawser end to a bollard.

BOLSTER. A cushion made of canvas or leather used to prevent chafe between ropes.

BOOM. A fixed or swinging spar rigged horizontally from a ship's mast or structure.

BOTTLESCREW. A device used to adjust any rigging equipment for length or tension. It consists of a sleeve contra-threaded at each end to take screws. As the sleeve is turned the two screws are drawn together.

BOW SHACKLE. See SHACKLE.

BULLDOG GRIPS. Screwed clamps which are used to hold the two parts of the end of a wire rope together to form a temporary eye.

CAPSTAN. A vertical drum situated on the forecastle of larger ships, powered by electricity or steam and used for heavy lifting work. (Fr. 'cabestan' from L. 'capistrare', to fasten with a rope.)

CARPENTER'S STOPPER. A portable patent stopper for use with wire hawsers.

CHAIN CHECK STOPPER. A device used to control a wire rope being paid out where a ring bolt is available.

CHEEKS. The sides of the shell of a block.

CHOCK-A-BLOCK. A term to describe the state of a tackle when both blocks are hauled up together. Also known as 'two blocks' and 'block and block'.

'CLAP ON'. An order to take hold of a rope or purchase for the purpose of hauling on it.

CLEAR. The inside width and length of a shackle.

CLEAT. A wood or metal fitment, having two arms, around which a rope may be secured.

CLENCHED SHACKLE. A shackle which is closed permanently by having the end of its bolt heated and hammered over.

CLUMP BLOCK. A special block with a large swallow which will take a rope of half its own size.

'COME UP'. An order given after taking the strain of a hauled tackle in order to belay the hauling part. Having hauled the tackle to the required limit, the hands hold steady. More hands hold the standing and running parts of the tackle tightly together. Once this is done, the order 'come up' is given when the hands having hauled bring up the hauling part and make fast.

COMPLAINING. Said of the sheave of a block when squeaking.

COSTON GUN. Used to make initial contact with another ship for the purpose of jackstay transfer. When fired, a light nylon line is passed over, the transfer gear is then attached and hauled over.

CROWN. The top of a block, where an eye or a hook is fitted. Also the part of a shackle opposite the jaws.

DECK CLENCH. A heavy metal fitting riveted to a deck for standing rigging, hawsers or cables which are subject to heavy strain.

DERRICK. A swinging boom which pivots to act as a jib on a crane, the heel of which pivots at the foot of a mast or the side of superstructure while the head is swung sideways by guys. The head is 'topped up' by a purchase called a 'topping lift' in order to plumb another lifting purchase over the weight to be lifted. The name comes from a 17th century hangman at Tyburn by the name of Derrick.

DISTANCE LINE. A line with different coloured flags bent to it which is used as a reference for keeping station by the receiving ship during a replenishment at sea operation. It is secured forward in the supply ship and kept in hand, taut, on the forecastle of the receiving ship.

DOUBLE WHIP. A purchase where a fall is rove through two single blocks with the standing part made fast near, or to, the upper block. The mechanical advantage is two.

DOWN-HAUL. A rope pulling downwards.

DRESSING LINES. Lines which are used for hoisting flags at close intervals for 'dressing ship'.

DUTCHMAN'S PURCHASE. A tackle used in reverse to take advantage of the velocity ratio; i.e. fast speed from a slow power source.

EYEBOLT. A steel eye, combined with a threaded or screwed bolt, used for attaching an eye to a deck or structure.

EYEPLATE. A steel eye, incorporated with a plate, for riveting or welding to a deck, deckhead or bulkhead. On board ship, eyeplates are fitted in convenient places to which lines or tackles may be secured.

FALL. The end of the rope of a tackle on which the pull is exerted.

FLEET. The span or scope of a rope or tackle.

FLEXIBLE STEEL WIRE ROPE. Rope which is used wherever a wire rope is to bend easily round the sheave of a block, etc. It is more flexible but weaker than steel wire rope for rigging.

FRENCHMEN. Left-handed loops placed in a coil of wire rope, necessary to counteract the twists formed when coiling down right-handed.

GARLAND. A strop or rope sling placed around a mast or spar with which to hoist or lift it.

GOOSENECK. A fitting by which the heel of a mast derrick is attached to a mast and upon which it pivots.

GUEST ROPE. A rope thrown down from a ship to a boat coming alongside, or to take a tow.

GUN TACKLE. Similar to a 'double whip' (but this term is used only for hoisting, see DOUBLE WHIP) used for purposes other than hoisting. The standing part is always made fast to one of the blocks. The name originates from the small tackle which was used to run out the old muzzle-loading gun carriages after they had been fired and recoiled.

GUY. The ropes holding a boom in position and also the ropes used to haul round and steady the head of a derrick. (Du. 'gei', rope attached to a sail, from OFr. 'guier', to guide.)

GYN. A temporary derrick made by lashing the heads of three spars together to form a tripod. As the spars are not moveable, it can only be used for a straight lift. (Fr. 'engin'.)

HAND OVER HAND. Hauling a rope quickly with alternate hands.

HANDY BILLY. A small tackle used for general purposes, with one double and one single block. When rove to advantage it gives a mechanical advantage of four.

'HANDSOMELY'. An order meaning slowly and with care, usually given when lowering.

'HAUL AWAY'. The order to haul on a rope steadily.

HAULING PART. The part of a rope used in a tackle which leads away from the assembly for hauling.

HAWSER. A large rope of over five inches in circumference. (Fr. 'hausser', to lift.)

HAWSER EYE. A wire rope which has a soft eye with a thimble seized into it after the eye splice is complete. It is used for hawsers and towing pendants.

HEAD. The upper end of a derrick or sheers.

HEAD LASHING. The lashing of spars together to form a gyn or sheers.

'HEAVE'. An order to give a strong pull.

HEAVY JACKSTAY. A wire rope passed between ships for the purpose of replenishment at sea. A traveller block is free to be hauled back and forth along the jackstay by inhaul and outhaul ropes.

HEEL. The lower end of a derrick or sheers.

HEEL TACKLES. Tackles placed at the heels of standing or swinging derricks, sheers, etc. and led to give support in all directions.

'HIGH ENOUGH'. The order to stop hoisting.

HOIST. A system designed for lifting, or the load to be lifted.

'HOIST AWAY'. The order to haul when a weight is to be lifted.

HORNS. The arms of a cleat around which a rope may be secured.

JACKSTAY. A hemp or wire rope suspended between two points to be used as supports. See LIGHT JACKSTAY and HEAVY JACKSTAY.

JACKSTAY FUELLING. The method of fuelling at sea from a supply ship by using flexible hoses suspended from a jackstay.

JACKSTAY TRANSFER. The operation of transferring stores, etc. from one ship to another whilst under way at sea by use of a jackstay.

JAWS. The space between the lugs of shackle.

JIGGER. A small tackle, in effect a luff tackle with a smaller fall, for general use. When fitted with a tail in the double block instead of a hook it is called a tail jigger. It had a mechanical advantage of four when rove to advantage.

LEADING BLOCK. A block used to lead a rope which is under strain clear of an obstacle to prevent chafing.

LEGGED SLINGS. Slings with each leg having one end secured to a common ring and the other with a hook or thimble eye. There can be two, three or four legs.

LIFTS. Standing rigging which holds a yardarm level.

LIGHT JACKSTAY. Used for the transfer of personnel between ships at sea. It is made up by the use of a 4-inch manilla rope, with a traveller block which is free to be hauled back and forth along the jackstay by inhaul and outhaul ropes.

'LIGHT TO'. The order to fleet a rope back along the deck to give enough slack to belay it.

'LOWER AWAY'. The order to lower a rope away steadily.

LOWER BOOM. A boat boom rigged from the ship's side at the after end of the forecastle. It is called a 'lower' boom because in the days of sail the lower studding sail booms were rigged as boat booms.

LUFF TACKLE. A purchase with a fall three inches in size or greater, consisting of a single and a double block, with the standing part of the fall made fast to the single block. The mechanical advantage is four if it is rove to advantage, otherwise it is three. So named from its original use for hauling down the tack of a fore-and-aft sail to tauten the luff (the leading edge of the sail). (Du. 'loef'.)

LUFF UPON LUFF. A luff tackle hooked into the fall of another to double the mechanical advantage.

LUGS. The ends of a shackle at the jaws.

MARTINGALE. A foreguy led down from the head of a standing derrick to prevent the head from springing upwards.

MAST DERRICK. A derrick which is rigged with the heel fitted to a gooseneck on a mast which also has topping lift fittings. (See DERRICK.)

MESSENGER. A heaving line when used to pass hawsers from ship to shore or vice-versa.

MOVING BLOCK. The block of a tackle which actually moves, as opposed to the 'standing block' which is fixed.

NIP. A sharp bend forced into a steel wire rope.

NIPPERS. A number of turns of rope around two hawsers as a temporary method of holding them together or for one hawser to haul another.

ON THE DIP. Said of a load, when being hoisted or lowered, slung in such a way as to tilt in order to pass through a hatch.

PARBUCKLE. A method of hauling up or lowering down a cask or other cylindrical object where it is not possible to use a tackle. A rope is middled around a standing object such as a post of bollard and the two ends are passed under the outboard ends of the object. The ends of the rope are then brought back up over the object to act as running parts for hoisting or lowering.

PENDANT. A length of rope or wire rope with a block or thimble spliced in one end which is used as an extension to a tackle.

PREVENTER. A rope employed to take the strain of another.

PREVENTER GUY. A standing guy fitted to a derrick to prevent it from swinging too far in a certain direction.

PRYPOLE. A spar used to form a strut, such as on the upright spar of a standing derrick as an alternative to a martingale to stop the head springing up. The centre spar of a gyn is a prypole.

PURCHASE. A rope rove through one or more blocks with mechanical advantage obtained according to the number of sheaves over which it passes. When there are two or more blocks involved in the purchase, it is usually called a tackle except when two double or two treble blocks are used when these are called two-fold and three-fold purchases. (OFr. 'purchaser', to gain.)

QUARTER BOOM. A boat boom rigged from the ship's side at the quarter, similarly rigged to a lower boom but shorter.

RIGGING SCREW. A screw fitting into an internally threaded sleeve with an eye at each end, used to adjust rigging for length or tension.

RIGGING SLIP. A quick release slip used for joining the end of a rope or chain to a fitting when the end may have to be cast off quickly.

RIGGING WARRANT. A warrant issued to a ship, by the yard at which she is fitted out, which gives details of all of the items of standing and running rigging.

RINGBOLT. See EYEBOLT.

ROPEWAY. An overhead jackstay of rope set between two sheers or gyns, along which a travelling block is hauled back and forth.

'ROUNDLY'. The order to haul or check a rope rapidly.

RUNNER. A rope rove through a single moving block.

RUNNING PART. The part of a rope used in a tackle which 'runs' between the blocks.

RUNNING RIGGING. Nowadays only seen as the guys of derricks, the purchases used permanently when working derricks or moving ropes in general used aboard ship. Once of course the term included all of the rigging used in hoisting, lowering or trimming sails and hoisting and striking yards. (ME 'riggen'.)

SCORE. The groove made in the cheeks of some blocks to take the strop.

SCREEN DERRICK. A derrick which is fitted to a ship's superstructure. (See DERRICK.)

SELVAGEE STROP. An untwisted skein of rope yarn marled together to form a strop, which is used for various purposes such as a sling for heavy weights. (From 'selvedge'.)

SHACKLE. A metal U shaped device, with a pin which screws through the jaws, used for joining purposes in rigging. It is called a 'straight shackle' when the sides are straight and a 'bow shackle' when the sides are curved. (ME 'schakel' from OE. 'sceacul', bond.)

SHEAVE. The wheel of a block which has a grooved rim to take a rope. Sometimes called a 'shiv', from the older name of 'shiver'.

SHEERS. (Also sheerlegs). A temporary derrick constructed with two spars raised at angle, lashed together where they cross and fitted with a tackle. (Du. 'scheren', to slip or move aside.)

SHELL. The main body of a block, housing the sheave and grooved around the outside to take the strop.

SHROUDS. Standing rigging giving a mast lateral support. The name comes from the days when ropes were not so strong and therefore many more supports were required making the mast appear as though wrapped in a shroud.

SIGNAL HALYARDS. The ropes used to hoist or lower the Ensign and signal flags, rove through sheaves in the truck of a mast or through blocks on a yard.

SINGLE WHIP. A fall rove through a single standing block. No mechanical advantage is obtained.

SLING. A rope attached to an object in order to hoist it. (OE. 'slingan'.)

SNATCH BLOCK. A single block with a hinged opening in the shell to allow the bight of a rope to be dropped in, thus avoiding having to reeve the rope through from its end.

SNOTTER. A single leg sling with an eye spliced in each end.

SOFT EYE. An eye spliced into the end of a wire rope without a thimble.

SPAN. A rope or wire rope which has each of its ends secured to fixed points, used to accommodate the standing block of a tackle when no convenient point is available.

SPANISH BURTON. A purchase employing two single blocks which has a mechanical advantage of four, but has a limited lift due to its arrangement.

SPANISH WINDLASS. A device used to achieve maximum tautness when seizing together two hawsers. Turns of the seizing are taken around a bar and then the bar is turned in the direction of the lay of the seizing by the use of a marline spike.

SPAR. The general name for any wooden item such as a boom, mast, yard, etc. (ME. 'sparre', pole.)

SPIDER BAND. A metal band at the head of a derrick which has eyes for the fitting of topping lift and guys.

SPLAY TACKLE. A tackle placed between the heels of the splayed out legs of a gyn or sheers.

STAGE. A plank, with 'horns' at each end, rigged with rope lanyards and used to support men when working over the ship's side or on superstructure.

STANDING BLOCK. The block of a tackle which is secured to the deck or other fitting.

STANDING DERRICK. A single upright spar stayed by rigging and having a tackle at its head for hoisting a load. It is used where no suitable crane or derrick is available aboard or ashore.

STANDING PART. The part of a rope used in a tackle which is secured to the block and does not move, as opposed to the running part between the blocks and the hauling part.

STANDING RIGGING. Shrouds and stays which are permanently in place.

STAYS. Wire ropes supporting a mast or spar forward and aft (forestays and backstays). (OE. 'stoeg'.)

STOPPER. A short length of rope used to take the strain of a hawser or large rope whilst it is being belayed.

STRAIGHT SHACKLE. See SHACKLE.

STROP. A rope spliced to form a circle, used for various purposes such as a sling for hoisting, or around a block for hanging it by. (ME., band or loop of leather or rope, from L. 'stroppus', band, strip, from Gk. 'strophus'.)

SWALLOW. The space between the sides of the shell of a block, into which the sheave is fitted.

SWINGING DERRICK. As in the case of a standing derrick, this is used where no suitable crane or derrick is available aboard or ashore. It is made up of two spars, one upright and the other secured by a snotter to the lower end of the first to form a swinging boom.

SWIVEL BLOCK. A block fitted with a swivel at the crown.

TACKLE. (Pronounced 'taycle'.) An arrangement of a rope and blocks for lifting objects and thereby obtaining mechanical advantage. (ME. 'takel - akin to MDu. 'takel', ship's rigging.)

TAIL. The bottom of a block.

TAIL JIGGER. See JIGGER.

TALURIT SPLICE. Not a splice in the proper sense, but achieving the same result when requiring an eye in the end of a wire rope. The end of the wire rope is threaded through a metal ferrule, passed around a thimble and then back through the ferrule to form the loop. The ferrule is finally gripped tightly in a press.

THIMBLE. An iron ring grooved on the outside to prevent steel wire rope from bending round too sharply when spliced into an eye.

THIMBLE EYE. An eye spliced around a thimble in the end of a wire rope.

THREE-FOLD PURCHASE. A tackle consisting of two treble blocks and used mainly in boat's falls. The mechanical advantage is seven if rove to advantage.

THUMB PIECE. A wooden projection screwed at the head of a spar when used as a standing derrick to prevent the topping lift and purchase from slipping down. An alternative is to position a rope collar on the spar like a whipping.

TOPPING LIFT. A purchase fitted to the head of a derrick to raise or lower it.

TOWING SHACKLE. A special long shackle which is used to take the end of a towing hawser and the tongue of a towing slip.

TRAVELLER. A ring sliding on a spar or rope.

TULIPS. Shoe links fitted by rivets to the ends of wire rope guardrails.

TURNING IN SCREW. A compression turn screw device used for breaking in a heavy wire rope around a thimble.

TWO BLOCKS. See CHOCK-A-BLOCK.

TWO-FOLD PURCHASE. A general purpose tackle consisting of two double blocks. The mechanical advantage is four if rove to advantage.

'WALK BACK'. The order to check a rope by walking back.

WARPING DRUMS. Drums fitted to a winch which are used for hauling ropes and hawsers.

'WELL'. The order to stop hauling or checking a rope.

WHIP. A fall rove through a single standing block for hoisting light loads.

WHIP UPON WHIP. Where a single whip is applied to the fall of another.

WINCH. A device used for hauling ropes, hawsers and running rigging which may be driven by electric or hydraulic power. A main horizontal shaft has warping drums at each end.

WIRE ROPE. Steel wire rope. It is normally made with six strands laid up right-handed around a hemp or jute heart. The strands are formed by twisting a number of small

21

TRADITIONAL TALLIES (NICKNAMES)

The Navy has always been a fertile source for nicknames and where applicable the traditional 'tally' is used almost without exception. A tally such as 'Sweeney' Todd after the barber may be obvious, as may be 'Dodger' Long (dodge along), but others may not be so because of the passage of time since their inception. For instance, 'Hoot' Gibson, a cowboy film star and 'Pedlar' Palmer, a boxer, both from long ago and neither well remembered.

'Dolly' Gray comes from 'Goodbye Dolly Gray', a popular song of the time of the Boer War; from other songs come 'Bill' Bailey and 'Nellie' Dean. There are those from the fictional detectives 'Sexton' Blake and 'Sherlock' Holmes, 'Jesse' James from the infamous American folk hero, 'General' Booth from the Salvation Army and 'Brigham' Young from the founder of the Mormons.

'Harry' Tate was one of the old music hall comedians and 'Harry' Freeman was really Henry Freeman, an 18th century warehouse owner on the Thames near Tower Bridge, well known for providing free beer for the porters who worked for him. 'Hookey' Walker is supposed to have derived from a London merchant, whose outstanding feature was a large hooked nose. However, 'Jim' Crow never did exist; this was once an American term for a negro.

As can be expected, some tallies have purely naval origins such as 'Tug' Wilson, an Admiral Wilson was once dissatisfied with a captain's anchoring of a ship and ordered a tug to bring him in. 'Johnny' Bone was at one time Admiral Cornwallis' boatswain, notorious for thieving and scrounging stores in order to build up his own ship's stocks. 'Wiggin', or the variation 'Wiggy', Bennett is said to come from an officer named Bennett who received a 'wigging' for his careless attitude. A 'wigging' was an old naval term for a reprimand.

'Tosh', for those with the name Gilbert, is believed to be an abbreviation of 'toshing' which was the act of stealing the copper sheathing from the hull of a ship. 'Chats', an old sailor's name for lice, is the tally given to those with the name of Harris. There is usually a tally to fit the more common names and if not then there is always 'Jagger' for a West Countryman, 'Janner' for a Cornishman and 'Geordie', 'Jock', 'Paddy', 'Taffy', 'Lofty', 'Tich' and 'Ginger'.

Here is a list of the most common tallies:-

Anderson	'Granny'	Bailey	'Bill'
Baker	'Pasha'	Bell	'Daisy'
Bennett	'Wiggin'	Bird	'Dicky'
Black	'Nigger'	Blake	'Sexton'
Bone	'Johnny'	Booth	'General'
Brown	'Bomber'	Casey	'Ginger'
Clark	'Nobby'	Coles	'Smokey'
Collins	'Jumper'	Craft	'Cheesy'
Crow	'Jim'	Day	'Happy'
Dean	'Nellie'	Evans	'Bandy'
Ewart	'Nobby'	Fisher	'Jackie'
Ford	'Florrie'	Freeman	'Harry'
French	'Froggy'	Gale	'Windy'
Gibson	'Hoot'	Gilbert	'Tosh'
Gray	'Dolly'	Green	'Jimmy'
Harris	'Chats'	Henderson	'Granny'
Hewitt	'Nobby'	Hinds	'Cosher'
Holmes	'Sherlock'	Howard	'Ginger'
Hughes	'Spike'	James	'Jesse'
Kelly	'Darby'	King	'Jerry'
Knight	'Bogey'	Lane	'Shadey'
Larsen	'Swede'	Lee	'Nancy'
Little	'Little'	Long	'Dodger'
Martin	'Pincher'	Miller	'Dusty'
Mills	'Timber'	Moore	'Pony'
Morgan	'Rattler'	Moyle	'Olive'
Murphy	'Spud'	Palmer	'Pedlar'
Parker	'Nosey'	Payne	'Whacker'
Rhodes	'Dusty'	Ring	'Jerry'

Short	'Jumper'	Steel	'Rusty'
Sullivan	'Spike'	Tanner	'Bob'
Taylor	'Buck'	Todd	'Sweeney'
Turner	'Topsey'	Vaughan	'Guy'
Walker	'Hookey'	Ward	'Sharkey'
Wells	'Kitty'	White	'Knocker'
Williams	'Bungy'	Wilson	'Tug'
Woods	'Slinger'	Wright	'Shiner'
Young	'Brigham'		

22

ROYAL NAVAL SLANG

In times past slang stood for words and expressions which Gypsies employed among themselves, to the bewilderment of everyone else. Today it serves as the watchwords or trademarks of ordinary people with similar tastes or occupations. However, it is doubtful if anyone can equal the slang vocabulary of the sailor. The reason for this extensive use of slang is that sailor language proper comprises words and expressions which may not on any account be replaced by shore-going terms. The sailor is forcibly reminded of the contrast between the language afloat and that used ashore and it is therefore not surprising that he attaches a vocabulary of his own to objects and situations of everyday life.

* * *

ACID. Sarcasm, criticism.
ACID DROP. Someone always arguing or quarrelling.
ACTING SCRAN. A substitution on the menu.
ADMIRAL'S BARGE. The personal aircraft of the Flag Officer Naval Air Command.
ADMIRAL'S HAM. Tinned or potted meat.
ADMIRAL'S MATE. A boastful know-all.
AFT WITH YOUR CAP OFF. To be taken before the Officer-of-the-Watch on the quarterdeck as a defaulter.
AGGIE WESTON'S. Agnes Weston's Sailors Rest. In 1876, Agnes Weston (later Dame) founded a 'Sailor's Rest' in Devonport, as part of her campaign to reform the hard drinking sailor of that port who spent most of their shore leave in the pubs. At her 'Sailor's Rest' the men were

able to have meals and lodging with recreation rooms provided. Temperance meetings were held, but the men were under no obligation to attend. The 'Rest' was so successful that in 1881 Agnes opened a second one in Portsmouth. Both of the old Sailor' Rests were bombed and destroyed during the Second World War, but have been rebuilt since. There are now also Rests at Rosyth, Gosport, and Plymouth.

AGGY. A grouser.

ALLIGATOR. Navigator.

ALL NIGHT IN. A full night's sleep with no interruption for watches.

ALL NIGHT IN WITH THE GUTS KICKED OUT. On the middle watch.

ALL OVERISH. Feeling ill.

ALL PARTS BEARING AN EVEN STRAIN. No problems, or for everyone to be 'pulling their weight'.

ANCHOR FACED. Someone keen.

ANCHOR ONE'S STERN, TO. To sit down.

ANDREW, THE. The Royal Navy. From Andrew Miller who was a legendary member of a press gang who was said to claim ownership of the navy because of the hundreds of men he had pressed.

ANOTHER BASH. Signing on for another engagement of service.

ARTICLE ONE, PARAGRAPH ONE. A reference to a non-existent part of Queen's Regulations and Naval Instructions meaning 'You should not have joined the Navy to begin with'. A reply to a complaint.

ASTERN OF STATION. Behind with one's work.

AWNING. Piecrust.

BABY'S HEAD. Meat pie.

BACK AND FILL, TO. To hesitate.

BACK TEETH AFLOAT. A desire to pee.

BACK TEETH AWASH. Intoxicated.

BACK WATER. A forgotten station or position. From an area of water unaffected by the tide.

BAD HAT. Someone with a bad reputation.

BAG MEAL. A packet of sandwiches supplied to men when working away from the ship.

BAG OF NUTS. Congratulations for a job well done.

BANANA BALANCER. Wardroom steward.
BANDAGE ROLLER. Medical assistant.
BARON. Someone with plenty of money.
BARRACK STANCHION. One who has spent a considerable time in barracks and, as suggested, is part of the fixtures.
BATS. Deck landing officer. From the hand markers, resembling table tennis bats, used for hand landing signals.
BATTLE BOWLER. Steel helmet.
BEACHED. An officer retired from the service.
BEACHER. A quick run ashore.
BEAKY. One who has a long nose.
BEATTY ANGLE. An officer's cap worn at an angle, emulating Admiral of the Fleet Sir David Beatty. Following a distinguished First World War career Admiral Beatty became First Sea Lord in 1919. He had a distinctive style of dress with his cap raked down over the left eye and a six button jacket (the dress regulations specifying eight).
BEDSTEAD. A ship's large radar aerial array.
BEEF CHIT. Wardroom menu.
BEING ON BARE NAVY. A wardroom mess existing on official rations.
BELAY IT. Shut up or stop it.
BELLS. Trousers. Originally bell shaped at the bottoms for ease of rolling up to scrub decks in bare feet, but not such a pronounced flare today.
BIBLE. The Manual of Seamanship.
BIBLE BOSUN. Chaplain.
BIG EATS. A meal ashore.
BILGE WATER. An unbelievable statement.
BIRDS. Missiles.
BISH. Chaplain.
BIT OF OLD ROPE. The naval equivalent of a 'piece of cake'; easy.
BLAST. A ticking off or a reprimand.
BLEAT, TO. To grumble.
BLOW THE GAFF, TO. To divulge a secret. From the of a ship identifying herself by hoisting her ensign at the gaff.

BLOW YOU JACK, I'M ALRIGHT. Said of one with selfish behaviour.

BLUE LINERS. RN duty free issue cigarettes, produced by the victualling department, each having a blue line along its length to stop them being smuggled and resold. The duty free issue of cigarettes is being discontinued and due to be phased out by 1991.

These originated in the early 1930s when a pensioner chief gunner's mate was given permission to set up a cigarette making machine in a lorry parked in Portsmouth Barracks. The men took their ration of 'Ticklers' tobacco (see TICKLERS) there and for a small fee had it made up into cigarettes. The business flourished and eventually a small factory was set up in the barracks. However, following the Second World War, HM Customs and Excise had the factory closed down and the Director of Victualling undertook to supply the cigarettes made up from 'Ticklers' direct to Supply Officers.

BLUEBELL. Metal polish; from the brand name of polish once in general use.

BLUES. Best uniform suits.

BOATS. (1) Boats officer.
(2) Submarines. These have always been called 'boats', even today at 18000 tons.

BOAT'S LEFT. In trouble. From being adrift from the ship when she sails, a most serious crime.

BOMBER BOATS. The name given to Polaris submarines by their crews.

BONE DOME. Flying or safety helmet.

BONE, TO. To scrounge or steal. From a boatswain by the name of Bone, who was notorious for appropriating ship's stores from other ships in order to build up his own stocks. He served in the flagship of Admiral Cornwallis during the Revolutionary War (1793-1801). When the commission ended, the Admiral is said to have remarked 'I trust Mr Bone, that you will leave me my bower anchors'.

BOOTIE. Abbreviation of BOOTNECK.

BOOTNECK. Royal Marine. A corruption of the earlier 'leatherneck' (see LEATHERNECK).

BOTTLE. Reproof or critisism. From an old naval saying 'a dose from the foretopman's bottle', which was a purgative given in all cases of sickness.
BOWS UNDER. Overloaded with work.
BOW WAVE. The seaman's cap mis-shapen so that the flat top has a curve.
BRAG RAGS. Medal ribbons.
BRASSED OFF. Fed up.
BRASS HAT. An officer of commander's rank or above, with reference to the gold oak leaves worn on the peak of the cap. (In the Army it means a staff officer).
BREAD BARGE. The wooden bread dish used in messes.
BREAK SHIP, TO. To desert, to go ashore without permission.
BREAK SURFACE, TO. To wake up. From a submarine submerged then breaking surface.
BRICK. A shell.
BRIG. Cells.
BROKE. An officer dismissed from the service. From an old naval court martial sentence 'to be broke and rendered unfit to serve His Majesty at sea'.
BRONZY-BRONZY. Suntanned.
BRONZY FOR LEAVE. To obtain that extra tan before going on home leave from foreign service.
BROUGHT UP WITH A ROUND TURN. To be stopped abruptly when doing something wrong. From a turn around a bollard stopping a boat.
BUCKSHEE. Free. (From Arabic.)
BUFFER. Chief Boatswain's Mate, the senior CPO.
BUFF UP, TO. To smarten up.
BUG RUN. A parting in the hair.
BUM BOAT. Usually a civilian boat plying to and fro in harbour. This once was actually 'bomb boat' and used to carry provisions and generally to act as a link with the shore. So called from 'bombard', a vessel in which beer was carried to soldiers on duty. In later years bumboats were the mens' only connection with the shore when in port at home or abroad, from which they could buy a great variety of articles.
BUM FREEZER. Naval officer's reefer jacket.
BUM NUTS. Eggs.

BUNCH OF BASTARDS. Tangled rope or line.
BUNDLEMAN. A married man. From the days when ratings were allowed to buy victuals at a cheap rate for their families and thus be recognised by the bundle of provisions they carried ashore.
BUNGHOLE. Cheese.
BUNG UP AND BILGE FREE. Relaxing in a horizontal position. Once the correct position for stowing rum casks.
BUNNY-MEAT. Vegetable.
BUNTING TOSSER. A radio operator (tactical), originally called a signalman, a rating responsible for hoisting signal flags. With reference to the name of the all wool cloth from which signal flags were once made.
BUOY HOPPING. Sailing a course from buoy to buoy.
BURBERRY. Raincoat. From the firm of Burberry who once supplied these.
BURBLING. Verbal rambling.
BURGOO. Porridge. Originally 'burgoo' was actually burnt bread boiled in water with sugar, which was the standard breakfast item in the navy until around the year 1825 when it was replaced by chocolate (see KYE).
BURN. A smoke.

Before 1862 Queen's Regulations and Admiralty Instructions forbade smoking in a ship of war, except in the galley.

BUTCHER. Surgeon.
BUY A WHITE HORSE, TO. To behave in a reckless manner.
BUZZ. A rumour. The term dates from the introduction of wireless into the RN. Wireless ratings were usually the first to hear details of any movements, etc.
CABOOSE. Pronounced 'caboosh'. A small cabin or compartment. Originally the galley in a ship.
CACKLE BERRIES. Eggs.
CAG, TO. To discuss or argue.
CAN SPANNER. Tin opener.
CANTEEN DAMAGER. Canteen manager.

Until the Royal Navy's Mediterranean Command was abolished in 1967, the canteen manager of a ship was usually of Maltese extraction. The Admiralty awarded the Maltese the concession to conduct a canteen in a warship as a reward for their support in the liberation of Malta from the French in 1814.

CAPTAIN OF THE HEADS. Rating detailed for cleaning the heads.

CAP TALLY. Cap ribbon.

CARRY BOTH SHEETS AFT, TO. To walk with the hands in the pockets.

CARRY THE CAN, TO. Take the blame.

CAT. Catamaran.

CATCH A CRAB, TO. To have an oar fouled in the water when boat pulling.

CHATS. Chatham. The dockyard and barracks which closed in 1984. Chatham had been a principle base and anchorage of the British navy since the reign of Henry VIII. The dockyard, founded later in 1570, was to become the most important in Britain until the expansion of Portsmouth in later centuries. Many great ships were built there, including *HMS VICTORY*.

CHATTY. Dirty rating.

CHEERILY. Smartly or quickly.

CHIEF. Senior engineer officer. Sometimes known as 'chiefy'.

CHIEF NIGHTINGALE. Chief Medical Assistant.

CHINESE WEDDING CAKE. Rice pudding.

CHINKY FOOT ROT. Athletes foot.

CHIPPY. A hull specialist of the marine engineering branch. Once the ship's carpenter.

In sailing days the carpenter was a warrant officer responsible for the hull, masts and spars of the ship and also for her boats. In battle his job was to plug any shot holes received and to take soundings within the ship to determine whether or not she was making water.

CHIT (or CHITTY). Any official paper, i.e. 'draft chit'. (Hindu 'chitti'.)

CHOCKER. Fed up.

CHOKE THE LUFF, TO. To satisfy hunger.

CHOP-CHOP. Hurry up.

CHOPPER. Helicopter.

CHUFFED. Pleased. (English dialect 'chuff', fat, proud, happy.)

CHUMMY SHIPS. Ships of the same squadron, flotilla or group.

CLACKER. Pastry.
CLEAN SHIFT. Clean underclothes.
CLEAR ONE'S YARDARM, TO. To absolve oneself from any blame.
CLEWED UP. Knowledgable.
CLUB SWINGER. A member of the physical training branch. 'Clubs' for short.
COCK SHIP. The most successful ship in a squadron or flotilla, usually in connection with a regatta.
CONKEY. One with a large nose.
COPPER-BOTTOMED. Reputable. From the sheathing of wooden ships' bottoms with copper as a protection against marine parasites. Being expensive it was only done by owners of substance and repute.
CORNED DOG. Corned beef.
CORPS, THE. The Royal Marines.
COUPLE OF WETS. A few drinks.
COWBOY'S BREAKFAST. Bacon and baked beans. (Originally U.S. Navy).
COW HITCH. A bend or hitch improperly tied which slips, or an unrecognised knot.
COWJUICE. Milk.
CRABBY. Dirty.
CRAB FAT. Ship's side grey paint.

Although prior to the 19th century there was no regulation regarding the paintwork of RN ships, the usual colour scheme was an all-over bright yellow with a broad black boot-topping along the whole length of the ship at the waterline. However, some ships were painted red or black. The Earl St. Vincent had all of his ships of the Mediterranean Fleet painted yellow and black in the traditional manner. Nelson developed this further by having his ship's sides chequered along the lines of gunports.

The Victorian colour scheme was for the hulls of ships to be painted black, the superstructure white and upper works a buff yellow. In 1903 the all over grey scheme was introduced.

CRABS. Lice.
CRASH THE SWEDE, TO. To sleep.
CROOK OF THE ROOK. Duty messman.

CROW. A rating always in trouble.
CRASH, TO. To sleep.
CRUSHERS. Regulating staff; ship's police.
CUDDY. Captain's cabin. In sailing ships this was the name of a cabin in the after part under the poop deck for the Master and his passengers and originally the cabin of a half-decked boat.
CUSHY NUMBER. An easy job.
CUSTARD BOSUN. A cook.
CUT AND RUN, TO. To escape. Originally this meant for a ship's cable to be cut in order to sail in a hurry.
CUT ONE'S PAINTER, TO. To die. A painter is the headrope of a boat used for securing and thus deemed to be a lifeline.
D. F. s. Duty free goods.
D. Q. s. Detention quarters; naval prison.
DALMATION PUDDING. Currant or raisin pudding.
DEAD MARINE. An empty bottle. Like a marine, it has done its duty and is ready to do it again.
DEAD MEN. Stray ropes' ends when hanging from aloft. From the once common execution method of hanging from the yardarm.
DECCO. A look.
DEEP SEA BEEF. Haddock.
DE-RATED. The punishment of losing one's rate. (The official term is 'dis-rated'.)
DEVIL DODGER. Chaplain.
DHOBI DUST. Washing powder. (To 'dhobi' is the naval term to wash clothes; indian for washerman.)
DHOBI ITCH. Irritation caused by insufficient rinsing when dhobying.
DIBDAB. An ordinary seaman.
DICKEY RUN. A quick run ashore.
DICKEY FRONT. White vest (shirt).
DIG IN, TO. To help yourself.
DIG OUT, TO. To work hard; to make an all out effort.
DIP, TO. To fail.
DIP IN, TO. To obtain a chance or a share.
DIP OUT, TO. To miss a chance or share, or to come off worse in any situation.
DIPPED. Reduced in rate (rank).

DISH UP, TO. To wash up dishes and clear up after a meal.
DISHED UP. Disrated, punished.
DITCH, TO. To throw away or discard.
DO A DINGER, TO. To dodge work.
DO A LOAF, TO. To slack during working hours.
DO A SUB, TO. To stand in for someone for duty.
DUB IN, TO. To report or inform on another.
DOCKYARD JOB. A big or heavy job. A sit-down job in the heads.
DOCKYARD MATEY. A dockyard worker. Sometimes 'dockie'.
DODGE. A deception to avoid work.
DODGE POMPEY, TO. To evade doing a job of work.
DODGER. A sweeper, or cleaner.
DOFF YOUR LID, TO. To be on defaulters. The cap is removed whilst the charge is being read and the judgement passed.
DOG. Dysentry.
DOGGIE. Officer's messenger, i.e. 'Captain's Doggie'.
DOGGO. Ugly.
DOGS. Dog watches.
DOME. Head.
DONKEY's BREAKFAST. Very badly performed or a mess.

Originally it was the term for a seaman's mattress in the days when it was made of straw.

DON'T COME THE ACID. Don't criticise or take advantage.
DON'T GET INTO A HANK. Keep cool.
DOUGHBOYS. United States sailors.
DOUGHY. In love.
DOUSE, TO. To put out (lights or fire).
DOWNER. A short sleep.
DRAFTY. The Naval Drafting Division.
DRAG THE PICK, TO. To go slow on a job.
DRILL, THE. The normal procedure.
DRINK. The sea.
DRIP, TO. To grumble or complain.
DRIVE, TO. To command a ship.
DRY RUN. A rehearsal.

DUFF. Any kind of pudding. (Mispronunciation of 'dough'.)
DUMMY RUN. A rehearsal.
DUNNAGE. Luggage. Originally this was the name for loose wood laid in the hold of a ship to raise the cargo above the bilge-water, or wedged between the cargo to keep it from rolling when stowed.
DUSTY. Supply rating. From the dust raised when removing stores from the hold.
DUTY DOG. Duty officer.
EX DART. An ex Dartmouth Royal Naval College officer.
FACE FUNGUS. A beard.
FALL OUT OF THE BOAT, TO. To become unpopular in the mess.
FALL OVER BACKWARDS, TO. To go to great lengths over something.
FANNY. Mess pot.

In 1867 the Royal Victualling Yard commenced issuing tinned mutton to Portsmouth warships on a trial basis but it did not find favour with the sailors. In the same year, Frederick Baker, a solicitor's clerk of Alton in Hampshire, enticed a nine year old girl named Fanny Adams away from her playmates and murdered her, dismembering her body. The new and unpopular meat issue was thereby dubbed 'Fanny Adams'. With a handle wired to the top, the meat tin lent itself to various domestic uses on board ship such as drawing the daily rum ration for the mess.

FATHER. The captain.
FERRET. Penis.
FETCHED UP. To be stopped suddenly, as when a vessel runs aground.
FEW WETS. A few drinks.
FIDO. Flight deck officer.
FIGGY DUFF. Suet pudding, not necessarily with figs.
FILL IN, TO. To thrash.
FILL YOUR BOOTS. Help yourself.
FILLY. Girl.
FISH. Torpedoes.
FISH HEAD. Royal Marines slang for a sailor.
FISH OUT, TO. To take out of the pockets.
FLAGS. Signalman.

FLAKERS. Exhausted or asleep.
FLANNEL. Bluff.
FLAP. Panic or confusion.
FLASH UP, TO. To light something. This was the term to light the furnace to raise steam in a ship.
FLAT ABACK. The seaman's cap when worn incorrectly on the back of the head.
'Lay all flat aback' was an order given in square-rigged ships to lay all sails aback to stop the ship's way through the water.
FLATTERS. A horizontal rest or a calm sea.
FLOATERS IN THE SNOW. Sausages and mashed potatoes.
FLOATING BARRACKS. A ship that rarely goes to sea.
FLOG THE CAT, TO. To complain.
FLOWER. A person with feminine tendencies.
FLYBOYS. Fleet Air Arm air crew.
FOULED UP. Unworkable. From fouled rope.
FRANKENSTEINED. Said of equipment which breaks down.
FRESHEN AWAY, TO. To run away.
FRESHERS. Fresh air.
FROG SPAWN. Sago.
FROM CLEW TO EAR RING. Said of something thorough and efficient.
FRUIT SALAD. Medal ribbons.
FULL DUE. For ever.
FULL FIG. Everything.
GALLEY GAZZETTE. An imaginary publication, said to be the source of information for rumour mongers.
GANNET. Greedy rating.
GARAGE. A covered refit dock.
GASH. Rubbish or spare, usually food.
GASH BIN. Rubbish bin.
GASH HAND. Rating spare with nothing to do.
GEN. The truth, genuine.
GET A ONE GUN SALUTE, TO. To be court martialled. A ship in which a court martial is to be held fires one gun at 0800 on the day, as a signal for the members of the court and the witnesses to attend.

GET ONE'S BUTTONS, TO. To be promoted to petty officer.
GET ONE'S HEAD DOWN, TO. To sleep.
GET THE CHOP, TO. To be terminated.
G.I. Parade Training Instructor. From Gunnery Instructor whose duties once included parade training.
GIB. Gibraltar.
GIPPO TUMMY. Upset stomach. 'Gippo' for Egyptian.
GLIM. A light.
GLITTER. Marmalade.
GO A BUNDLE, TO. To be enthusiastic about something.
GOBBIE. A coastguard.

Until 1923 HM Coastguard Service was administered by the Admiralty and manned by pensioners of the Royal Navy. The Service was transferred to the Board of Trade and in 1949 to the Ministry of Transport.

GOFFER. A wave breaking over the ship.
GOFFERS. Soft Drink.
GO FOREIGN, TO. To go to foreign parts.
GOING ASTERN. Said of someone who places his cap on his head back to front by mistake; with the name on the cap tally to the rear.
GOLD BRAID. Senior officers, from the gold braid worn on the uniform cap.
GOLDFINCHES. Officers, from the gold lace worn on the sleeves.
GOLDEN RIVET. An imaginary rivet which young green new entries are asked to find in a ship.
GOLDFISH. Tinned herrings.
GONE ALOFT. Died.
GONE OFF HIS TROLLEY. Lost his reason. A 19th century term which comes from the barrel of a gun having been thrown off its trolley.
GONGS. Medals.
GOOD HAND. One of good repute.
GOOFERS. Off watch hands spectating an aircraft taking off or landing on.
GOON BAG. Aircrew survival suit.
GO OUTSIDE, TO. To leave the service.
GO ROUND THE BUOY, TO. To have an extra helping of food.

GOSSY. Gosport.
GOT EARS ON IT. Something stolen. See RABBITS.
GO UP THE STRAITS, TO. To go to the Mediterranean. With reference to the Straits of Gibraltar.
GRABHOOKS. Fingers.
GRAVEL GRINDER. Parade Training Instructor.
GRAVEYARD WATCH. The middle watch from 0001 to 0400.
GREEN. Naive.
GREENIES. Members of the weapons and electrical engineering branch. Once, officers wore coloured cloth between the gold lace of rank in order to distinguish between branches; that for the electrical branch was green.
GREEN RUB. An undeserved rebuke.
GREEN 'UN. A wave washing up on board.
GREY FUNNEL LINE. The Royal Navy.
GRIFF. News, information.
GRIPPO. Something free.
GROG BLOSSOM. A red nose.
GRUB SPOILER. Cook.
GUFF. Nonsense.
GUFF UP, TO. To replenish.
GULPERS. A mouthful. A term from the days of rum issue which was discontinued in 1970. The daily 'tot' was often irregularly used as payment in kind for favours granted on a scale of 'lighters', 'sippers', 'gulpers' or 'grounders' (the whole tot), dependent upon the size of the favour. The leading hand of the mess, who measured out the tots, was always given sippers by each member.
GUNNELS UNDER. Overloaded with work (or drink). From 'gunwhale', pronounced 'gunnel', the top edge of a boat's side.
GUNS. Gunnery officer.
GUT ROT. Cheap booze.
GUZZ. Devonport. The name comes from 'guzzle' as a reference to the good food associated with the West Country. Men returning from sea, following a long voyage on poor victuals, could always be assured of plenty to eat and drink when putting into that port.

HANG ON TO THE SLACK, TO. To wait for something to happen.
HALF MAST. Trouser legs which are too short.
HAPPY SHIPS. Ships with good relations between officers and men.
HARD LYERS. Hard lying money.
HARDLY OUT OF THE EGG. Immature.
HARD SCRAN. Bad luck.
HARD TACK. Ship's biscuits; not a general issue now of course, but still used for emergency rations for ship's boats.

Biscuit was issued in the navy from the very earliest times as a substitute for bread. The road leading to the biscuit bakery in the Deptford victualling yard was called 'Hard Tack Lane'. (See also SOFT TACK.)

HARRY FREEMANS. Everything provided free. Henry (not Harry) was an 18th century warehouse owner of Tooley Street, near Tower Bridge, who provided free beer for the porters who worked for him. From this came an old cockney saying 'drinking at Freeman's quay'.
HARRY TATES. Any irregular naval formation or 'private' navy. Harry Tate was a music hall comedian who performed a sketch with a motor car on which nothing worked properly. He appeared in the first ever Royal Variety Command Performance in 1912.
HAUL ONE'S WIND, TO. To get out of trouble.
HAVE A BASTARD ON, TO. To be grumpy.
HAVE A SAD ON, TO. To be unhappy.
HAVE A WEED ON, TO. To air a greivance.
HEAVE, TO. stop.
HEDGEHOG. Veal.
HENS AND BITCHES. Bends and hitches.
HERRINGS IN. Herrings in tomato sauce.
HOLD YOUR WATER. Be patient.
HOGWASH. Nonsense. Also the sea.
HOIST IN, TO. To understand.
HOOCH. Poor quality alcoholic drink. Short for 'hoochinoo', spirits made by the Hoochinoo Indians of Alaska.
HOOK. Anchor.
HOOK ROPE PARTY. A party to give the decks a final clear up before inspection.

HOOKEY. Form of address to a leading seaman.
HOOSH. Stew.
HONEYMOON. The period of working up a ship ready for service.
HORSE. Form of address to someone whose name is not known.
HOTTERS. Hot water.
'I'M INBOARD. The equivalent of 'I'm alright Jack'. Provided the speaker's own welfare is assured, then everything is fine.
IN DOCK. In hospital.
IN EVERYBODY'S MESS, BUT NOBODY'S WATCH. Said of a plausible but work-shy man.
IN THE DITCH. Overboard.
IN THE DRINK. In the sea.
IN THE RATTLE. Placed on defaulters, on a charge.
IN THE REPORT. In the Captain's report as a defaulter.
IN THE SPUD LINE. Pregnant.
IRISH HURRICANE. A flat sea.
IRISH MAIL. Sacks of potatoes.
IRISH PENNANT. A loose rope or line left hanging.
JACK. Term for a rating.
JACK DUSTY. A rating of the stores branch dealing with victualling. It comes from the old term for the purser's assistant who was known as 'Jack of the dust' because he was employed in the bread room from where the daily flour issue was made.
JACK-ME-HEARTY. One who makes a nuisance of himself ashore, i.e. wine, women and song.
JACK-ME-TICKLER-PAPER. An old salt, or one who acts like one. See TICKLER.
JACK NASTYFACE. A nickname for a seaman who is disliked by his shipmates. Derived from the pen name of a seaman who exposed bad conditions in the Royal Navy in the early 19th century.
JACK STROP. A name for a troublemaker, a boaster or one who is conceited.
JACK TAR. Used to describe a seaman in a derogatory sense. 'Tar' was once the affectionate name given to a seaman, derived from their practice of tarring canvas clothes to make them waterproof.

JAGGER. A Cornish rating.
JAM BOSUN. Victualling officer.
JAN or JANNER. A West Countryman.
JANKERS. Punishment.
JANKERSMAN. A hand undergoing punishment.
JAUNTY. Master at Arms. This originated in the early 19th century. French prisoners of war aboard the British prison hulks called the Master at Arms 'le gendarme', which in turn became copied phonetically by the British seamen as 'Johnny Damn' which later became 'johndy' and finally 'jaunty'.
JENNY. Wren.
JEW. Tailor.
JIMMY or JIMMY-THE-ONE. The First Lieutenant.
JOCKEY. Any piece of food, especially cheese, added to one's plate.
JOLLIES. Royal Marines. In 1664 a new regiment of 'sea soldiers' was formed, known as the Duke of York and Albany's Regiment of Foot or 'Admiral's Regiment' (after Charles II's brother, the Duke of York and Lord High Admiral). Many were raised from the Trained Bands of the City of London and, on account of their cockney cheerfulness, received the nickname 'jollies'.
JOLLY. Organised recreation or an easy job.
JOLLY JACK. A term for the civilian conception of a sailor.
JONAH. A bringer of bad lack.
JOSE. Nickname for a Maltese.
JOSS. Luck. (Chinese.)
JOSSMAN. Master-at-Arms.
JOSS-PIECE. Lucky charm.
JUDY. A woman.
JUNKET BOSUN. A steward.
KILLICK. The rating of leading seaman. The badge of rate worn on the left arm is a fouled anchor. A killick is a small anchor.
KIP, TO. To sleep.
KEY OF THE KEELSON. A mythical object referred to when playing a prank on a new entry. The new boy is sent to the keyboard sentry to ask for the 'key of the keelson'. A keelson is a stringer bolted to the inside of a

ship's keel to provide additional strength and to support the floor.

KYE. Soluble drinking chocolate.

In 1825 cocoa was introduced into the navy as a substitute for burgoo (burnt bread, boiled in water with sugar) served with biscuit for breakfast. As it required three to four hours of boiling, the cook had to make an early start! It was replaced by a soluble chocolate in 1832 which was made in the Royal Victoria Victualling Yard at Deptford. The chocolate was made with cocoa beans from Grenada, Trinidad and Guayaquil in certain fixed proportions. The beans were roasted, crushed, mixed with sugar and arrowroot, pressed, then stamped out in large thick slabs, The ingredients remain unchanged up to the present day. Generally served on watch at night or in cold weather.

KYE BOAT. Kye pot.

LAID ON. Arranged.

LAND CRABS. Hands of a shore establishment.

LASHINGS. Lots of.

LASH UP. A temporary or badly performed job.

LEATHERNECKS. Royal Marines. The corruption 'boot neck' is more commonly used, this only occasionally. Derived from the leather tongue they once wore at the junction of the collar of their tunics.

LEDGER BOSUN. Writer (clerk).

LEND A HAND, TO. To assist.

LID. Cap.

LIMERS. Lemonade (formerly lime-juice) issued in hot weather.

LINED UP. To be paraded as a defaulter.

LITTLE F. The Lieutenant-Commander (Flying) in an aircraft carrier or air station.

LOAFERS. Malingerers.

LOAFING. Of gear left sculling (lying) about.

LOAFING STATIONS. Men in shore establishments awaiting drafts to ships.

LOFTY. Name for anyone tall.

LONG TOM. A paint brush lashed to a broom handle, used for painting in spots difficult to reach. Originally the name for a forty-two pounder gun captured from a

French ship in 1798 and sold to America. It was also the name for a naval gun used by the British in the Boer War.

LOOK OUT FOR. To act as a substitute on duty.

LOSE THE NUMBER OF ONE'S MESS, TO. To die.

LURK, TO. To impose on someone's kindness.

LUSH UP, TO. To treat.

MAJOR. The senior Royal Marines officer on board.

MAKE ONE'S NUMBER, TO. To report for duty or introduce oneself in a new mess.

Every ship is assigned four alphabetical signal letters in the International Code for identification purposes. A ship using the four letters by hoisting alphabetical signal flags is known as 'making her number'.

MALTA DOG. Mediterranean dysentry.

MALTESE LACE. Frayed edges of clothing, i.e. cuffs.

MATEY SHIPS. Ships of the same squadron or group who are on particularly friendly terms.

MATLOW. Sailor. From the French 'matelot'.

MED. Mediterranean.

MESSDECK DODGER. Messdeck sweeper; the hand detailed for duty to clean the messdeck.

MESSDECK LAWYER. Someone outspoken on sailor's rights.

MONEY JACKET. The jacket worn by officers and petty officers. Originally it was the name given to a thick close-fitting serge jacket worn by seamen on watch at night or in rough weather.

MISS THE BOAT, TO. To be late.

MOTHBALLS. Said of a ship in reserve. Such a ship is placed into a state of preservation by various means, usually with the machinery and armament 'cocooned' against moisture.

MOTHER CAREY'S CHICKENS. Stormy Petrels; small seabirds.

MUCKSTICK. Rifle (from musket).

MUDHOOK. Anchor.

MUNGY. Food. (From Fr. 'manger', to eat.)

MUSCLE BOSUN. Physical training instructor.

NEATERS. An undiluted mixture. A term from the days of the rum issue which was discontinued in 1972. Chief and petty officers were issued 'neaters' but junior rates were issued 'grog', i.e. one part rum to three parts water.

The rum ration for officers was abolished in 1881 and the only entitlement thereafter was on the order to splice the mainbrace.

Originally the navy's rum was obtained from Jamaica, later it became a blend of rums imported from Barbados, Demerara and Trinidad. In the victualling yards it was broken down by the addition of water, from its original 140 degrees over-proof to a strength of 95.5 degrees under proof before issue to ships.

NAV-O or NAVVY. The navigating officer.

NAZZER. Meat bone.

NELSON'S BLOOD. Rum. From the old story of how the body of Lord Nelson was brough back to England in a cask after the battle of Trafalgar. In fact the body was preserved in brandy, not rum.

NIGGERS IN THE SNOW. Prunes and rice.

NO BADGE A.B. An able seaman who has lost his long service and good conduct badges through misconduct.

NODDY SUIT. The NBC (Nuclear, Biological and Chemical) protective suit.

NO GREAT SHAKES. No great trouble.

NOO. Scotland.

NOR' EASTER. Not entitled (N.E.) for pay due to forfeiture for misconduct.

NOT MY PART OF SHIP. Not my responsibility or duty.

NOT ON MY SLOP CHIT. The same as 'not on my part of ship.'

NOT OUT OF THE EGG. Inexperienced.

NOZZERS. New entries; recruits. The term is said to have come from *HMS GANGES*, the boys training establishment at Shotley which closed in 1976. The boys under one instructor named Parker were known as 'Nosey's boys'.

NUKES. Nuclear submarines (ex US Navy term).

NUMBER ONE. The First Lieutenant.

NUMBER ONES. Best uniform with gold badges.

NUTS AND BOLTS. Stew with meat and vegetables.

NUTS AND BOLTS WITH AN AWNING. Steak and kidney pie.

NUTTY. Confectionery, whether or not it contains nuts.
O.D. An ordinary seaman.
OFF THE BEAM. Inaccurate.
OGGIN. The sea. From 'ogwash.
OLD HANDS. Experienced, long serving.
OLD MAN. The commanding officer.
OLD SHIPS. Sailors who have previously sailed together in the same ship.
ONE BADGEMAN. A hand with one long service and good conduct badge.
ONE EYED STEAK. A kipper.
ONE HAND FOR THE SHIP AND ONE FOR ONSELF. A naval motto, used generally when working in precarious position such as painting over the ship's side.
ON ONE'S JACK. Alone.
ON THE BOOKS. On a ship's or establishment's strength.
ON THE DOT. Punctual.
ON THE PUTTY. Aground.
ON THE RUN. Adrift from the ship; deserted.
To 'run' is a term dating back to the press gang days; no leave was ever given for fear of men 'running'.
ON THE STRENGTH. A member of the ship's company.
ON THE TROT. Successively, i.e. two watches on the trot.
ON YOUR SLOP CHIT. A threat that an article of service property lost or damaged will be paid for.
OOZUM BIRD. An unidentified bird.
OPPO. Friend.
OPPOSITE NUMBER. Someone having the same duties as oneself in the other watch.
OUTSIDE. Out of the navy.
OVER A BARREL. No way out of a predicament. From securing a man to a gun barrel for flogging.
OVER THE WALL. In detention quarters (naval prison).
OWNER. The commanding officer.
PANIC STATIONS. Ready for an emergency.
PAPER NAVY. Administrative branches.
PART BRASS RAGS, TO. To dissolve a friendship. See RAGGIES.
PART CABLE, TO. To die.
PARTY. Girl friend.
PASH. Love letter.

PASSED OVER. Overlooked for promotion.
PEA DOO. Pea soup.
PEA DOO MEDAL. Long service and good conduct medal which is awarded for 15 years service (or in slang terms 'for 15 years undetected crime'), first introduced in 1830. Pea doo, being slang for pea soup, is thus associated with decorations which are said to 'come up with the rations'.
PEEPERS. Eyes.
PERISHERS' COURSE. The submarine commanding officers qualifying course. The course was originally called the periscope school.
PICK. Anchor.
PICK UP ONE'S HOOK, TO. To become rated leading seaman. From the anchor in the badge.
PICTURISE, TO. To be put in the picture; to be informed.
PIER HEAD JUMP. Joining a ship just as she is about to sail.
PIGS. General term of disdain applied to officers by ratings.
PIG STICKER. Bayonet.
PILOT. The navigating officer.
PINK GIN. Gin and bitters.
PIT. Bed.
PLATE WASTE. Uneaten food on a plate.
PLENTY OF SHOTS LEFT IN HIS LOCKER. Plenty of arguments left to satisfy his case.
PLUM DUFF. Christmas pudding.
PLUMBER. Junior engineering officer.
PLUMBER PILOT. Test pilot.
POMPEY. Portsmouth Naval Base.
POND. The Atlantic Ocean.
PONGO. A soldier. After the mule on the North West Frontier.

There is an old naval saying: 'messmate before shipmate, shipmate before stranger, stranger before dog, dog before soldier. It originates from the 18th century when the soldier's lot was far worse than that of the sailor.

PORT AND STARBOARD OARS. Knives and forks. These did not become official issue for the lower deck until 1907; prior to this only spoons were supplied.
POSTIE. A rating in the ship's mail office.
POTMESS. A stew.

POTTED DOG. Steamed pudding.
PRACTICE FISH. A practice torpedo, fitted with a dummy warhead which 'blows' from compressed air at the end of its run in order to float for retrieval.
PRESS GANG SHOW. An officer ordered to represent his ship at a boring civil function.
PUSH THE BOAT OUT, TO. Stand a round of drinks.
PUSSAR. The equivalent of 'pukka' to denote superative correctness.
PUSSER. Entirely service minded. Pronunciation of purser, later paymaster and today supply officer.
PUSSER BUILT. One who always obtains his uniform requirements from 'pusser'. It also means one who sticks rigidly to the regulations at all times.
PUSSER SHIP. A smart disciplined ship.
PUSSER'S. Belonging to the navy.
PUSSER'S CRABS. Service issue boots.
PUSSER'S DIRK. The seaman's knife.
PUSSER'S GREY. Ship's side grey paint.
PUSSER'S HARD. Service issue soap.

Until 1810 the seaman did not see soap and after that date he had to pay for it.

PUSSER'S ISSUE. Service issue clothing, food, tobacco, etc.
PUSSER'S LOAF. Ship's bread.
PUSSER'S MEDAL. Food stain on clothes.
PUSSER'S WAGON. A warship.
PUT IN AN OAR, TO. To express an opinion.
PUTTY. Ship's painter. Also sea bed.
PYSOE. Said of one who is mean and tight-fisted. From the obsolete Scottish 'pyster', to hoard up.
QUEEN BEE. The senior WRNS officer.
QUIET NUMBER. An easy job.
QUICK BURN. A quick cigarette.
RABBIT RUN. A 'run' ashore to buy presents.
RABBITS. Presents. Also anything made on board with materials from service stores with the object of landing it for one's own use.

St. Mary's Island, reclaimed marshland, was purchased by the Admiralty for the Chatham dockyard extension programme which commenced in 1862. The island was inhabited by large colonies of rabbits, the removal of which was regarded as poaching. However, rabbits did find their way out of the dockyard concealed in kitbags and other luggage. See also TUCK ITS EARS IN.

RABBITTING. Talking.

RAGGIE. Friend. Formerly seamen provided their own cleaning gear and if two men shared their cleaning rags it was a sign of trust and friendship.

RAILINGS. False teeth.

RAISE THE WIND, TO. To raise money.

RANG A FEW BELLS. Stirred a few memories.

RATE OF KNOTS, A. Very fast.

RATED UP. Advanced or promoted.

RECOMMEND. Praise.

REAL RUB. The real problem.

RED DICK. Frankfurter sausage.

RED DUSTER. The Red Ensign worn by British merchant ships.

READ LEAD. Tomato sauce.

RHINO. Money.

RINGER. Officer, depending on rank; 'two ringer', 'two and a half ringer', etc.

ROCK, THE. Gibraltar.

ROCKING THE BOAT. Upsetting things.

ROCKET. Reprimand.

ROLL ON MY NINE. A remark made by someone wishing away his (service) time.

ROPED IN. Compelled to 'volunteer'.

ROSE GARDEN. Minefield.

ROUGHERS. Rough sea.

ROUND ROBIN. A joint complaint. The name originates from a document, signed by a number of individuals, which had the names radiating from the centre so that no name headed the list.

'Round robins' are against regulations. Any man having cause for complaint of injustice or illtreatment may obtain redresss by requesting, through the proper channels, 'to state a complaint'.

ROYAL. Used to address a Royal Marine whose name is not known.

ROYALS. Royal Marines.

RUB. Loan. This comes from the term 'rubbing out chalks' which meant paying debts. In sailing days, debts were chalked up on the bulkhead and when settled they were rubbed out.

RUB UP. Refresher course.

RUN ASHORE. Short leave, from either ship or shore establishment.

RUN IN. Placed on defaulters.

SAHA. Goodnight. From Maltese.

The RN once had a long association with Malta. Whilst under Napoleon's occupation, the island was captured by the British in 1799 and confirmed as under British rule by the Treaty of Paris in 1814. From that time RN ships used the Grand Harbour in Valetta as the headquarters of the Mediterranean Fleet. Upon the introduction of steam, dockyard facilities were built which were considerably enlarged in the early part of this century.

Malta suffered heavy air raids during the Second World War, 34 ships were sunk in the harbour alone, with all five dry docks out of action by 1942. For gallantry during this time the island was awarded the George Cross. After the war the dockyard was completely repaired and updated, but was transferred to private ownership in 1959. The island continued as a naval base until the Mediterranean command was abolished in 1967 and the station closed.

SAILING CLOSE TO THE WIND. Cutting it fine.

SANDSCRATCHER. A seaman rating (by other branch rates). This comes from the practice in days of old when seaman cleaned the wooden decks with sand and holystone.

SANDY BOTTOMS. Empty tea-pot.

SAWBONES. Surgeon.

SCATTERS. Diarrhoea.

SCHOOLIE. Education officer.

SCONCE. Head.

SCRAMBLED EGG. Reference to the gold oak leaves worn on the peaks of caps of officers of commander's rank and above.

SCRAN. Food.

SCRAN BAG. Said of an untidy person. The 'scran bag' is the 'bag', or other place, where lost items of clothing found 'sculling around' are collected.

SCRATCH. Captains secretary.

SCRIBE. Writer (clerical branch).

SCULLING AROUND. To wander about aimlessly, or loose gear rolling around with the movement of the ship.

SCUPPERED. Dead.

SEA BOOT FACE. Someone gloomy. With reference to the dull finish on the rubber boot.

SEA DADDY. An experienced seaman detailed to instruct young hands. Often applied to the officer in charge of midshipmen.

SEA LAWYER. One more given to questioning orders than readily obeying them.

SEA ROVERS. Herrings.

SEA TIME. Service afloat.

SEE OFF, TO. To cheat or defraud.

SENIOR. The senior engineer officer's second in command.

SET. A full beard and moustache, which is the only permitted 'growth'.

SHARP END. The bow of the ship.

SHAVE OFF. An exclamation of surprise.

SHEER OFF, TO. To depart.

SHERWOOD FOREST. The missile compartment in a Polaris submarine. The missiles are stowed upright in green painted launching tubes.

SHIP IT GREEN, TO. To run into trouble. Specifically to have the sea breaking over the foc'sle of a ship.

SHIP ONE'S SWAB, TO. To be promoted to sub-lieutenant from midshipman. With reference to removing the midshipmans' distinctive white patches from the jacket collar.

SHITEHAWKS. Gulls.

SHONKY. A mean messmate who will drink, but avoid paying his round.

SHOOTING A LINE. Telling a tall story.

SHOVE IN YOUR OAR, TO. To interrupt a conversation.

SICK BAY. Sick berth. In 1798, Admiral the Earl St. Vincent when C-in-C Mediterranean, ordered that a sick berth be prepared in each ship of the line. This was to be situated under the foc'sle with a roundhouse enclosed for the use of the sick. The rounded shape of the bow resembled the bay window of a room.

SICK BAY COCKTAIL. A dose of medicine.

SICK BAY GOOSE. Bedpan.

SICK BAY SHACKLE. Safety pin.

SICK BAY TIFFY. Medical assistant. 'Tiffy' from artificer.

SIN BOSUN. Chaplain.

SINKERS. Dumplings.

SINK IT, TO. To drink it.

SIPPERS. A sip. (From the days of the rum issue, see GULPERS).

SITTING ON A DRAFT CHIT. About to be drafted to another ship.

SKATE. One who is often 'in the rattle' or a shirker.

SKERS. Name for anyone bearded. (After part of the word 'whiskers').

SKIN. Good looking, usually a female.

SKIPPER. The commanding officer.

The master of a merchant ship is sometimes known as a skipper and always in the case of a fishing vessel. (Du. 'scipper' from 'scip', ship).

SKY ARTIST. Psychiatrist.

SKY HOOK. An imaginary hook which, if only it existed, would make a job easier. Used as the expression 'could do with a skyhook.'

SKYLARKING. Fooling around. In Victorian days 'skylarking' was a form of 'follow my leader' played up and about the rigging by junior officers. From the practice of young sailors who used to come down from the rigging by sliding down the stays. 'Lark' is a corruption of the Old English 'lac', to play.

Up to the beginning of the 20th century, on long voyages the pipe 'hands to dance and skylark' would be made to encourage dancing as a form of exercise. The hornpipe was particularly suitable for the cramped conditions because of the small space it required.

SKY PILOT. Chaplain.

SLAP IN FOR, TO. To make a request, e.g. for leave.

SLIDE. Butter.

SLIDE AND GLITTER. Marmalade on buttered toast.
SLIP ONE'S CABLE, TO. To die.

To 'slip the cable' is to allow a ship's anchor cable run out when there is not time to weigh the anchor.

SMACK IT ABOUT. Hurry up with the job.
SMALLEY. Small or little.
SMALLEY PORSH. Small portion.
SMIGGET. A good looking messmate.
SNAFU. A mix up. Abbreviation of 'situation normal and all fouled up'.
SNAKE PIT. A rough bar or place of entertainment.
SNAGS AND MASH. Sausages and mash.
SNORKERS. Sausages.
SNOTTY. A midshipman. From the allegation that the 'young gentlemen' used their sleeves instead of their handkerchiefs and that buttons once wore on the cuffs were placed there to discourage the practice.
SNOWBALL HITCH. A badly made bend or hitch that will not hold.
SOAKED. Severely punished.
SOAP AND FLANNEL. Bread and cheese.
SOD'S LAW. Unfortunate things that always happen at the worst time and in the wrong place.
SOD'S OPERA. Ship's concert, abbreviation of 'Ship's Own Dramatic Society'. Usually includes from rock groups to dancing girls, all drawn from officers and ratings aboard.
SOFT NUMBER. An easy job.
SOFT TACK. Bread.

At the turn of the century, Admiral John Fisher became Commander-in-Chief of the Mediterannean Fleet and was responsible for quite a number of improvements to the living conditions of his men. One of these was the substitution of fresh bread for the traditional ship's biscuit (known as 'hard tack') and had bakeries installed in some of the larger ships of the fleet. In 1904 Fisher became First Sea Lord and within a few years all large ships had bakeries as standard installations. (See also HARD TACK.)

SOFTERS. Soft soap.
SOLID. Said of someone stupid.

SOLDIERS. Wardroom slang for Royal Marines in the mess.
SPANKING ALONG. The ship steaming fast.
SPARKED OUT. Unconcious.
SPARKS. Communications rating.
SPIN A YARN, TO. To tell a story.
SPIN IT CLEAN OFF THE REEL, TO. To tell a yarn smartly.
SPITHEAD NIGHTINGALE. The boatswain's call.
SPITHEAD PHEASANT. A kipper.
SPLICED. Married.
SPRINGER. Physical training officer.
SPROG. An infant. (Not a recruit as the RAF slang.)
SPOTTED DOG. Currant or raisin pudding.
SPUN-YARD TRICK. An underhand trick.
SQUARE NUMBER. An easy duty or posting.
SQUARE ONE'S OWN YARDARM, TO. To put oneself in the right without regard for others.
SQUARE YARDS, TO. To agree with someone.
SQUEEGEE BAND. A band with improvised instruments, e.g. comb and paper, etc. (A squeegee is an implement used for clearing water from decks.
STAFFY. Staff officer.
STAG. Sentry duty.
STAID HAND. An experienced hand.
STARVED DOG. The appearance of a ship's side due to the shrinking of the steel plates between frames as they cool after welding.

The first all welded British warship was the minesweeper *SEAGULL*, launched at Devonport dockyard in 1937. Following on from this, towards the end of the Second World War the Admiralty decided to use welded, in place of riveted, hull construction for destroyers, and ultimately to introduce all-welded ships of all types.

STEAM, TO. To work at high pressure.
STICKY BUN. Not necessarily a 'sticky' bun, but generally any form of individual cake or pastry.
STOKES. Engineering rating. From the old title of 'stoker' during the days of coal fired boilers, itself still used as a generic term for engineering ratings.
STONE FRIGATE. Barracks or shore establishment.

It was not until the later 19th century that barracks for the Royal Navy were built. Up to that time hulks were used to provide accommodation. When the new barracks were built they were known as 'stone frigates' and are still so called today.

STOP A BOTTLE, TO. To receive a reprimand. See also BOTTLE.

STOP CACKLING. An order to 'pipe down' in the ranks.

STOW IT. Shut up.

STRAIGHT OFF THE HORNS. Tough meat.

STRANGLE A BARON, TO. To accept hospitality.

STRIKE IT DOWN, TO. To drink heavily.

STRIPEY. Name for a three-badgeman, i.e., one who has three long service and good conduct badges.

STRONGERS. Any strong mixture such as cleaning water, etc.

STROPPY. Obstreporous, trouble making.

SUB, TO. To substitute for another's duty.

SUBBIE. Sub-lieutenant.

SUCK A FISH'S TIT, TO. To attempt the impossible.

SURFACE, TO. To wake up.

SWAB. A useless individual.

SWAIN. Coxswain.

SWALLOW THE ANCHOR, TO. To leave the service.

SWEATING NEATERS. Worried.

SWEEPERS. Minesweepers.

SWINDLE SHEET. Expenses sheet.

SWING ROUND THE BUOY, TO. To hold on to a 'soft number'. Indicative of a ship having an easy time in harbour swinging round the buoy.

SWING THE HOOK, TO. To be idle.

SWISH DISH. An attractive girl.

TABLE MONEY. An allowance to flag officers for the upkeep of their personal mess.

TAKE AN EVEN STRAIN, TO. Not to jump to conclusions without thinking.

TAILOR MADES. Commercially manufactured cigarettes.

TAKEN AFT. Taken before the officer of the watch as a defaulter which, in harbour, would be aft to the quarterdeck.

TAKE IN TOW, TO. To pick up a girl.

TAKE ON BOARD, TO. To understand; to comprehend.
TAKE THE HOOK, TO. Accept promotion to leading seaman. See HOOKEY.
TANKY. A Seaman who helps 'Jack Dusty' with daily issues. From his original connection with the old-time master who in sailing ships was responsible for the storage of the hold, including the beer and fresh water casks.
TAP UP, TO. To ask someone for a loan.
TAR. Sailor. From the 19th century sailors who wore black shiny hats believed to have been painted with tar.
TATTIE OGGIE. Cornish pasty.
TAUT HAND. A good sailor; efficient, smart.
TAUT SHIP. A well disciplined and efficient ship.
TEA BOAT. Tea pot or trolley.
TEA LEAF. Thief. Ex cockney rhyming slang.
TEA'S WET. The tea is ready.
TEETH AWASH. Drunk.
TEL. Communication rating. From Telegraphist.
THICKERS. Strong tea.
THREE BADGEMAN. A rating with three long service and good conduct badges.
TICKLERS. Tinned tobacco and cigarettes rolled from it. In 1908 when jam became an official issue item to the RN, it was supplied by a London firm called Tickler and company. At that time a new short service engagement was introduced, in order to provide a fleet reserve; for men to serve for seven years active service and five in the reserve. Old timers suggested that the new short service men could not be expected to eat proper sailors' food and that the new jam issue was obviously intended for them. Both the jam and the new men became known at 'ticklers'. Shortly afterwards, tinned tobacco became available for those who wanted it instead of leaf tobacco. Again, the old hands said that the fancy tobacco was only for the 'ticklers' and so it was called 'ticklers' tobacco.
TIDDY OGGIE. Cornish pasty.
TIDDLY. Anything smart, e.g. 'tiddly' suit. From tidily.
TIED UP. Married.
TIFFY. Artificer. Also for any assistant, e.g. sick bay tiffy.
TIN FISH. Torpedo.
TIT. Any operating button.

TOMBOLA. Bingo.
TOMBSTONE. Mess menu.
TONSIL SNATCHER. Medical officer.
TONSIL VARNISH. Tea.
TOOTH PICK. Officer's sword.
TOOTHY. Dental officer.
TOUCH ONE IN THE BUNT, TO. To remind someone forcibly of something.
TOWNIE. Someone from the same home town. Addressed as 'towns.'
TRADE. The submarine service.
TRAIN SMASH. Tinned tomatoes.
TROOP, TO. To take someone before the Officer-of-the-Watch as a defaulter.
TROOPS. A wardroom term for ratings.
TROT BOAT. A duty boat plying between ship and shore.
TROUGH. Dining table.
TRUNKY. Electrical artificer. From the trunking in a ship housing electrical wires.
TUCK ITS EARS IN. Heard when going on leave with a bulging suitcase. See RABBITS.
TURKEYS. Royal Marines. From the red tunic worn by the Royal Marine Light Infantry before amalgamation with the Royal Marine Artillery in 1923 to form 'The Royal Marines'.
TURN IN, TO. Go to bed.
TURN TURTLE, TO. For a ship or a boat to capsize.
TWO BADGEMAN. A rating with two long service and good conduct bades.
TWO BLOCKS. Completely dissatisfied with conditions. From two blocks on a tackle coming together.
UCK. To remove something. See UCKERS.
UCKERS. A form of ludo, popular in the navy for many year's, with the object of 'hucking' the opponents' counters from the board instead of the usual progress to base.

'Hucking' is an old navy term which, in the wooden ship days, meant to scrub the barnacles off the bottom whilst in graving dock.

ULLAGE. Useless. Originally the residue left in a cask or barrel.
UNDERGROUND PHEASANT or MUTTON. Rabbit.

UNDER YOUR LEE. Under your protection.
UNHOOK, TO. To borrow something without the owner's permission.
UP HOMERS. Homely hospitality given to men away from home.
UP THE LINE. Home on leave.
UP THE SMOKE. In London.
URK. A rating always in trouble.
VARNISH. Tea.
VICARAGE. Chaplain's cabin.
VICTUALLED UP. Plenty of food and drink.
VIOLETS. Onions.
WALEY. Whale Island at Portsmouth, originally the Gunnery School HMS EXCELLENT and now known as NELSON (Whale Island).

The island was in fact once two small islands, called on the chart 'Waley', which the Admiralty bought in 1853. The land between the two islands was reclaimed and the whole extended to become known as 'Whale Island'.

WALLABIES. Australians.
WALLAH. The operator of a small unofficial shop or stand.
WARM THE BELL, TO. To be early, e.g. to relieve the watch. In the days when time was measured on board ship by a half-hour sandglass, it was believed that if the glass was warmed then the neck would expand and allow the sand to run through faster, thus making the watch pass more quickly.
WASHING. Signal flags.
WASH OUT, TO. To countermand an order or instruction. This comes from the days when signalmen recorded messages on a slate and 'washed them out' before recording new ones.
WATER BEWITCHED. Weak tea.
WATERLINE. Waistline.
WATERLOGGED. Drunk.
WEIGHED OFF. Punished or reprimanded.
WET. A drink.
WET AS A SCRUBBER. Simple.
WET ONE'S STRIPES, TO. For a newly promoted officer to stand a round of drinks in the wardroom.

WET THE PLUE, TO. Make the tea.
WHALES. Sardines.
WHEATIES. Breakfast cereals.
WHITE HORSES. Foam on wave crests.
WHITE FRONT. The uniform white flannel vest.
WHITE RAT. A sneak and a tell-tale.
WINDY HAMMER. Pneumatic riveter or paint stripper.
WINGS. The Commander (Air) in an aircraft carrier or air station.
WINGER. Usually used to refer to the younger of two close friends. Addressed as 'wings'. Originally it referred to a young seaman or boy who had been under the care ('wing') of an old seaman who 'showed him the ropes' and looked after him ashore and aboard as far as possible.
WITH A CLEW UP. Dead.
WOOLEY PULLEY. The service issue navy blue heavy wool jersey.
WORK YOUR TICKET, TO. To deliberately disobey the regulations in an attempt to obtain a discharge from the service.
WORMS IN READ LEAD. Spaghetti in tomato sauce.
WRAP UP, TO. To finish.
WRENNERY. WRNS quarters.
WRINKLE. A smart way of doing something, or perhaps of dodging it.
WRITE ONE'S NAME ASTERN, TO. To steer an eratic course.
YAFFLE, TO. To eat.
YELLOW JACK. The 'Q' for quarantine flag, which is plain yellow, flown by all vessels with infectious disease aboard. This is also the term for yellow fever.
YELLOW PERIL. Smoked haddock.
ZIZZ. Sleep. From the speech balloon in comic cartoons.
ZIZZ PUDDING. A heavy suet pudding.
ZULU TIME. Greenwich mean time.

23

THE LANGUAGE OF THE SEA ASHORE

As a child, I can remember hearing the expressions 'let the cat out of the bag' and 'no room to swing a cat'. At the time, visualising a poor animal being bagged or swung around by its tail seemed to me to be very strange and cruel ideas. Both sayings come from days gone by which were indeed cruel, but have nothing to do with the domestic tom; they refer to the cat-o'-nine-tails, once used to administer floggings in the fleet.

Because of our country's great maritime heritage, nautical words and expressions colour our language. The meanings of many are obvious; we 'shove our oar in', 'rest on our oars', 'swim with the tide' and can either 'miss, 'rock' or be 'in the same boat'. When the business is 'on the rocks', it is 'all hands to the pumps' and with a new man 'at the helm' the company 'weathers the storm'. However, there are a good many sea terms which have become colloquial expressions, the original meanings of which have become forgotten with the passage of time. For example, we use an Old English term for the deck of a ship when we 'board' a bus or train.

The following collection has been researched and brought together with the hope that the reader may be enlightened, indeed perhaps surprised, with the nautical connections. Quite a number come from different eras of the Royal Navy's history, giving some interesting glimpses of our naval past. Others are from the Merchant Service, while some were once common to all seafarers. Many originate from the days of sail; working terms which, by the early part of this century had all but disappeared, but seem assured to live on into the future as part of our language.

* * *

A1. First class.

In Lloyd's register of shipping, A1 was the mark of a wooden ship of the first class. 'A' referred to the quality of her hull and '1' to the quality of her equipment. Incidentally, 'Lloyd's', the headquarters of the London underwriters and insurance brokers, is so called from Lloyd's coffee house which was their original meeting place.

ALL AT SEA, TO BE. To be completely confused.

This refers to the complexity of seamanship and navigation, with the suggestion that a landlubber put to sea would find life difficult.

ALL FAIR AND ABOVE BOARD. Utterly fair and nothing hidden.

'Board' was an old term for the upper deck of a ship, from the Old English 'bord' meaning table. Things 'above Board' were on or above the upper deck and so open for all to see. (See also GO OVERBOARD and GONE BY THE BOARD).

ALL IN THE WIND. In the lap of the gods.

This is the term for a sailing vessel when she is going about and is head to wind with all sails shivering.

ALL MY EYE AND BETTY MARTIN. Without foundation or fact. The story of the origin of this saying possibly is 'all my eye'. It goes as follows:

A sailor once entered a church where a service was in progress and sat next to a lady who was praying out loud. Afterwards, when asked how he had enjoyed the service, he remarked that it had been all nonsense; for the lady alongside him had said it was 'all me eye and Betty Martin'. What the lady had really said was 'A mihi, Beate Martin' ('Oh help me, blessed Martin'.)

ALOOF, TO BE. To be at a distance, though within view; keeping away from.

Originally, to sail as close to the wind as possible. To 'stand aloof' was to keep to windward of another vessel. (Du. 'loef', windward.)

ANCHOR, TO. Used ashore, the term means to secure something firmly, for example, 'anchor' points for car seat belts.

In its original form, to anchor is to hold a ship fast in the water by grappling the bottom with an anchor.

AS BOLD AS BRASS. A brash character.

Originally an old naval term, from the brightwork on board a ship which is really only for show.

AT LARGE. Not under constraint.

From the sailing term, which means sailing free with the wind abaft the beam.

BARGEPOLE. As in the expression 'wouldn't touch it with a bargepole'.

This is from the long heavy pole, iron shod and used aboard barges for fending off from other vessels and obstructions.

BARGE, TO. To move heavily or clumsily.

From the slow, heavy movement of a barge.

BEAM ENDS, TO BE ON ONE'S. To be in extreme embarrassment or in a precarious position.

A ship is said to be on her beam ends when she is lying over on her side with her beam and decks perpendicular.

BEAR DOWN, TO. To apply pressure.

The term once meant to sail toward an enemy, or another ship, rapidly from windward.

BEAR UP, TO. To keep one's spirits up.

A sailing expression meaning to bear the tiller to windward in order to keep the vessel's head away from the wind, accepting an easier course to leeward.

BEDLAM. A place of uproar.

At the beginning of the 19th century, one in a thousand men were being discharged from the navy as insane. This figure, compared with one in seven thousand in the whole country, was high due to several reasons. A regular half pint of rum per day, frequent floggings and continual knocks from heavy gear, all contributed. Such was the problem that the navy had it's own lunatic asylum, the Bethlehem Royal Hospital in Moorfield, London, commonly known as 'Bedlam'. Today this old hospital houses the Imperial War Museum.

BETWEEN THE DEVIL AND THE DEEP BLUE SEA. No choice.

In wooden ships the 'devil' was a seam between the hull timbers near the keel. To be working between this and the waterline was to be in a precarious position. (See also DEVIL TO PAY.)

BETWIXT WIND AND WATER. In a dangerous situation.

The part of a sailing ship 'betwixt (between) wind and water' was that below the waterline which was exposed when the ship heeled over under the pressure of the wind. There was, of course, great danger if a shot struck there.

BILGE. A term sometime used to describe oratory rubbish.

The bilge is the part of the bottom of a ship, either side of the keel, which meets the sides. Being the lowest part of the hull, it is where any waste water collects.

BITTER END. The limit.

In sailing ships, the 'bitts' were wooden centre-line bollards to which the anchor cable and certain ropes were belayed. When they were run out almost to the limit, they were said to be nearing the 'bitter end'. (Bitt from ON. 'biti', beam.)

BLACK LIST, ON THE. To be remembered for one's misdemeanours.

To be 'on the black list' was a form of punishment in the Royal Navy during the 19th century, which entailed waking earlier than the rest of the ship's company and working after 'pipe down' at night. Meals had to be taken on the upper deck under the eye of a sentry and work had to be carried out during proper mealtimes. This punishment was later modified to become 'number 10A'.

BLAZER. The name for a coloured jacket.

Before the days of authorised uniform for ratings of the Royal Navy, a few ship's captains dressed some of their crews in special 'rigs' for prestige purposes. The captain of *HMS BLAZER* (Captain J. W. Washington, RN) had his boat's crew dressed in blue and white striped guernseys.

BLOOD IS THICKER THAN WATER. Said when helping for fellowship's sake.

In 1859 Britain and France were at war with China and on 25th June a force of small British gunboats, under the command of Rear Admiral Hope, was attacking the powerful Peiho forts. Booms across the river proved impassable and the boats came under heavy fire. After several hours, not enough men remained to man the guns and those that were left were exhausted.

The senior American naval officer present was Commodore Josiah Tattnall from Georgia who, in his younger days, had fought the British in the War of 1812. Although a neutral, he decided to go in to offer help to bring out the wounded. In doing so, his boat also came under fire and his coxswain was wounded, but he managed to get alongside Hope's flagboat and went on board. Hope gratefully accepted the offer and his thanks to Tattnall was replied to with the words 'blood is thicker than water'.

Tattnall returned down river for a steamboat which he used to tow boats carrying wounded to safety. Hope, although wounded himself, remained to direct the battle to the end, but eventually the attack had to be called off. The Royal Navy did not forget this act of kindness. Some years later, having fought as a Confederate in the American Civil War, Tattnall fell on hard times and a fund for him was subscribed to by British naval officers.

BLOOD MONEY. Reward money.

During the 19th century this was the term for the £20 which the Admiralty paid to the officers and men of the Coastguard Service for each smuggler captured and convicted. Also known as 'blood money' was the £5 per head paid by the Admiralty to the crew of a ship for the sinking of an enemy vessel.

BLOWER. Telephone.

This comes from the voice pipes once used for communication within a ship. The cover would be removed and the caller would blow down it to attract the attention of the person at the other end.

BLOW THE GAFF, TO. To divulge information.

A gaff is a short spar which rides on the afterside of a mast and which carries the ensign halyards. The saying comes from the practice of a ship identifying herself by hoisting her ensign at the peak of the gaff.

BORN WITH A SILVER SPOON. Indicative of a well-off person.

This was an old naval saying to indicate the 'young gentlemen' who, through birth or connection, were able to enter the Royal Navy without examination, being assured promotion. They were also said to have entered the navy 'through the cabin windows'. Those less fortunate entered 'through the hawseholes' and, promoted by merit, were said to have been 'born with a wooden ladle.'

BOWING AND SCRAPING. Bowing to authority.

'Scraper' was the nickname given to the naval officer's cocked hat when this was part of full dress. 'Bowing and scraping' was the term for the removal of headgear as a mark of respect.

BRACE OF SHAKES, A. Quickly, almost immediately.

An old sailing term which denoted a moment of time which could be measured by the shaking of a sail as a ship came into the wind.

BREAK THE BACK, TO. To master something.

A saying which comes from the expression 'to break the back' of a ship, meaning to break the keel.

BULLY BEEF. A slang name for tinned corned beef.

The process for the canning of meat was invented by Nicholas Appert, a French chef, being called 'boeuf boulli.' Marketed under this name in England by the firm of Donkin and Hall, it was tried out experimentally in RN ships on the East and West Indies stations in 1813. It eventually became a standard item in the navy's ration scale as a substitute for salt beef on one day a week.

BURN ONE'S BOATS, TO. To act irrevocably, leaving no means of retreat.

The crew of a ship in danger with no boats would obviously have no means of escape.

BY AND LARGE. Meaning 'on the whole' or 'all things considered'.

'By' and 'large' were sailing terms. 'By' meant 'close hauled' which is the set of the sails when 'beating' to windward. 'Large' meant 'running free' with the wind astern. 'By and large' was sailing under any condition of wind.

CAP IN HAND. Subservient.

Derived from the 19th century salute to an officer by the removal of the hat.

CHANGE TACK, TO. To try a different idea for doing something from the one currently in progress.

To change tack is for a sailing vessel to change on to a different course when working to windward.

CHEESCUTTER. The name for a cloth cap, where the front of the top is sewn down to the peak.

Originally the slang name for a naval officer's peaked cap.

CHOCK-A-BLOCK. Filled to capacity.

A term for the state of a tackle when the moving and standing blocks are hauled close together. Originally it was 'block and block.'

CLEAN BILL OF HEALTH, A. Used to describe state of health following a medical examination.

A 'bill of health' is a certificate issued by a consul or port authority. It certifies that a ship is sailing from a place where there is no contagious disease and that none of her crew, at the time of her departure, were infected with such a disease. This constitutes a clean bill of health. A foul bill of health indicates disease in the port or among the crew.

CLEAN SLATE, A. Meaning that the past is forgotten and a new start may be made.

The expression comes from the days when a slate was used in order to record courses steered and distances run during a watch at sea. At the end of the watch, the details were transferred to the deck log and the slate wiped clean.

CLEAR OFF, TO. To go away.

An old nautical term meaning to depart.

CLINCH. To seal a contract.

Originates from the fastening of heavy lines to objects to secure them. It was also the term for turning over the ends of copper nails to secure planking to the frame of boat.

CLOSE QUARTERS, AT. Close or near to.

'Close quarters' were barriers of wood erected across the decks of sailing merchant ships through which to fire muskets. These were necessary to repel boarders from enemy privateers.

COCKPIT. Usually known as the control position of an aircraft.

In sailing ships of war this was a part of the lower deck which was used as a hospital in action. (Ashore, it was an enclosed area where game cocks fought.)

COME DOWN A PEG, TO. To lose credit in a person's estimation or, to reduce one's demands in what one is charging, asking or expecting.

From the old practice of rendering honours to a person by hoisting a ship's flag. This was done by pegs which were raised according to the rank of the person to be honoured. These could be lowered if it was found that they had been raised too high.

CON, TO. To lead someone into an action.

To 'con' is to direct a vessel by giving specific orders to the helmsman. (Fr. 'conduire', to guide.)

CRACK ON, TO. To pretend.

A term from sailing days when, to give the enemy the impression that a ship was fast, more sails were set.

CRAFT. As in 'aircraft' and 'spacecraft'.

'Craft' is the term for all small vessels, but in Old English it meant skills and wisdom. In Middle English it was applied to particular skills, among seamen it was skill in handling boats. By a curious sidestep the word later came to mean the boats themselves. Now it has soared into the sky and further.

CUT AND RUN, TO. To escape.

In the days of sail, in an emergency, the hemp cable attached to the ship's anchor was cut in order to get to sea quickly. The Spanish Armada 'cut and ran' when they were threatened by fireships in Calais Roads. It originated with the method used by square rigged ships to get under way speedily, which entailed stopping furled sails with rope yarns which could be cut quickly to let the sails fall.

CUT LITTLE ICE, TO. To make little impression.

Wooden ships could make little progress in pack ice.

CUT OF ONE'S JIB, THE. The description of a person's appearance.

A sailing ship's nationality could be told at a distance by the cut of her sails. A ship was often identified by her jibs. These were triangular sails carried in front of her foremast, which varied in size and number.

DECK. One speaks of a top 'deck' of a bus. Also used as a verb meaning to array or decorate.

A deck was originally the platform covering the whole or part of a ship's hull, but now refers to all horizontal 'floors' in a ship. (Du. 'dek', roof or covering.)

DEVIL TO PAY, THE. Something awkward or difficult.

In wooden sailing ships, the seams between the hull timbers were caulked (filled) with oakum (old rope fibre) and then filled with pitch. This operation was known as 'to pay' (from the French 'poix', meaning pitch). The upper outboard strake, or the garboard seam nearest the keel, was referred to as the 'devil' by the caulkers. There was very little space to reach this seam with a caulking iron, making it a difficult one 'to pay'.

The seam was also the most difficult to keep above the water to caulk when a ship was 'careened.' 'Careening' was the operation of turning a ship over on to her side, by hauling down on the masts with ropes to expose her bottom.

DOGSBODY. A general assistant.

Once naval slang for a junior officer.

DOUBLE DIAMOND. A well known beverage.

A double diamond is an old nautical decorative knot, usually made on the bight of a rope.

DRAW THE LINE, TO. To set a limit.

An old naval expression, particularly with regard to conduct.

DRUNK AS A LORD. See PICKLED.

EDGE AWAY, TO. To gradually move away from someone or something.

An old nautical term meaning to increase the distance gradually from a coast or other object.

EVERY MAN JACK. Everyone included.

'Man jack' was once a Merchant Navy term for seamen as distinct from ship's boys.

FAG END. Cigarette end.

This was originally the piece remaining in a ship when a rope carried away (snapped).

FIGUREHEAD. A person at the head of an organisation.

At one time ships of the Royal Navy had carved busts or full length 'figures' mounted in the 'head' or bow.

FIRST RATE. Of the highest excellence.

This comes from the division of naval ships into six 'rates', according to the number of guns they carried, which was introduced by Anson when he was First Lord of the Admiralty in the 1750's. The most powerful ships, with three decks of cannon, were the first rates with 100 guns or more (like *HMS VICTORY*) and the second rates with between 90 and 98 guns. These first and second rates were fairly rare and were often used as flagships of senior officers. The third rates, with between 64 and 68 guns and usually two deckers, were the work horses of the fleet.

First, second and third rates were considered powerful enough to lie in he forefront of battle and were therefore known as 'ships of the line'. Among the lesser rates was the frigate, used as fast escort, scout or messenger and armed with between 28 and 40 cannon.

FLASH IN THE PAN. To make a short lived impression.

Originally it was the powder in the firing pan of a flintlock gun failing to ignite the charge in the chamber.

FLEET, A. Often used as a collective term for buses, taxis, lorries, etc.

A fleet is a navy or a squadron of ships. The Royal Navy for instance, consisting of officers, men, ships and shore establishment, is known under the general term of 'The Fleet'. (OE. 'fleot', a number of ships.)

FLOGGING (OR WORKING) A DEAD HORSE. Doing something for nothing.

A 'dead horse' was once a slang term which referred to the advance of pay given to seamen, before the start of a voyage, with which they could purchase clothing, etc. required for the trip. 'Working a dead horse' meant working for the first month without pay, because that had already been drawn and spent. At the end of the first month, it was at one time customary to hoist a canvas effigy of a horse up into the rigging.

FLOTSAM. Sometimes used to describe a person as floating, in a derogatory sense.

It is actually the floating wreckage of a ship or cargo. (OF. 'flotaisson', a flooding.)

FLYING SQUAD. A special unit within the Metropolitan Police used to deal with extraordinary and special emergencies.

The Royal Navy created a 'Flying Squadron' in 1870 which was sent on a world wide deployment lasting two years, mainly engaged in duties of 'showing the flag'.

FORGE AHEAD, TO. To progress with strength.

An old sailing term, which meant to move ahead rapidly under 'press of canvas' (all sails set and drawing well).

FREEZE THE BALLS OFF A BRASS MONKEY. Extremely cold.

This is a corruption of the 17th century term 'freeze the balls of a brass monkey'. A 'monkey' was a brass cannon and in freezing temperatures the iron cannon balls and the brass cannon shrank at different rates, making the cannon inoperable.

FREIGHT. Transported goods.

The word comes from the Old French 'fret', meaning a ship's cargo.

GASKET. The packing used for sealing the glands in engines and pumps.

Originally, 'gasket' was the name for a flat plaited cord which was fastened to a ship's yard and used to furl or tie the sails to the yard. Early steam engines and pumps used plaited hemp for packing. (From the F. 'garcette', cat o' nine tails.)

GET DOWN TO BRASS TACKS, TO. To get down to the basics of a problem.

Originally a Merchant Navy term, from the brass tacks which were used to secure linoleum down to the decks.

GET THE WIND UP, TO. To be frightened.

Whistling on board ship has for centuries been considered by sailors to be unlucky. In days gone by a superstition existed that, because of its likeness to the sound of the wind, to 'whistle down the wind' would actually raise it, thereby causing gales and possible shipwreck.

GET TO GRIPS, TO. To tackle a problem.

This originlly was the term for approaching close to an enemy ship.

GET YOUR FINGER OUT. Hurry.

This was once the order given to a gunner to remove his finger from the venthole of a muzzle loading canon whilst it was being loaded. The hole was sealed by this method to prevent gas in the gun chamber mixing with air and igniting.

GIVE A WIDE BERTH, TO. To avoid, or to keep well clear of, someone or something.

A maritime term used to indicate a clearance of danger.

GIVE WAY, TO. To yield, as in road traffic.

'Way is the movement of a ship through the water. A ship 'gives way' to another according to the 'Rules of the Road'.

GLAD RAGS. Best clothes.

A mid 19th century term for seamen. At that time they went ashore dressed in brightly coloured clothes.

GO ON STRIKE, TO. To withdraw labour.

In the 18th century, seamen occasionally revolted against harsh conditions by lowering, i.e. 'striking', a ship's sails. Thus they went on 'strike'.

GO OVERBOARD, TO. To be enthusiastic about something.

Overboard means to have gone 'over the board', that is over the deck and into the sea. (See also ALL FAIR AND ABOVE BOARD and GONE BY THE BOARD.)

GO WITH THE STREAM, TO. To do as people around one do.

As a vessel going with the tidal stream.

GOING GREAT GUNS. Going strong, going well.

This comes from 'blowing great guns and small arms', an old maritime term for a heavy gale or a hurricane.

GONE BY THE BOARD. A chance missed or an item lost.

'By the board' was a term meaning close to the deck. When a mast was broken off close to the deck level, it was said to have gone by the board. (See also ALL FAIR AND ABOVE BOARD and GO OVERBOARD.)

GROGGY. Tipsy; moving uneasily.

From 'grog', the name for the rum which was once issued daily to the men of the Royal Navy. So called from the nickname 'Old Grog' of Admiral Vernon from his wearing a grogram cloak. About 1745 he ordered that the hitherto neat rum issued to his men be diluted with water.

HALF SEAS OVER. A semi-drunken state.

A maritime term of the same meaning.

HARD TO FATHOM. Difficult to understand.

Derived from the difficulty to taking soundings in deep water. A fathom is a nautical measure of six feet, used before metrification for measuring the depth of water.

HARD UP. Financially embarrassed.

From the 19th century seamens' term 'hard up in a clinch and no knife to cut the seizing', which meant being in trouble with no means of extricating oneself.

HARING ALONG. Moving at great speed.

This was once the term for a fully rigged sailing ship making speed with all sails set.

IN HIS BEST BIB AND TUCKER. Smartly dressed.

Originally a naval term for a sailor in his best uniform.

IN THE DOLDRUMS. Depressed.

The doldrums is an area of low pressure near the equator between the trade winds, having calms and light variable winds alternating with squalls, heavy rains and thunderstorms.

IN THE OFFING. Something which is attainable; in sight.

Offing is the distance a ship keeps away from the shore to avoid hazards, i.e. within sight of land.

IN THE RED. In debt or overdrawn.

This was originally a naval slang expression which meant to be in debt to the crown, as debtor balances were recorded in the naval pay ledger in red ink.

IN THE WAKE OF. Following immediately behind.

A wake is the name of the track which a ship leaves when under way, formed by the meeting of the water behind. Wake is an old Norse word, meaning a track through the ice.

JACK KNIFE. A clasp knife.

Originates from the name of the large clasp knife with a horn handle once carried by seamen. 'Jack' is an old term for a sailor.

JACK OF ALL TRADES. Someone who can turn their hand to anything.

An old term for an able seaman who was 'able' to carry out any task in the ship.

JUNK. Rubbish.

Junk was the name given to pieces of old rope used for making mats, fenders, oakum for filling the seams of ships, etc. It was also the term applied to the salt beef issued, because of its resemblance to old rope.

KEEP A WEATHER EYE OPEN, TO. To keep a close watch or observation.

This comes from the nautical expression 'to keep one's weather eye lifting', meaning to keep one's eye looking in the direction of the wind from which the changes in the weather come.

KNOCK THE GILT OFF THE GINGERBREAD, TO. To disillusion.

Much of the cost of building warships was once met by the King and at that time it was customary for the builder to include a great deal of ornamentation. The stern and quarter galleries were elaborately carved and gilded, being described by the seamen as 'gingerbread work'. Damage to these parts in battle was termed as 'knocking the gilt off the gingerbread'.

KNOW THE ROPES, TO. To know the method or way of doing things.

Originally a nautical expression meaning to know the methods of seamanship.

LAID UP. Sick in bed.

From the 'laying up' of a ship out of commission, in reserve.

LEG. As in 'leg' of a journey, meaning section or stage.

A 'leg' was the distance a sailing vessel sailed on a single tack.

LET THE CAT OUT OF THE BAG, TO. To divulge a secret.

The expression comes from the days when floggings were administered in the navy and refers to the cat-o'-nine-tails which was kept in a red baise bag. The 'cat' was not removed from the bag until the offender was secured to the gratings, thus beyond the possibility of a reprieve. (See also NO ROOM TO SWING A CAT.)

LIMEYS. An American slang name for the British.

Originally this was the American slang name for British seamen, because of the regulation lime-juice they had to drink in an attempt to combat scurvy. The medical profession had long been baffled by the fact that some ship's companies were attacked by scurvy, whilst others were not. Probably because of the confusion between lemon-juice which was the most effective preventative, and lime-juice which contained only half the ascorbic acid of the lemon. Also, lemons had gradually been replaced by limes which the navy could obtain plentifully in the West Indies.

So it continued, until at the end of the last century the best opinion held that there was no effective anti-scorbutic. Polar expeditions of the time, including Scott's to the Antarctic, suffered badly. It was not until 1917 that the specific anti-scorbutic vitamin C was isolated. Lime juice was replaced by vitamin pills in the Royal Navy in the 1930's.

LOG BOOK. An official diary of events.

From the book of the same name which contains the official record of the daily events of a ship's voyage. So called from the old method of measuring speed through the water, by the use of a log attached to a line, thrown overboard at the bows and timed for its arrival at the stern. Speed and other data such as time, wind, etc. were written to a 'log board' for subsequent transcription into the log book.

LOGGERHEADS, TO BE AT. To quarrel.

The expression comes from the instrument once used for heating pitch for 'paying' the seams of ships. This was made up of two large iron spheres, one each end of an iron bar. One of the spheres was heated and then placed into the pitch bucket to melt the pitch. A hot loggerhead was a thing to keep away from.

LONG SHOT. A decision made on long odds or risks.

From the firing of a gun at extreme range and hoping to score a hit.

LOOPHOLE. A way or means of escape.

Originally a hole in the bulkhead of a ship or in a wall through which small arms were discharged.

MAINSTAY. Chief support.

In a sailing ship this was a rope to stay the mainmast. It was the largest and most important stay in a ship (HMS VICTORY's was 19 inches in circumference) and was usually a four-stranded cable-laid rope.

MAKE A HASH OF IT, TO. To make a mess of a task.

This is a naval term which comes from 'hash', which was the name for left-overs cooked in another dish.

MAKE HEADWAY, TO. To progress.

'Headway' is the term applied to the ahead movement of a ship under way through the water.

MAKE UP LEEWAY, TO. To make up a deficiency.

A nautical expression meaning to make good the amount of deviation of a ship in lateral drift to leeward (the direction towards which the wind blows).

MONEY FOR OLD ROPE. Something gained for little or nothing.

Old rope was once sold to dealers for the manufacture of paper boards.

MOONLIGHTER. One who has more than one job.

This was originally a smuggler who landed his goods at night.

NAVY BLUE. The recognised name for a particular shade of dark blue.

The colour of dark blue for naval uniform was chosen by George II, supposedly after admiring the riding habit of that colour worn by the Duchess of Bedford.

NIPPERS. A slang term for children.

Until the 19th century, the hemp anchor cable was worked on the main deck of a ship but, because of its thickness and weight, was unsuitable to be worked around the capstan direct. A smaller, endless rope, called a 'messenger', was passed around the capstan and led forward by blocks in line with the cable. The messenger was bound to the anchor cable by short lengths of rope called 'nippers', thus enabling the cable to be hove in as the capstan turned. Boys, or men, also called nippers, put on the rope nippers at the hawsehole, walked aft with the cable until it reached the hatch, then took off the nippers to run forward to bind the cable again.

NO ROOM TO SWING A CAT. An expression to describe a cramped space.

This refers to the cat–o'–nine–tails, once used in the navy to administer floggings. In 1871 flogging in the Royal Navy was suspended in peacetime and in 1879 suspended in wartime; it is still only suspended, not abolished!

NO SHOT IN THE LOCKER. All money is spent.

This comes from sailing days, when ammunition aboard warships was stowed in lockers. Once the lockers were empty of shot, a ship could no longer fight.

NOSEY PARKER. One who interferes with others' affairs.

In 1797 two large scale mutinies took place in the Royal Navy, due to dissatisfaction among seamen with regard to the grimness of naval life. The first, at Spithead, was a peaceable affair led by reasonable men; Earl Howe was sent to Portsmouth to talk the mutineers and a settlement was agreed.

However, at the same time there was similar unrest at the Nore, at Sheerness. A man called Richard Parker, believed to be the original 'Nosey Parker', was made leader, but he was a self important man who misused his forces and eventually antagonised his supporters. These mutineers intended to sail away from the country, but were thwarted by Trinity House lifting all navigation buoys. All eventually surrendered and Parker was hanged.

OLD HAND. An experienced person.

'Hand' being the term for a seaman.

ON AN EVEN KEEL. A stable situation.

Said of a ship in a stable condition. The keel is the lowest longitudinal member on which a ship is built up.

ON OPPOSITE TACKS, TO BE. To be at cross purposes.

'Opposite tacks' means more than one vessel sailing together in company, but not on the same tack. (See ON THE RIGHT (OR WRONG) TACK.)

ON THE MAKE. To 'feather' one's nest.

Originally an old sailing term meaning making the desired course when tacking.

ON THE RIGHT (OR WRONG) TACK. Employing the right (or wrong) method.

A 'tack' is a sailing vessel's direction in relation to the wind. To tack is to work a vessel to windward, changing course alternately from starboard tack to port tack (with the wind on the starboard and port sides respectively).

ON THE STOCKS. Said of a project on which work has already commenced.

A 'stock' is the frame on which a ship rests whilst being built. (OE. 'stocc', trunk.)

ONE VOLUNTEER IS WORTH TEN PREST MEN. To find one who is willing to do a job is better than having to force others.

In the days of the press gangs, each 'prest man' was advanced the sum of one shilling prest money (the King's shilling). This method of recruitment was forced upon the navy by the fact that the fleet was never kept up to strength in peacetime. Faced with sudden emergencies, there were never enough volunteers forthcoming. (Prest from F. 'prester', to loan.)

OUT OF TRIM. Physically unfit.

The 'trim' of a vessel is the distribution of any load so that she rides in the water to the best advantage. 'Out of trim' is the term to describe a ship whose cargo is not properly trimmed.

OVER A BARREL. No way out of a predicament.

From securing a man over a gun barrel for flogging.

PICKLED. Drunk.

Alludes to the pickling of Lord Nelson's body in brandy for transport back to England after the Battle of Trafalgar. 'Drunk as a lord' also originated from this source.

PILOT. As a pilot of an aircraft.

The original meaning of 'pilot' was a steersman, especially one qualified to conduct ships into or out of harbour or along particular coasts, channels, etc.

PIPING HOT. A description of freshly cooked hot food, straight from the pot or oven.

The term comes from the traditional custom of 'piping' the men to meals in the Royal Navy with the Boatswain's pipe.

PLAIN SAILING. Easy, straightforward.

The 'plane' charts, which were in use during the 16th century, were drawn on the assumption that the earth was flat, even though by then navigators knew it was not. When the first Mercator chart was produced in 1569, the chartmaking problem of drawing meridians as parallel lines without distorting the navigational process was solved.

However, for more than a century after, most navigators continued to use plane charts, even though this caused errors in longitude calculations. This method was known as 'plane' or 'plain' sailing. Since this form of chart did not involve any calculation to convert departure in difference of longitude, it was obviously easier.

POSH. Wealthy.

Actually an abbreviation of 'Port Out and Starboard Home'. The letters 'P.O.S.H.' were once printed on the tickets of the more wealthy first class passengers travelling in P & O ships to and from India. To avoid the intense heat when passing through the Indian Ocean, these passengers were berthed in the specified side of the ship, sheltered from the sun.

POUR OIL ON TROUBLED WATERS, TO. To pacify, act as peacemaker.

A method used in cases of distress, when it is necessary to bring a boat alongside a ship in a heavy sea. Oil is allowed to drip from a container, called an oil bag, into the sea to form a slick and prevent waves from breaking.

PRESSED INTO, TO BE. To be forced into an action.

From 'press', to compel men to join the navy. (See also ONE VOLUNTEER IS WORTH TEN PREST MEN.)

PULL TOGETHER, TO. To work harmoniously.

It is essential that the oarsmen of a pulling boat pull together, following the stroke oar (the leader or time keeper), to keep a smooth steady motion through the water.

PUT ABOUT, TO BE. To be anxious, annoyed, in a flurry, turned around.

From the term for turning a ship around.

PUT THROUGH THE HOOP, TO BE. To be put to the test.

In a sailing warship, netting ran around the outboard sides of the upper deck in which the mens' hammocks were stowed to act as shot stoppers and to provide protection against splinters in action. If the ship were sunk, any hammocks going overboard made convenient life-rafts for survivors. To perform these functions effectively, hammocks had to be lashed up tightly. One of the duties of the master's mates was to pass each man's hammock through a hoop each morning to check the tightness.

RACK AND RUIN. Loss of fortune.

'Rack' is a variant of 'wrack', a former spelling of wreck.

RIG UP, TO. To fix hurriedly in an improvised manner.

The 'rig' of a sailing ship was the manner in which her sails were worn, depending on the class of ship. A 'jury rig' was improvised sailing gear 'rigged up' to enable a damaged ship to reach port.

ROUND THE BEND. Abnormal behaviour.

From the 'bend' of a rope.

ROUGH PASSAGE, A. A time of difficulty or hardship.

A ship is said to have a rough passage when experiencing difficulties through bad weather.

RUN THE GAUNTLET, TO. To brave critisism.

A corruption of the old naval punishment 'to run the gantlope', introduced in the mid 18th century and awarded to men convicted of theft. The offender had to make his way between two ranks of men, all of whom were armed with a rope's end with which to hit him. In addition, the Master–at–Arms held a sword to the offender's breast to prevent him from moving too quickly. It was abolished in 1806.

SAIL CLOSE TO THE WIND, TO. To take risks.

To sail with the wind too close to the bow can be dangerous.

SCOUSE. A term for a Liverpudlian.

A name derived from 'lobscouse' which was a naval dish consisting of salt beef stewed with vegetables and biscuits. It was particularly popular in merchant ships manned from Liverpool.

SHEET ANCHOR. Dependability and security. Winston Churchill once called the Royal Marines 'The country's sheet anchor'.

A sheet anchor is the anchor carried in reserve by a ship, ready for immediate use in an emergency.

SHIPSHAPE AND BRISTOL FASHION. Something done in a correct and proper manner.

In the 18th century, Bristol was the second most important commercial port in the country. The docks were not constructed there until later in 1804, and so in those days the high range of tides there necessitated ships berthed alongside being left high and dry at the fall of the tide. Because of this, ships regularly trading into Bristol had to be of specially stout construction.

SHOT ACROSS THE BOWS. A verbal warning.

Prize rules required that a vessel be ordered to stop by visual signals, with a token shot being fired 'across the bow' if necessary.

SHOW A LEG. An awakening call.

In the days when women were allowed to sleep on board warships, they were allowed to 'lie in.' The call 'show a leg' was made to see that it really was a woman who was enjoying the privilege. The full cry was 'show a leg or else a purser's stocking'.

SKEDADDLE, TO. To scamper off or to run away.

An early 19th century seaman's term for sneaking away from a working party.

SKYSCRAPER. A name for a tall building.

In sailing days this was the name of a triangular sail set above the skysail.

SLOPPY. Careless or untidy.

From 'slops', originally the wide baggy breeches worn by seamen and later to become all of the items made available to men on repayment out of their wages.

SLUSH FUND. A fund for financing bribery and corruption.

An old naval term for the small illegal fund raised in ships from the misappropriation and sale of rope ends, grease, etc., used to pay for such items as an extra rum ration.

SON OF A GUN. A rascal.

The expression first came into use as a definition of a boy born as the result of a temporary mess-deck liason, in the days when women were allowed on board warships. Since gangways had to be kept clear, births had to be managed in the spaces between the broadside guns.

There was also the saying, 'Begotten in the galley and born under a gun. Every hair a rope yarn, every tooth a marlin spike, every finger a fish-hook and his blood right good Stockholm tar'.

SPIN A YARN, TO. To tell a tall story.

From the days when sailors were set to produce spun-yarn from old rope. As this spun yarn had little strength, it was not used for rope but for caulking seams. Thus the term was used in a derogatory sense in the phrase 'to spin a yarn', meaning to tell a tale that was not reliable.

SPRING A LEAK, TO. For a vessel containing liquid to develop a leak.

The expression originated from the occasional tendency for the hull planking of a ship to 'spring'; to break free of its fastenings to the timbers.

STEER CLEAR, TO. To avoid trouble.

From the steering of a ship.

STEM THE TIDE, TO. To oppose a force and successfully make progress against it.

The original meaning of 'stem' was to urge the stem of a vessel against the tide of current and just be able to make headway.

STRANDED. Left without resources.

'Stranded' is when a vessel is drifted or run aground on a strand, shore or beach. 'Strand', still occasionally used, is the old English word for shore.

SWING THE LEAD, TO. To shirk, not to pull one's weight.

Before the advent of electronic sounding devices in ships, the depth of shallow water was obtained by the use of a weighted line called a 'lead line'. This line was marked at various fathom measurements along its length by a series of knots, pieces of bunting and leather strips. The weight, called the 'lead' and hollow in the bottom part, was filled with tallow so that mud, stones, etc. could be picked up to ascertain the nature of the sea bottom for anchoring purposes.

The 'leadsman', situated in the 'chains' on the forecastle, would swing the lead by its line to obtain momentum, before releasing it to drop into the water ahead near the bow. When the ship had caught up with the lead on the bottom, bringing the line into a vertical position, the leadsman was able to observe the mark near the surface and call out the sounding. The expression 'to swing the lead' comes from the leadsman's action of going through the motions of taking soundings without actually sounding.

TAKEN ABACK, TO BE. To be suddenly surprised.

A term from the days of sail which meant when, through a shift of wind or bad steerage, the wind came in front of the square sails and laid them back against the masts. The ship's onward course would be instantly stayed and she would have sternway on, which was very dangerous in a gale.

TAKE THE CAN BACK, TO. To take the blame.

It was once the custom in some dockyards to employ a boy to fetch beer from a local public house. This boy was invariably blamed if accounts were unpaid or cans not returned.

TAKE THE WIND OUT OF ONE'S SAILS, TO. To verbally deflate, to anticipate another or to gain a clever advantage over a competitor.

Henry VIII issued an order that no junior captain should 'take the wind out of his admiral', meaning to cross to windward and take the wind out of his sails.

TAKE YOUR HAT OFF TO SOMEONE, TO. An expression of admiration.

This originated from a speech given by Admiral-of-the-Fleet Sir John Jellicoe when paying respect to the Harwich Striking Force during the First World War; 'The officers and men serving out of Harwich earn and deserve all the leave they receive and, what is more, whenever I meet them I'll take off my hat and I won't expect a salute in return'.

TELL IT TO THE MARINES. Said of a story which requires qualification for truth.

Pepys, relating to Charles II in 1664 some stories told him by the Captain of *HMS DEFIANCE*, mentioned that fish flew. This the courtiers refused to believe, but an officer of the Maritime Regiment of Foot, Sir William Kellegrew, said that he too had seen this remarkable occurrence. The King, after looking at the Colonel's weatherbeaten face, turned to Pepys and said 'From the very nature of their calling, no class of our subjects can have so wide a knowledge of seas and lands as the officers and men of our loyal Maritime Regiment. Ere ever we cast doubts upon a tale that lacks likelihood we first 'Tell it to the Marines'.

THREE SHEETS IN THE WIND, TO BE. To be half intoxicated.

A 'sheet' is a line used for trimming a sail to the wind. The meaning of this expression therefore, is that even if a man had three sheets with which to trim his sail, he would still have difficulty in maintaining a steady course.

TIDE OVER, TO. To get over or surmount.

A term from sailing days, meaning to make progress against a contrary wind by working the tides. 'Tiding over' was common for ships proceeding east down the English Channel, because of the prevailing south-westerly wind. A ship would beat to windward, relying on the strength of the west running tide. When the tide turned, the ship would anchor until the next west running tide and then continue to windward again.

TOE THE LINE, TO. To conform, to follow the rules.

This old naval expression comes from the practice of utilising the pitch seams between wooden deck planking to ensure that the lines of men fallen in for inspection were straight. Originally, the expression was 'toe the pitch'.

TOLD OFF, TO BE. To receive a verbal reprimand.

This is naval language, meaning to be detailed off for a duty.

TON. A measure of weight.

The word comes from the 16th century practice of taxing merchant ships according to the number of 'tuns' (wine casks) that a ship could carry in her hold. Even today, a merchant ship's tonnage is calculated on capacity; dividing the useable interior volume by 100. It has really nothing to do with the actual weight of the vessel.

Because warships are assumed to be fully loaded and ready for battle, naval tonnage is a measure of the vessels weight, calculated on the Archimedes principle of displacement of weight in water.

TOUGH AND GO. A near thing.

An old term which means for a vessel to just touch on a sandbank; not quite running aground.

TURN A BLIND EYE, TO. To know what is happening, but to ignore it.

From Admiral Nelson's action at the Battle of Copenhagen. Nelson was second in command of 18 ships-of-the-line under Admiral Sir Hyde Parker. He urged Parker to be allowed to attack the Danish fleet, of some 18 vessels protecting the City of Copenhagen, with ten ships-of-the-line and ten frigates. Parker agreed and held the rest of the fleet in reserve to the north while Nelson proceeded.

As the fleets became heavily engaged, three of Nelson's ships became stranded and out of range. This concerned Parker; he was so anxious that the outcome would be a defeat for which he would be held responsible, that he hoisted the signal 'Discontinue the action'.

Nelson realised that from his flagship in the middle of the battle, he was better placed to judge the situation than Parker was. He placed his telescope to his blind eye and said to his flag captain 'You know Foley. I have only one eye; I have a right to be blind sometimes. I really do not see the signal. Keep mine for closer battle flying'.

Some two hours later the battle was over and the bulk of the Danish fleet destroyed.

UNDER HATCHES, TO BE. To be in a state of depression or poverty.

From the old term describing men confined below decks.

UNDER WAY. Proceeding.

The term for a ship which has 'way' on and is moving through the water.

WALLOP. A resounding blow.

This originates from the destruction of French ports by Admiral Wallop in the region of Henry VIII.

WASHOUT, A. Something useless.

From the days when signal messages between ships were read and taken down on a slate. After the message had been noted, it was washed off the slate.

WATCH. The name for a wrist or pocket clock.

In 1758 James Harrison had perfected an accurate clock (later called a chronometer) as an aid to calculating longitude, by lunar observation in conjunction with the difference in time to that at Greenwich. Captain James Cook was one of the first users of such an instrument on his second voyage of exploration. He referred to it in his journal as a 'watch machine', watches being the division of time on board ship.

WHEN ONE'S SHIP COMES HOME. When one's fortune is made.

This refers to a trader waiting for his ship to return laden with goods.

WHEN THE BALLOON GOES UP. The beginning of trouble.

Of relatively recent origin, this expression came from the 1914-18 War. When observation balloons were sent up from RN ships fitted with them, this was the first visible sign of an operation.